Current
Directions
in
CHILD
PSYCHOPATHOLOGY

READINGS FROM THE
ASSOCIATION FOR
PSYCHOLOGICAL SCIENCE

Current Directions

in

CHILD PSYCHOPATHOLOGY

EDITED BY

Kenneth A. Dodge

Duke University

Allyn & Bacon

Boston • New York • San Francisco
Mexico City • Montreal • Toronto • London • Madrid • Munich • Paris
Hong Kong • Singapore • Tokyo • Cape Town • Sydney

Series Editor: Michelle Limoges
Editorial Assistant: Lisa Dotson
Marketing Manager: Kate Mitchell
Production Supervisor: Patty Bergin
Editorial Production Service: TexTech International
Manufacturing Buyer: JoAnne Sweeney
Electronic Composition: TexTech International
Cover Designer: Kristina Mose-Libon

Library of Congress Cataloging-in-Publication Data

Current directions in child psychopathology / edited by Kenneth A. Dodge. —1st ed.
    p. cm.
  ISBN-13: 978-0-205-68013-9
  ISBN-10: 0-205-68013-5
  1.   Child psychopathology. I. Dodge, Kenneth A.
  RJ499.C87 2010
  618.92'89—dc22

                                                   2009015755

10 9 8 7 6 5 4 3 2 1   13 12 11 10 09

Allyn & Bacon
is an imprint of

ISBN-10: 0-205-68013-5
www.pearsonhighered.com ISBN-13: 978-0-205-68013-9

Contents

Current
Directions
in
CHILD
PSYCHOPATHOLOGY

Introduction

Perhaps the most important and dramatic development in the field of child psychopathology ever occurred at the turn of the twenty-first century with the discovery of the gene-by-environment interaction effect in predicting child psychopathology outcomes. Using large community samples followed across childhood, Caspi et al. (2002) found that the experience of physical maltreatment by one's parents in the first five years of life predicts later conduct disorder, but only among children who carry a genetic polymorphism in monoamine oxidase—A (MAOA). A year later, Caspi et al. (2003) found that the experience of life stressors predicts later major depressive episodes, but only among children who carry a genetic polymorphism in a serotonin gene 5HTT. These findings have transformed the field of child psychopathology because they signal a resolution to the nature-nurture debate, and they offer a rapprochement between those scholars who have emphasized the genetic causes of disorder and those scholars who have emphasized environmental causes. No longer is nature pitted *against* nurture, as if one factor will "win out" over the other. Rather, the answer is "yes" to both factors in an interdependent way.

The challenge is now on for researchers to discover *how* genes and environments interact, transact, and mutually support each other in the development of psychopathology. Most of the major discoveries in the field in the past decade have involved a growing understanding of the processes and mechanisms through which these factors operate in concert. This has been a theoretically rich and empirically dizzying decade for child psychopathologists who seek understanding of how some children, and not others, grow up to experience mental illness. So, too, most of the articles selected for this volume represent efforts to articulate theories and provide empirical findings of how genes and environments operate in tandem in the development of the various child disorders including externalizing disorders, internalizing disorders, and neurodevelopmental disorders.

We now understand that genetic effects often operate indirectly, by coding for proteins that alter the way that some children's brains experience, respond to, and act on the external environment. Children not only respond to the environment, they also elicit particular reactions from the environment based on their prior characteristics. The environment, in turn, acts on the child by altering the child's biological processes. These biological processes, in turn, lead to child psychopathology. In this way, processes such as hormonal secretions, neural synapses, and autonomic reactions mediate the impact of the environment on children's development.

One implication of the gene-environment interaction effect is that the environment must be conceptualized and measured in more precise ways than in the past. The first section of this reader summarizes innovative examples of environmental variables that have an impact on child psychopathology, including violence in the family and community, qualities of the interparental relationship, parental and residential stability, siblings, mentors, and parental discipline strategies, especially spanking. All of these factors influence the onset or course of child psychopathology and may be influenced by the child as well. The second section addresses the question of how environmental variables "get under the skin" of the child to affect child psychopathology outcomes. Environmental stressors such as trauma and problematic parent-child interactions lead to enhanced stress reactivity in brain regions known to regulate responses to stress. One specific mechanism is the release of corticotropin-releasing factor in response to childhood trauma. These concepts are integrated with a model of how exposure to stressors enhances biological sensitivity to context, which sets up a child to respond to later challenges in ways that characterize child psychopathology.

The third section includes descriptions of how genes moderate the impact of the environment on child psychopathology. Concepts such as "interplay" and "plasticity for affective neurocircuitry" summarize interactions, reciprocal effects, and transactions between the child and the environment. The notion is advanced that not only are children susceptible to environmental influences, but some children are genetically disposed to be more susceptible than others.

The fourth and fifth sections summarize how these concepts and findings on developmental processes have been applied to disorders of externalizing behavior and neurodevelopment, respectively. The fourth section describes models of the development of conduct disorder, adolescent risk taking, and school dropout, with implications for prevention, intervention, and public policy. The fifth section describes recent models of autism, learning disabilities, and attention deficit disorders.

Understanding processes in the development of child psychopathology paves the way to novel clinical interventions and public policies to treat or prevent disorders. Innovative approaches described in the pages of this volume include training children's executive attention processes to combat attention deficit disorder, shaping the environments of adolescents so that their tendency to take risks does not lead them toward rash mistakes and precarious outcomes, and rethinking public policy's role in parents' spanking of their children. Although exciting, these interventions have not yet proven so successful that they have transformed society. Perhaps the next decade will identify stories of how a psychological understanding of the development of child psychopathology has been used to shape interventions and policies that transform not only science but also society.

Section 1: Environmental Factors That Lead to Child Psychopathology

Although it has long been known that environments contribute to children's adjustment and psychopathology, the field has been hampered by inadequate conceptualization of these factors and poor measurement of variables. The articles in this section describe progress that has been made on both of these fronts.

In the past, environments have been conceptualized mainly in terms of socioeconomic advantage or disadvantage. Although this feature continues to be important in children's development, richer models emphasize the environment as a stressor and a model for behavior. The stressor can be acute, as in trauma, or chronic, as in exposure to community violence on a daily level. Stress effects can come from obvious sources such as family violence but also previously ignored sources such as the frequency of residential moves. Stress effects also cumulate. Environmental models for behavior likewise come from obvious sources such as interparental relationships and spanking but also from previously under-emphasized sources such as siblings and mentors.

One feature of many environmental variables is multi-finality. That is, the impact of an environmental variable is diffuse and wide-reaching. It can lead to one form of psychopathology in one child but a different form in another child. For example, exposure to interparental conflict can lead to aggressive behavior or anxiety, to conduct disorder or depression and substance abuse. This characteristic suggests the importance of considering multiple outcomes in the same study and points toward child factors as possible moderators of the effect of the environment.

The measurement of environmental variables has been improved dramatically in the past decade, leading to a richer data base of environmental impacts. For example, the study of residential instability had been neglected because the very objects of inquiry (i.e., families that move frequently) are the ones most likely to attrite from studies across time. Improved methods of tracking families and retaining them in studies has led to a better understanding of the role that this stressor plays in the development of psychopathology.

Children's Exposure to Violence in the Family and Community

Gayla Margolin[1] and Elana B. Gordis
University of Southern California

Abstract

Exposure to family and community violence is linked with aggression, depression, post-traumatic stress symptoms, and academic and cognitive difficulties. It has the potential to permeate many dimensions of children's day-to-day lives and to erode possible sources of social support. Although the literature focuses on deleterious outcomes, many children fare well in the face of exposure to violence. Research attending to developmental processes, the co-occurrence of multiple forms of violence, and psychobiological mechanisms will clarify why outcomes are better for some children than for others. Greater understanding of children's risk and resilience in the face of such exposure will inform intervention efforts.

Keywords

children; child abuse; interparental violence; community violence; risk and resilience

Violence is a public-health problem, and children are particularly vulnerable to its effects. Besides being a leading source of injury, violence takes a toll on more subtle aspects of functioning, such as cognitive, behavioral, social, and emotional functioning. Disruption in these domains can affect children's progression through typical developmental processes, with the nature of the impact dependent on the timing, type, and chronicity of the exposure to violence. Violence affects children even if they are not the direct victim but have a close relationship with the victim.

Because exposure to violence typically occurs in familiar settings, the safe havens of family and community are marred by danger. Parents have not been able to prevent the violence and may be the perpetrators, the victims, or themselves affected in ways that compromise their caretaking. Distressing consequences of violence may include breakup or relocation of the family or repercussions following disclosure of abuse. Children living with violence may also experience family conflict and other life stresses, such as poverty, parents' unemployment, or parents' substance abuse and psychopathology. In an iterative fashion, these life stresses increase the risk for continued violence, and violence increases the likelihood of these stresses.

SCOPE OF CHILDREN'S EXPOSURE TO VIOLENCE

Definitions

Violence is defined in many different ways in the research on its effects on children. Major categories of violence that have been investigated are (a) child maltreatment, including physical abuse, sexual abuse, and neglect; (b) aggression between parents; and (c) community violence, including direct victimization and witnessing of violence. Despite high rates of co-occurrence among exposure to different types of violence (Appel & Holden, 1998; Margolin & Gordis, 2000), published works have typically examined child abuse, domestic violence, and community violence separately.

A key issue is the wide range of severity in the violence that children observe or experience. Some forms of severe aggression, such as beatings or use of weapons, can be traumatic to the victim and to observers. Other forms of aggression, such as pushing or shoving and corporal punishment, are considered normative by much of society. In samples drawn from the population at large, low-severity aggressive behaviors may suffice as the criterion for violence. Other studies compare people recruited from shelters, treatments, or child protective services who have been exposed to violence with people who have not received such services. In these studies, the violence-exposed groups typically have experienced severe, injurious behaviors. However, lower-severity aggressive behaviors may have occurred in both groups.

Rates of Exposure

Estimates of the rate of children's exposure to violence vary because of different definitions and methods of data collection. Using official and unofficial reports of professionals working with children, The National Center of Child Abuse and Neglect (NCCAN) estimated that approximately 23 per 1,000 children are victims of maltreatment, including physical abuse, sexual abuse, and neglect (Sedlack & Broadhurst, 1996). Rates of severe physical abuse, based on national studies of the population at large, are 49 per 1,000, or five times the NCCAN estimate (Straus, Hamby, Finkelhor, Moore, & Runyan, 1998). Straus (1992) extrapolated that each year more than 10 million U.S. children witness physical aggression between their parents. Rates of community violence are generally based on interviews or surveys with children and sometimes corroborated by parents. Richters and Martinez (1993) reported that exposure to community violence is quite common, with at least one third of children victimized and more than 90% witnessing violence at least once during their childhoods. With the majority of children having some type of violence exposure, researchers need to distinguish between severe and mild exposure and between chronic and one-time events.

EFFECTS OF EXPOSURE TO VIOLENCE

Short-Term Effects

Although each type of violence has its own literature, studies have shown some common short-term effects. (For a detailed review of the effects of family and community violence, see Margolin & Gordis, 2000.) Children who are exposed to violence of any kind may exhibit behavioral disorders such as aggression and delinquency; emotional and mood disorders such as depression and anxiety; posttraumatic stress symptoms such as exaggerated startle, nightmares, and flashbacks; health-related problems and somatic symptoms such as sleep disturbances; and academic and cognitive problems. Some forms of violence tend to have specific consequences. For example, sexual acting out sometimes is a specific consequence of sexual abuse. However, exposure to other forms of violence also may lead to this problem, but the connections are not as theoretically salient, and not all of the connections have been investigated.

Exposure to family and community violence is linked with aggressive behavior. One of the theoretical perspectives that explains this link is social learning theory, according to which children learn from the aggressive models in their environments. Additionally, victimization may compromise children's ability to regulate their emotions, and as a result they may act out aggressively. Sexual abuse, physical abuse, and exposure to violence between parents and in the community have all been linked to aggression, with links particularly well documented for physical abuse.

Considerable literature documents links between exposure to violence and problems such as depression and anxiety. A child may interpret violence at home and in the community to mean that the world is unsafe and that he or she is unworthy of protection. This interpretation may engender helplessness and lead to negative self-perceptions. Community violence also is linked to anxiety and depression, though one methodological issue is that studies of community violence frequently include intrafamilial as well as extrafamilial violence.

Posttraumatic stress symptoms and posttraumatic stress disorder (PTSD) are important consequences of exposure to violence because they can impair social and behavioral functioning. Many children who do not meet diagnostic criteria for PTSD may experience troublesome symptoms. Physical and sexual abuse, community violence, and exposure to domestic violence are linked with posttraumatic stress symptoms, with links particularly well documented for sexual abuse. The degree to which exposure leads to posttraumatic stress symptoms in children may vary with the intensity of the violence and the degree to which the violence has lasting effects on the people most important to them (e.g., witnessing a stranger being punched vs. seeing a parent being assaulted vs. being directly victimized).

Family violence and community violence also relate to academic and cognitive difficulties, possibly through their impact on psychological functioning. For example, PTSD and depression may interfere with learning and with the ability to perform well in the classroom. Neglect has a particularly negative impact on academic and cognitive performance.

Long-Term Effects

A few prospective studies in this area have explored whether exposure to violence during childhood increases the likelihood of either perpetrating or being the victim of aggression during adulthood. In a 20-year prospective study by Ehrensaft et al. (2003), children who were exposed to violence between their parents subsequently were more likely to perpetrate violence against an adult partner and to be treated violently by an adult partner than were children who were not exposed to violence; children who were physically abused had an increased rate of injuring a partner. However, Kaufman and Zigler's (1987) early review of prospective studies concluded that although a history of abuse increases the rate of abuse toward children from 5% to approximately 30%, 70% of children exposed to violence do not become abusive adults. Moreover, Widom (1998) concluded that childhood victimization increases the risk of criminal behavior and other mental health problems, but the "cycle of violence is not deterministic or inevitable" (p. 226).

KEY DIRECTIONS FOR RESEARCH

The variability across children in the effects of exposure to violence is largely unexplained. Many children do not exhibit negative outcomes at the time they are studied. For example, using meta-analytic procedures to combine statistically the results of 118 studies on children's exposure to domestic violence, Kitzmann, Gaylord, Holt, and Kenny (2003) found that 63% of child witnesses to violence were doing worse than nonwitnesses, whereas 37% were doing comparably or better.

The fundamental question remains: Why do some children show negative outcomes and other children appear to be more resilient? Although early research primarily examined the outcomes associated with violence, research recently has begun to explore the mechanisms that explain these outcomes.

Developmental Processes

An important consideration is how exposure to violence alters the typical developmental course. For example, risk taking typically increases in adolescence, but studies need to examine whether risk taking differs between teenagers who have and have not been exposed to violence. It is possible, for instance, that exposure to violence is associated with increased, prolonged, or earlier onset of risk taking. Moreover, researchers need to identify the developmental processes underlying linkages between exposure to violence and later developmental problems. If the short-term effects are exhibited in emotional dysregulation, cognitive difficulties, and disruptions in important relationships with caregivers, these effects may increase risk for subsequent failure in two key developmental tasks: establishing a supportive peer network and effective work habits at school. Disruption of these tasks places the adolescent at risk for further problems, including school failure, depression, involvement with deviant peers, substance abuse, and delinquent behaviors.

A developmental perspective highlights the following types of questions: Does early exposure to violence trigger more profound disruption in development than later exposure? Does exposure have delayed effects, and do delayed effects occur regardless of whether the exposure continues? The study of developmental processes could identify developmental periods of particular vulnerability, as well as periods amenable for intervention.

In addition to having direct effects, exposure to violence compromises interpersonal relationships that are the fabric of children's daily lives. Social support is a key buffer against the negative effects of violence. Because parents are key sources of social support, the disrupted parenting associated with family violence may exacerbate negative effects of exposure to violence (Margolin, Gordis, & Oliver, in press). More generally, children exposed to violence may be sensitized to hostile interactions and may have difficulty negotiating peer conflicts. These interpersonal difficulties can rob children of social support and increase their risk for associating with deviant peers.

Exposure to Multiple Forms of Violence

Research findings have not yet clarified whether exposure to multiple types of violence increases the risk of negative effects (Kitzmann et al., 2003). Exposure to multiple types of violence may increase risk because it tends to be associated with a higher frequency of exposure and increased seriousness of violence. Alternatively, exposure to multiple forms of violence may increase risk because it reflects severe disruptions in parent-child relations, particularly if the child both witnesses aggression between his or her parents and is directly maltreated.

Moreover, children who both observe aggression between their parents and are directly victimized may perceive aggression and conflict as particularly threatening, and consequently develop difficulty regulating their own emotions and hypervigilance to cues associated with interpersonal conflict. We (Gordis, Margolin, & John, 1997) found that parent-to-child hostility exacerbated the effects of aggression between parents on children's distress during family discussions. Investigators need to explore whether children become more reactive to aggression when they both observe it in their parents and are themselves directly victimized.

Because families are made up of interconnected subsystems (e.g., marital, parent-child), violence in one family subsystem can spill over into other family subsystems. Although personality and genetic factors can predispose someone to behave aggressively with multiple family members, a family systems perspective suggests that one type of violence exposure can overwhelm a family system, deplete emotional and physical resources, and lower thresholds for aggression in other family subsystems. We (Margolin & Gordis, 2003) found that an accumulation of aversive family circumstances, such as high financial stress and high parenting stress, renders families vulnerable to aggression across multiple subsystems. Additional research is needed to identify factors that allow conflicts and aggression to spread from one family subsystem to another.

Psychobiological Approaches

An important recent development is the focus on both biological and psychological consequences of exposure to violence (e.g., De Bellis, 2001). Children who have been exposed to violence may experience dysregulation of the hypothalamic-pituitary-adrenal (HPA) axis, the stress response system. This system involves the release of a series of hormones, resulting in the secretion of cortisol from the adrenal glands. Researchers have found links between exposure to violence and levels of cortisol both in nonstressful situations and in response to a stressor. However, the direction of dysregulation is inconsistent, with research showing both higher and lower cortisol levels in children exposed to violence. The variability of findings may reflect different types of response to stress. Emerging

9

research additionally suggests that different types of dysregulation of the HPA axis may correspond to different types of behavioral problems in children. Much remains unknown about this complex and important stress-response system.

Exposure to violence may also cause disturbances in physical and sexual development. Stress may lead to elevations in certain gonadal hormones. Some researchers suggest that these effects may result in the early onset of puberty and elevated levels of sexual behavior often linked to sexual abuse. Moreover, factors associated with increased sympathetic nervous system activity (the "fight or flight" response), including hormone and catecholamine neurotransmitter activity, appear to suppress immune function and may even damage brain cells in the hippocampus, which is important in memory functioning. Researchers also have found alterations in patterns of growth hormone response in abused children. These disturbances may cause disturbances in patterns of physical growth.

Another new research direction is the application of twin studies to examine the effects of violence exposure. A nagging concern with earlier literature on exposure to violence is that genetic links may account for outcomes assumed to be environmentally influenced. However, researchers recently have found that exposure to family violence contributes over and above the effects of genetic influences to various outcomes, such as IQ (e.g., Koenen, Moffitt, Caspi, Taylor, & Purcell, 2003). Thus, accumulating evidence indicates that exposure to violence has an effect on behavior that goes beyond the effects of shared genes.

Many questions remain for psychobiological research. What is the normal developmental course of relevant biological systems, and how are these systems altered by exposure to violence? How do these systems relate to maladaptive emotional and behavioral functioning? Most important, what aspects of the psychobiological variables are amenable to interventions that would improve outcomes, and how can psychobiological consequences of exposure to violence inform treatments for violence-exposed children?

CONCLUSION

Data repeatedly indicate that exposure to family and community violence compromises the development of some but not all children. Explanatory models of individual and contextual factors that either buffer against or exacerbate the effects of violence are needed. Individual factors for these models include cognitive, behavioral, emotional, and biological resources available to the child. Relevant contextual dimensions include family, community, and cultural factors that influence children's interpretation of and reactions to violence.

Although previous research has emphasized what is wrong with children who have been exposed to violence, a focus on children's successful adaptation is equally important. Resilience to such exposure is a function of how children manage and cut short negative chain reactions, for example, through effective problem solving, supportive responses from family or peers, and opportunities for success at school. Resilience, however, is not a fixed characteristic, but changes across time and circumstances. Protective factors may be more accessible to children as they mature; alternatively, chronic exposure to violence or exposure to severe violence may erode protective factors.

Children's exposure to violence frequently goes unnoticed and unattended by parents and by professionals who work with children. Parents typically underestimate their children's exposure to violence and may even be unaware of abuse in the home. Children exposed to violence tend to exhibit symptoms associated with common types of maladjustment. Thus, professionals may not be aware when violence plays a role in the etiology of those symptoms. Detailed information about the range of consequences related to exposure to violence and the factors that influence those consequences will help to identify children who may be at risk for negative outcomes. Moreover, little is known about whether standard treatments for childhood disorders are effective in the context of exposure to violence. Models for understanding risk and protective factors in the child and his or her social context will inform interventions for violence-exposed children.

Recommended Reading

Cicchetti, D., & Toth, S. (1995). A developmental psychopathology perspective to child abuse and neglect. *Journal of the American Academy of Child and Adolescent Psychiatry, 34,* 541–564.
Cicchetti, D., & Toth, S. (1997). *Rochester Symposium on Developmental Psychopathology: Developmental perspectives on trauma: Theory, research, and intervention.* Rochester, NY: University of Rochester Press.
Margolin, G., & Gordis, E.B. (2000). (See References)
Repetti, R.L., Taylor, S.E., & Seeman, T.E. (2002). Risky families: Family social environments and the mental and physical health of offspring. *Psychological Bulletin, 128,* 330–366.
Trickett, P.K., & Schellenback, C.J. (1998). *Violence against children in the family and the community.* Washington, DC: American Psychological Association.

Acknowledgments—Preparation of this article was supported by Grant 99-8412 from the David and Lucile Packard Foundation and by National Institutes of Health Grant K23HD041428.

Note

1. Address correspondence to Gayla Margolin, University of Southern California, Department of Psychology, SGM 930, Los Angeles, CA 90089-1061; e-mail: margolin@usc.edu.

References

Appel, A.E., & Holden, G.W. (1998). The co-occurrence of spouse and physical child abuse: A review and appraisal. *Journal of Family Psychology, 12,* 578–599.
De Bellis, M.D. (2001). Developmental traumatology: The psychobiological development of maltreated children and its implications for research, treatment, and policy. *Development and Psychopathology, 13,* 539–564.
Ehrensaft, M.K., Cohen, P., Brown, J., Smailes, E., Chen, H., & Johnson, J.G. (2003). Intergenerational transmission of partner violence: A 20-year prospective study. *Journal of Consulting and Clinical Psychology, 71,* 741–753.

Gordis, E.B., Margolin, G., & John, R.S. (1997). Marital aggression, observed parental hostility, and child behavior during triadic family interaction. *Journal of Family Psychology, 11,* 76–89.

Kaufman, J., & Zigler, E. (1987). Do abused children become abusive parents? *American Journal of Orthopsychiatry, 57,* 186–192.

Kitzmann, K.M., Gaylord, N.K., Holt, A.R., & Kenny, E.D. (2003). Child witnesses to domestic violence: A meta-analytic review. *Journal of Consulting and Clinical Psychology, 71,* 339–352.

Koenen, K.C., Moffitt, T.E., Caspi, A., Taylor, A., & Purcell, S. (2003). Domestic violence is associated with environmental suppression of IQ in young children. *Development and Psychopathology, 15,* 297–311.

Margolin, G., & Gordis, E.B. (2000). The effects of family and community violence on children. *Annual Review of Psychology, 51,* 445–479.

Margolin, G., & Gordis, E.B. (2003). Co-occurrence between marital aggression and parents' child abuse potential: The impact of cumulative stress. *Violence and Victims, 18,* 243–258.

Margolin, G., Gordis, E.B., & Oliver, P. (in press). Links between marital and parent-child interactions: Moderating role of husband-to-wife aggression. *Development and Psychopathology.*

Richters, J.E., & Martinez, P. (1993). The NIMH Community Violence Project: I. Children as victims of and witnesses to violence. In D. Reiss, J.E. Richters, M. Radke-Yarrow, & D. Scharff (Eds.), *Children and violence* (pp. 7–21). New York: Guilford.

Sedlack, A.J., & Broadhurst, D.D. (1996). *Third National Incidence Study of Child Abuse and Neglect.* Washington, DC: U.S. Department of Health and Human Services, National Center of Child Abuse and Neglect.

Straus, M.A. (1992). Children as witnesses to marital violence: A risk factor of lifelong problems among a nationally representative sample of American men and women. In D.F. Schwarz (Ed.), *Children and violence: Report of the Twenty-Third Ross Roundtable on Critical Approaches to Common Pediatric Problems* (pp. 98–109). Columbus, OH: Ross Laboratories.

Straus, M.A., Hamby, S.L., Finkelhor, D., Moore, D.W., & Runyan, D. (1998). Identification of child maltreatment with the Parent-Child Conflict Tactics Scales: Development and psychometric data for a national sample of American parents. *Child Abuse and Neglect, 22,* 249–270.

Widom, C.S. (1998). Child victims: Searching for opportunities to break the cycle of violence. *Applied & Preventive Psychology, 7,* 225–234.

This article has been reprinted as it originally appeared in *Current Directions in Psychological Science*. Citation information for this article as originally published appears above.

Children's Emotional Security in the Interparental Relationship

Patrick T. Davies[1] and Meredith J. Woitach
University of Rochester

Abstract

In response to the societal premium placed on understanding the difficulties faced by children from high-conflict homes, emotional security theory aims to understand precisely how and why interparental discord is associated with children's psychological problems. One of its main premises is that interparental discord increases children's vulnerability to mental illness by undermining their sense of safety or security in the context of the interparental relationship. In this article, we highlight the main assumptions of a new ethological formulation of emotional security theory and its predictions and findings regarding the organization, precursors, and consequences of individual differences in children's emotional insecurity. We conclude with a synopsis of the value of the new formulation for future work.

Keywords

interparental conflict; child coping; child psychopathology

Conflict between parents is a significant public health concern by virtue of its prevalence and threat to children's mental health. Most families have some degree of interparental conflict. However, when such conflict contains escalating hostility, violence, unresolved endings, or disengagement, it creates a toxic environment in which children are particularly likely to be concerned for their own safety and the welfare of their family (Cummings & Davies, 1996). Moreover, exposure to these destructive forms of interparental conflict increases children's risk for many psychological problems including depression, anxiety, aggression, and social problems (Grych & Fincham, 2001). Emotional security theory (EST) was developed by Davies and Cummings (1994) to address precisely how and why interparental discord is associated with negative trajectories in children's mental health. (For other theories of marital conflict, see Grych & Fincham, 2001.)

EST postulates that, within the emotion-laden context of interparental conflict, a prominent goal for children is maintaining a sense of protection, safety, and security. Thus, a primary thesis is that witnessing destructive interparental conflict increases children's vulnerability to psychological problems by undermining their ability to preserve emotional security within various family relationships. Our objective in this article is to provide a synopsis of a new, ethological formulation of EST that seeks to understand the adaptive or survival value of children's reactions to family discord within the context of evolutionary history.

THE SUBSTANCE OF EMOTIONAL SECURITY

Consistent with attachment theory (Hilburn-Cobb, 2004), EST accepts the notion that the deleterious effects of parenting difficulties (e.g., unresponsiveness, intrusiveness, low warmth) on children's psychological adjustment can be explained, in part, by children's difficulties in using parents as sources of protection and support within the parent–child attachment relationship. As a result, children's quality of attachment to parents is also regarded as a key mechanism accounting for the greater vulnerability of children exposed to destructive interparental conflict. For example, interparental conflict may increase attachment insecurity through its co-occurrence with greater parental hostility, rejection, disengagement, and intrusiveness (Paths 1 and 2 in Fig. 1). Likewise, Path 3 in Figure 1 illustrates that witnessing frightening (e.g., hostility, aggression) and vulnerable (e.g., distress, fear) caregiver behaviors during interparental conflict may directly undermine children's confidence in their parents as sources of security (e.g., Frosch, Mangelsdorf, & McHale, 2000).

However, EST differs from attachment theory in arguing that maintaining security is a salient goal in other family relationships as well. As shown in Path 4 of Figure 1, children's patterns of security in the interparental and parent–child relationships are regarded as interrelated, but distinct systems (Davies, Harold, Goeke-Morey, & Cummings, 2002). Prior theoretical papers, however, have failed to elucidate how and why these systems differ. To address this issue, an ethological reformulation of EST theorizes that stressors within the context of family relationships activate distinct behavioral systems that developed and persisted based on their success in promoting survival over evolutionary time (Davies & Sturge-Apple, 2007). Within the parent–child relationship, the psychological

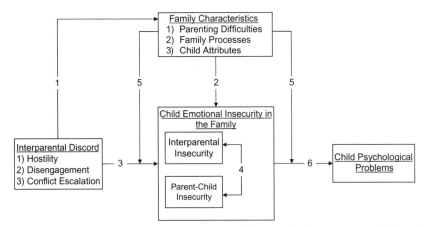

Fig. 1. An emotional-security-theory depiction of how and why interparental discord increases children's adjustment problems in the family system. Together, Paths 1 and 2 indicate that interparental conflict may increase attachment insecurity through its association with other forms of parenting and family difficulties. Path 3 illustrates that prolonged exposure to interparental conflict may directly increase children's insecurity in both the parent–child and interparental relationships. Path 4 shows that children's experiences with insecurity in the interparental and parent–child relationships are interrelated, but also distinct. Path 5 illustrates that interparental conflict has different implications for children's experiences with security, depending on negative and positive characteristics in the broader family system. Path 6 shows that insecurity in family relationships lays the foundation for social, emotional, cognitive, and physical health problems.

goal of felt security is primarily achieved through the attachment system. In times of distress or threat, maximizing the sensitivity and protection of one's caregiver is the central behavioral goal of the attachment system (Bowlby, 1969). Children have access to a large repertoire of attachment behaviors to achieve this behavioral goal and the psychological goal of felt security—behaviors including expressions of distress, bids for comfort, proximity seeking, and increased monitoring of the attachment figure. These behaviors indicate the activation of the attachment system and are important signs of security in the parent–child relationship.

In contrast, children's concerns about security in the face of interparental conflict largely reflect the operation of the social defense system. Evolutionary theory postulates that the social defense system developed throughout our history as a species to minimize threats posed by other members of family and social networks. Recurrent threats are theorized to have put selective pressure on the development of a behavioral system capable of efficiently identifying and responding to social signals that signal potential threat (e.g., yelling, dominant posturing). Although families in humans' evolutionary past differed from contemporary families in some ways (e.g., living in extended families or clans), a similarity is that most if not all families are headed by dominant adults who carry disproportionate power in shaping the structure, stability, and safety of the family unit. Because relationship difficulties between these adults increase exposure to threat, the social defense system and its behavioral goal of protecting oneself from interpersonal harm is posited to organize children's patterns of response to interparental conflict. As a result, a different and distinct repertoire of protective strategies is required to preserve a sense of security in the interparental relationship than is involved in preserving security in the parent–child attachment relationship. Specific indicators of concerns about security in the interparental relationship include fear, distress and vigilance, fight behaviors (e.g., mediating the conflict, siding with one parent, aggression), flight and camouflaging activities (e.g., avoidance, inhibiting overt emotions), social de-escalation strategies (e.g., comforting, pacifying parents), and heightened perceptual sensitivity to identifying threatening stimuli accompanying interparental conflict. Thus, exposure to interparental conflict should yield a higher incidence of these patterns of responding than of behaviors that primarily serve the attachment system (e.g., comfort or proximity seeking).

Although thorough scientific tests of this new hypothesis will require the development of measurement batteries that more precisely distinguish between attachment and defense variables, existing studies provide tentative support for distinction between the systems. For example, parent reports in daily home diaries revealed that a high percentage of children exhibited fear, flight (e.g., left the room), fight (e.g., took sides), and social de-escalation (e.g., tried to make peace) behaviors in response to interparental conflict (Garcia O'Hearn, Margolin, & John, 1997). Moreover, as Figure 2 shows, latent variable analyses (which examine whether measures of variables correspond with their proposed theoretical constructs) provide support for the assumption that social defense responses reflecting insecurity in the interparental conflict (e.g., fear, involvement, negative representations) and attachment behaviors within the parent–child relationship

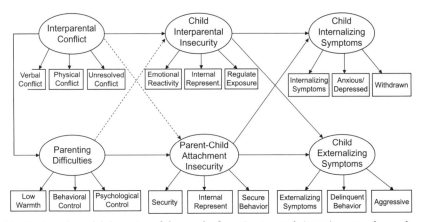

Fig. 2. A path model depiction of the results from Davies et al. (2002) testing the mediational role of child security in family relationships in the link between interparental conflict and parenting difficulties and child psychological symptoms. *Interparental conflict* = parent reports of verbal conflict, physical conflict, and unresolved conflict. *Parenting difficulties* = parent reports of low warmth, poor behavioral control (e.g., monitoring), and psychological control (e.g., guilt induction). *Child interparental insecurity* = aggregated parent and child reports of children's emotional reactivity to interparental conflict and their regulation of exposure to interparental discord (i.e., involvement and avoidance responses) and children's reports of their internal representations of interparental problems. *Parent–child attachment insecurity* = child reports of behaviors indicative of their attachment security, child internal representations of doubt about parents as supportive figures, and parent reports of secure behaviors in parent–child relations. *Child internalizing symptoms* = child reports of their own internalizing symptoms, parent reports of child anxious and depressed behavior, and parent reports of child withdrawal. *Child externalizing symptoms* = child reports of their externalizing symptoms (i.e., aggression, delinquency) and parent reports of child delinquent and aggressive behaviors. Solid arrows reflect significant paths between variables, whereas dotted arrows reflect estimated paths that were negligible in magnitude.

cohere into distinct latent constructs of interparental insecurity and parent–child insecurity, respectively (Davies et al., 2002).

INTERPARENTAL SOURCES OF VARIATION IN CHILDREN'S SECURITY

A history of exposure to destructive forms of interparental conflict is theorized to play a primary role in the development of stable individual differences in children's security in the interparental relationship. High-conflict homes are proposed to sensitize children to concerns about security because conflicts are prolonged, increase the likelihood of future conflicts, spill over to affect parent–child relationships, and jeopardize the stability and structure of the family unit (see Path 3 in Fig. 1). Thus, concerns about security and the activation of social defense behaviors likely serve an adaptive function, preparing children to identify and cope with potential dangers and safeguarding them against threat in the context of interparental conflict. For example, sensitivity to the beginning stages of an argument and the rapid capacity to cope through flight and fight (e.g., involvement) behaviors may reduce children's exposure to the escalation and spread of interparental hostility in high-conflict homes. In support of the role of interparental conflict in models of child insecurity, analyses have shown that interparental conflict is a more consistent predictor of concurrent and subsequent signs of child insecurity (e.g., distress, avoidance, involvement, negative representations) than parenting difficulties are (Davies et al., 2002; Davies, Sturge-Apple, Winter, Cummings, & Farrell, 2006; see Fig. 2).

An evolutionary perspective helps identify conflict properties that are most likely to promote children's insecurity in the interparental relationship. A common assumption is that aggressive, angry, and fearful displays held primacy in detecting imminent peril in prehistoric environments. Consequently, the development of a biologically hard-wired sensitivity to expressions of anger and fear is theorized to provide an adaptive solution to the threats faced across evolutionary time (Bowlby, 1969; Hofmann, Moscovitch, & Heinrichs, 2004). In applying it to our model, witnessing intense anger, aggression, or fear between adults, particularly two attachment figures, may be especially likely to pose a threat to children's emotional security. In partial support of this hypothesis, children who witnessed violent interparental conflict were more likely than children who witnessed no conflict or verbally aggressive conflict to exhibit distress, avoidance, and alliance-formation, according to parent diary reports (Garcia O'Hearn et al., 1997). However, no studies have distinguished between exposure to interparental anger, fear, and other conflict properties (e.g., parental dysphoria) in models predicting children's signs of insecurity. Therefore, precisely identifying destructive properties of conflict remains an important research direction.

FAMILY SOURCES OF VARIATION IN CHILDREN'S EMOTIONAL SECURITY

Other family characteristics, beyond interparental conflict, may also modulate child worries about security in the interparental relationship (Davies & Cummings, 2006). Although natural selection likely equipped individuals with many ways of coping with threats in the family, choice of strategy is thought to hinge on how interparental conflict fits into the broader family ecology (Ellis, Jackson, & Boyce, 2006; Gilbert, 2001). First, as illustrated by path 2 in Figure 1, family characteristics may play an important role as predictors of children's security even after taking into account interparental conflict styles. For example, the availability of support in the broader family unit may foster the development of necessary developmental skills and capacities, such as regulation of emotions, self-confidence, and self-efficacy, for maintaining a sense of security in the face of interparental difficulties. Supporting this prediction, Davies et al. (2006) found that observations of parental warmth continued to predict lower levels of children's distress in response to interparental conflict even after taking into account interparental conflict as a predictor of children's distress reactions to the conflict.

Second, path 5 in Figure 1 reflects the proposition that interparental conflict has different implications for children's preservation of security depending on characteristics of the broader family system. In evolutionary terminology, stability and support in the family system suggests that the possibility of harm is negligible, even in the wake of danger cues that accompany interparental discord. In contrast, experiencing recurrent family threats without opportunities for solace or escape is proposed to amplify the sensitivity of the social defense system. Thus, signs of fragile family functioning (e.g., parent psychopathology, family distress) may intensify the negative consequences of interparental discord for children's insecurity. In supporting these predictions, Davies et al. (2002) found that interparental conflict was a stronger predictor of a composite of signs of child insecurity (e.g., distress, avoidance, involvement, and negative appraisals) when children also experienced high family instability and low levels of emotional expressiveness and relationship satisfaction in the interparental relationship.

THE UNFOLDING CONSEQUENCES OF EMOTIONAL SECURITY

The final pathway (#6) in Figure 1 proposes that insecurity in family relationships lays the foundation for problems in socio-emotional, cognitive, and physical domains of functioning. Within the parent–child attachment literature, the role of attachment insecurity as a distinct risk factor for child psychopathology is well-established (Hilburn-Cobb, 2004). Recent research has shown that emotional insecurity in the interparental relationship is also a significant predictor of increases in children's psychological problems over time (Cummings, Schermerhorn, Davies, Goeke-Morey, & Cummings, 2006; Harold, Shelton, Goeke-Morey, & Cummings, 2004). However, the validity of EST as a model that cannot be subsumed within attachment theory hinges, in part, on demonstrating that emotional insecurity in the interparental relationship is a unique risk mechanism predicting children's psychological problems even after taking into account attachment insecurity. In the first study to test this proposition, Davies et al. (2002) found that children's insecurity in the interparental relationship and attachment insecurity were each uniquely associated with concurrent levels of adolescent internalizing symptoms (e.g., depression, anxiety) and externalizing symptoms (e.g., aggression, delinquency; see Fig. 2). In a more powerful longitudinal test, a recent study also showed that children's negative perceptions of the consequences of interparental conflict for themselves and their families significantly predicted subsequent declines in children's school adjustment even after including their negative perceptions of the parent–child relationship as a predictor in the model (Sturge-Apple, Davies, Winter, Cummings, & Schermerhorn, in press).

FUTURE DIRECTIONS

Our reformulation of EST generates a number of questions for future research. Evolutionary accounts underscore the multiplicity of strategies within the social defense system that can be flexibly enlisted to defend against interpersonal threat. The implication is that there are substantial variations in the ways different children experience and express their insecurity. Thus, one key direction is to refine and test pattern-based schemes that attempt to distinguish between children based on their unique profiles of responding to conflict across multiple response domains (e.g., subjective distress, overt distress and vigilance, involvement, negative internal representations). Our application of evolutionary models of the social defense system highlights a new system for distinguishing between novel patterns of reactivity to interparental conflict that reflect distinct types of insecurity (Davies & Sturge-Apple, 2007). For example, some children may exhibit a camouflaging pattern of insecurity, characterized by an inhibition of behavioral displays of distress, despite experiencing high levels of subjective alarm and apprehension. In contrast, other children may express insecurity through the demobilizing strategies of disengagement, worry, dysphoria, anhedonia, helplessness, and self-blame (Gilbert, 2001). Because evolutionary models suggest that each pattern of insecurity is associated with specific configurations of family antecedents and developmental consequences, identifying pattern-based approaches may help advance an understanding of the pathways between family characteristics, children's patterns of insecurity, and their psychological adjustment.

Addressing how insecurity in the interparental relationship develops into broader patterns of psychological maladjustment is a critical research direction. EST proposes that the prolonged operation of the social defense system produces changes in neurobiological (e.g., neuroendocrine hormones and sympathetic nervous system functioning), neuropsychological (e.g., self-regulation, reasoning, and problem-solving capacities), psychological (e.g., emotion regulation), and attention processes that ultimately undermine children's mental health. In keeping with regulatory depletion models (Baumeister, Vohs, & Tice, 2007), concerns about security may deplete a common reservoir of self-regulatory resources, thereby creating deficits in other challenging domains of developmental functioning (e.g., inhibitory control, self-regulation, attention, academic activities). The first attempt to empirically test a component of this model supported the hypothesis that attention problems partially explain the link between children's insecurity in the interparental relationship and their adjustment difficulties (Davies, Woitach, Winter, & Cummings, in press). However, outside of this study, no studies have explored why insecurity in the interparental relationship increases children's vulnerability to mental health problems.

In closing, it is important to note that theory and research on models of interparental conflict have a great deal of potential in informing health initiatives that improve children's mental health. Given the evidence indicating that security in the interparental relationship is distinct from parent–child security in its substance, origins, and developmental consequences, the goal of improving parent–child relationship processes in many public health programs is unlikely to address the needs of children who have concerns about their safety and security when parents have disagreements. Although it is premature to offer authoritative recommendations for treatment and policy, we argue that programs focusing on interparental relationship processes are a necessary part of alleviating the burden of child mental illness. Research on interparental discord will also be an important guide in (a) establishing techniques for screening and identifying children at greater risk for experiencing mental illness in discordant homes, (b) delineating targets and goals of intervention and prevention programs, and (c) formulating evidenced-based treatment tools (see Davies, Winter, & Cicchetti, 2006).

Recommended Reading

Cummings, E.M., Schermerhorn, A.C., Davies, P.T., Goeke-Morey, M.C., & Cummings, J.S. (2006). (See References). A representative paper describing two empirical studies that provide longitudinal tests of emotional insecurity as an explanatory mechanism in the link between interparental conflict and child adjustment.

Davies, P.T., Harold, G.T., Goeke-Morey, M., Cummings, E.M. (2002). (See References). A monograph presenting a relatively comprehensive, highly accessible overview of the primary assumptions of emotional security theory and four empirical studies designed to test the primary hypotheses of the theory.

Davies, P.T., & Sturge-Apple, M.L. (2007). (See References). This review provides a theoretical reformulation of the emotional security theory within an evolutionary and ethological framework.

Grych, J.H., & Fincham, F.D. (Eds.). (2001). (See References). An edited volume providing a thorough, wide-ranging analysis of the state of empirical, theoretical, and clinical work on children's functioning in high-conflict homes.

Johnston, J.R., & Roseby, V. (1997). *In the name of the child: A developmental approach to understanding and helping children of conflicted and violent divorce*. New York: Free Press. Provides a highly accessible and vividly descriptive, clinical account of how children cope and function in the context of high levels of interparental conflict.

Acknowledgments—Patrick Davies was supported by the National Institute of Mental Health during the preparation of this article (Projects 2R01 MH57318 and R01 MH071256).

Note

1. Address correspondence to Patrick Davies, Department of Clinical and Social Sciences in Psychology, University of Rochester, Rochester, NY 14627; e-mail: patrick. davies@rochester.edu.

References

Baumeister, R.F., Vohs, K.D., & Tice, D.M. (2007). The strength model of self-control. *Current Directions in Psychological Science, 16,* 351–355.

Bowlby, J. (1969). *Attachment and loss. Vol. I: Attachment*. New York: Basic Books.

Cummings, E.M., & Davies, P. (1996). Emotional security as a regulatory process in normal development and the development of psychopathology. *Development and Psychopathology, 8,* 123–139.

Cummings, E.M., Schermerhorn, A.C., Davies, P.T., Goeke-Morey, M.C., & Cummings, J.S. (2006). Interparental discord and child adjustment: Prospective investigations of emotional security as an explanatory mechanism. *Child Development, 77,* 132–152.

Davies, P.T., & Cummings, E.M. (1994). Marital conflict and child adjustment: An emotional security hypothesis. *Psychological Bulletin, 116,* 387–411.

Davies, P.T., & Cummings, E.M. (2006). Interparental discord, family process, and developmental psychopathology. In D. Cicchetti & D.J. Cohen (Eds.), *Developmental psychopathology: Vol. 3. Risk, disorder, and adaptation* (2nd ed., pp. 86–128). New York: Wiley & Sons.

Davies, P.T., Harold, G.T., Goeke-Morey, M., & Cummings, E.M. (2002). Children's emotional security and interparental conflict. *Monographs of the Society for Research in Child Development, 67,* 1–129.

Davies, P.T., & Sturge-Apple, M.L. (2007). Advances in the formulation of emotional security theory: An ethologically-based perspective. *Advances in Child Behavior and Development, 35*, 87–137.

Davies, P.T., Sturge-Apple, M.L., Winter, M.A., Cummings, E.M., & Farrell, D. (2006). Child adaptational development in contexts of interparental conflict over time. *Child Development, 77*, 218–233.

Davies, P.T., Winter, M.A., & Cicchetti, D. (2006). The implications of emotional security theory for understanding and treating childhood psychopathology. *Development and Psychopathology, 18*, 707–735.

Davies, P.T., Woitach, M.J., Winter, M.A., & Cummings, E.M. (in press). Children's insecure representations of the interparental relationship and their school adjustment: The mediating role of attention difficulties. *Child Development*.

Ellis, B.J., Jackson, J.J., & Boyce, W.T. (2006). The stress response systems: Universality and adaptive individual differences. *Developmental Review, 26*, 175–212.

Frosch, C.A., Mangelsdorf, S.C., & McHale, J.L. (2000). Marital behavior and the security of preschooler–parent attachment relationships. *Journal of Family Psychology, 14*, 144–161.

Garcia O'Hearn, H., Margolin, G., & John, R.S. (1997). Mothers' and fathers' reports of children's reactions to naturalistic marital conflict. *Journal of the American Academy of Child and Adolescent Psychiatry, 36*, 1366–1373.

Gilbert, P. (2001). Evolutionary approaches to psychopathology: The role of natural defences. *Australian and New Zealand Journal of Psychiatry, 35*, 17–27.

Grych, J.H., & Fincham, F.D. (Eds.). (2001). *Interparental conflict and child development: Theory, research, and application*. New York: Cambridge University Press.

Harold, G.T., Shelton, K.H., Goeke-Morey, M.C., & Cummings, E.M. (2004). Marital conflict, child emotional security about family relationships and child adjustment. *Social Development, 13*, 350–376.

Hilburn-Cobb, C. (2004). Adolescent psychopathology in terms of multiple behavioral systems: The role of attachment and controlling strategies and frankly disorganized behavior. In L. Atkinson & S. Goldberg (Eds.), *Attachment issues in psychopathology and intervention* (pp. 95–135). Mahwah, NJ: Erlbaum.

Hofmann, S.G., Moscovitch, D.A., & Heinrichs, N. (2004). Evolutionary mechanisms of fear and anxiety. In P. Gilbert (Ed.), *Evolutionary theory and cognitive therapy* (pp. 119–136). New York, NY: Springer Publishing.

Sturge-Apple, M.L., Davies, P.T., Winter, M.A., Cummings, E.M., & Schermerhorn, A. (in press). Interparental conflict and children's school adjustment: The explanatory role of children's internal representations of family relationships. *Developmental Psychology*.

This article has been reprinted as it originally appeared in *Current Directions in Psychological Science*. Citation information for this article as originally published appears above.

Beyond Quality: Parental and Residential Stability and Children's Adjustment

Emma K. Adam[1]

School of Education and Social Policy, Northwestern University

Abstract

In identifying environmental factors affecting children's development, researchers have typically focused on the quality of children's home or family environments. Less attention has been paid to environmental stability as a factor influencing children's well-being. This is partially due to outdated notions of children's living arrangements and to the fact that children in the least stable environments are often the hardest to involve and retain in research. Recent research suggests that there are associations between the degree of environmental instability and difficulties in adjustment, such that children exposed to higher levels of family instability (e.g., more frequent separations from parent figures and more frequent residential moves) show worse adjustment across a variety of developmental domains. Although there is still uncertainty regarding the causal direction of these associations (does instability cause children's problems or do the problems cause instability?), the sources and consequences of family instability clearly deserve greater attention in future research on child and adolescent adjustment.

Keywords

parental separation; residential mobility; adjustment

Children's home or family lives have long been considered a primary environmental context influencing their cognitive, social, emotional, behavioral, and physical development. Although modern-day developmental theories also recognize the important influences of genetic factors and extrafamilial factors on children's outcomes, these variables have been found to have much of their effect through their influence on children's home environments (Collins, Maccoby, Steinberg, Hetherington, & Bornstein, 2000).

Many aspects of children's family environments have been studied. These variables include family structure or composition, family economic and learning resources, and the quality of parent-child relationships (Collins et al., 2000; Linver, Brooks-Gunn, & Kohen, 2002). Even when measured at multiple time points, however, these variables are typically treated as providing a "snapshot" of the quality of a child's home environment at each time. Rarely has the degree of change in children's home environments over time been treated as the primary variable of interest in research on child adjustment.

FAMILY INSTABILITY AS THE VARIABLE OF INTEREST

As many of us are aware from our own lives, family circumstances are not static. We move, change jobs, get sick, separate from romantic partners, and lose loved ones. For most people, these are relatively infrequent events. For others, change is a frequent and even defining feature of their home lives. Recent research has demonstrated that the degree of family instability children are exposed to is a strong predictor of their developmental adjustment (Ackerman, Kogos, Youngstrom, Schoff, & Izard, 1999; E.K. Adam & Chase-Lansdale, 2002).

Many family-instability variables can be studied, including changes in marital status and household composition, separations from parent figures, changes in physical residence, and episodes of antisocial behavior or mental or physical illness in the family. Because many of these events occur more often for low-income families than for families with more economic resources, family instability has been proposed as one mechanism explaining the associations between poverty and negative child outcomes (Ackerman et al., 1999; Linver et al., 2002).

In this review, I focus on two indicators of family instability that Chase-Lansdale and I investigated in a recent study of a sample of low-income adolescent girls: residential moves and separations from parent figures (E.K. Adam & Chase-Lansdale, 2002). *By residential moves,* I mean physical changes of residence, including moves that adolescents make either with their families or on their own. *By separations from parent figures,* I mean major separations[2] from any adults the child considers "parental."

Residential moves and separations from parent figures are both highly disruptive events in children's lives, and both are relatively easily quantified. These events are not uncommon, particularly in low-income populations. Among the girls in our study, 15% had experienced at least one separation from a mother figure, and 42% had experienced at least one separation from a father figure. They had lived with a range of 1 to 5 parent figures in their lifetime and had experienced from 0 to 6 major parental separations. The numbers of residential moves experienced in the past 5 years ranged from 0 to 10. Such events are not restricted to low-income families, however—16% of the U.S. population moved the year these data were collected (Faber, 1998).

SEPARATIONS FROM PARENT FIGURES AND CHILDREN'S ADJUSTMENT

Interest in separations from parent figures emerged from research on how loss of a parent affects children's mental health, as well as from research on the effects of divorce on children. In an early instability study, K.S. Adam, Bouckoms, and Streiner (1982) found that suicidal adolescents and adults were more likely to have experienced the loss of a parent through death, divorce, or separation, and to have experienced a generally disorganized, unpredictable home life, than were nonsuicidal individuals who were the same age and gender and similar in demographic background. Although early research treated divorce as a one-time event, later researchers noted that divorce is often associated with multiple changes in family structure, including the loss of the father from the home and subsequent remarriages and divorces of the mother. Studies found that multiple changes in a mother's partners have a cumulative negative effect on her children's social, emotional, educational, and behavioral outcomes (Capaldi & Patterson, 1991; Kurdek, Fine, & Sinclair, 1994).

Prior research has focused primarily on changes in children's contact with their fathers, rarely acknowledging that children experience major separations from their mothers as well. In our sample of adolescent girls, Chase-Lansdale and I found that as the number of separations from parent figures increased, adolescents showed higher levels of adjustment problems on an index measuring cognitive, emotional, academic, and behavioral functioning (E.K. Adam & Chase-Lansdale, 2002). (See Fig. 1.) Separations from mother figures and father figures were both significantly and independently related to the girls' adjustment. Separations from temporary (less than 2 years) and long-standing (more than 2 years) caregivers, and those occurring early in childhood, in middle childhood, and during adolescence, all had significant effects on adjustment. The effects of separations were independent of family demographics and the quality of current relationships with parents and peers, as well as neighborhood environments.

How and why might separations from parent figures have these effects? Attachment theorists have long argued that children's feelings of security are strongly determined by their internalized perceptions of the availability of their primary caregivers. Although threats to the availability of caregivers have their most visible effect in infants, such threats provoke profound feelings of anxiety, anger, and despair throughout childhood and adolescence, and therefore have implications for emotional health (Kobak, 1999). Kochanska (2003) also provided evidence that the internalized history of mutual positive emotion and trust between a parent and child ("mutually responsive orientation") is an important basis for conscience.

What happens when this internalized sense of emotional security and mutual trust is disrupted by a major separation from a parent? Negative implications for emotional health and behavior could be expected. What happens if a child experiences this kind of disruption repeatedly? An anecdote illustrates one possible answer. A child living in foster care, who had lived with five different caregivers

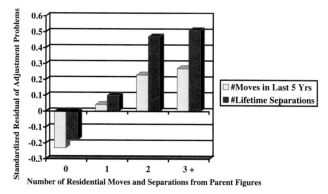

Fig. 1. Adolescents' adjustment problems as a function of two indicators of environmental instability: number of residential moves in the previous 5 years and number of separations from parent figures. The standardized residual measure of adjustment controls for household demographics and quality of the current environment, so that any effects of those variables are removed. Reprinted with permission from E.K. Adam and Chase-Lansdale (2002). Copyright 2002 by the American Psychological Association.

before the age of 6, was told: "You are a wonderful and special girl." She responded: "Then why does everybody leave me?" The violation of trust involved in the repeated loss of caregivers has implications not only for perceptions of other people, but also for perceptions of the self.

At the same time that the child is experiencing the emotional impact of a separation, he or she may also be losing an important source of social support. He or she may also experience dramatic changes in daily routines and reductions in the quality of care provided by the remaining adult or adults in the household.

RESIDENTIAL MOBILITY AND CHILDREN'S ADJUSTMENT

Sociological and epidemiological research on residential mobility has shown that a high rate of residential moves predicts social-emotional, behavioral, and educational problems, even when controlling for family characteristics contributing to a greater likelihood of moving (Pribesh & Downey, 1999; Wood, Halfon, Scarlata, Newacheck, & Nessim, 1993). In our study, the number of moves adolescents had experienced in the prior 5 years was positively associated with the number of adjustment problems they had (see Fig. 1), and this association was independent of the effects of separations from parent figures, family demographic characteristics, and the quality of the adolescents' current environments (E.K. Adam & Chase-Lansdale, 2002).

Researchers interested in explaining the effects of residential moves on children have proposed that these effects are due to the loss of familiar physical environments, activities, and routines; the loss of social-support networks; or decreases in parents' well-being and parenting quality. One study (Pribesh & Downey, 1999) found evidence that children's loss of prior social connections is indeed an important mechanism. Characteristics such as the age or sex of the child, family structure, and parental support have been found to moderate the effects of moves on children (Simmons, Burgeson, Carlton-Ford, & Blyth, 1987).

THE CAUSALITY PROBLEM

Clearly, the associations between family instability and children's and adolescents' adjustment problems can be explained in various ways. There is still considerable debate regarding the causal direction of these associations. Rather than family instability causing children's problems, children's adjustment problems may be the cause of family instability, or preexisting characteristics of families and communities may cause both family instability and adjustment problems. Evidence exists, for example, that children of couples who later divorce exhibit problematic behavior prior to the divorce (Cherlin, Chase-Lansdale, & McRae, 1998), that mothers who change partners tend to have preexisting personality attributes that contribute to unstable relationships (Capaldi & Patterson, 1991), and that families who move more frequently have more disadvantages than other families prior to their moves (Pribesh & Downey, 1999). Researchers strive to measure and statistically control for such possibilities, but adequate data have not always been available to rule out these alternative explanations. Experimental research on non-human primates, however, has shown that random assignment to high levels of social disruption results in an array of serious social, emotional, and physical health problems (Kaplan, 1983). At a minimum, the current findings indicate that high levels of separations from parent figures and residential moves are important markers that may be used to identify children at high risk for adjustment problems so that intervention efforts may be targeted toward them.

WHY HAS FAMILY INSTABILITY NOT RECEIVED MORE ATTENTION?

There are several reasons why family instability has not received much research attention thus far. First, there has been a reliance on cross-sectional studies, which are poor tools for studying change. Second, much psychological research has been conducted with middle-class families, who tend to have relatively low levels of instability. Third, studies often select traditional family types as a means of "control," thus automatically excluding children with unusual or changing family experiences. Fourth, narrowly worded questions about family, such as questions that ask about only biological parents rather than all potentially important adult figures, may fail to illuminate the complexity and changeability of children's family lives. Finally, families with the highest amount of instability are often the hardest to recruit, track, and retain in research.

CUMULATIVE INSTABILITY INDICES

In my research, the independent effects of residential moves and separations from parents on adolescent adjustment were assessed. Other researchers have added together multiple instability factors to form a single index (Ackerman et al., 1999) and tested the effect of this cumulative measure of instability. Whether it is more informative to cumulate or to separate different aspects of family instability remains to be determined. Arguments can be made for both approaches. Cumulative indices describe the total degree of instability children are exposed to, and may therefore produce stronger effects, but separate instability indicators could illuminate the processes by which particular instability factors relate to specific outcomes.

The cumulative perspective suggests that normative changes that take place during individual development, such as those associated with puberty, also are important aspects of instability and may increase the impact of external events. Simmons et al. (1987) found that early adolescents coping with several life changes concurrently (including normative changes and other less typical events) were at high risk for problematic outcomes. They suggested that adolescents need an "arena of comfort" involving continuity in at least some spheres of their lives. This notion of arena of comfort could be easily extended to explain the effects of instability on younger children and adults during periods of developmental transition.

FOCI FOR FUTURE RESEARCH

Numerous issues remain to be examined in future research on the effects of instability on children; the following recommendations should be considered.

First, future studies should use prospective longitudinal data, preferably from representative samples including the full range of socioeconomic and family circumstances. Whether the effects of instability vary across different socioeconomic, racial-ethnic, and other subgroups needs to be explored. Second, a wider range of instability variables should be examined. Any variable contributing to disruption, unpredictability, or chaos in a child's life is a reasonable candidate. Such variables should be examined both independently and as part of a cumulative instability index, and the impact of the developmental timing of each instability event should be considered. Third, the interaction between the quality and stability of children's environments needs to be examined. Is a stable but low-quality environment better than a typically high-quality one punctuated by occasional disruption? Does previously having experienced a high-quality home environment buffer the individual from the effects of later disruption?

Fourth, physiological and physical health outcomes should be examined. Animal research and research on human stress physiology show that predictability and control are important variables determining the organism's ability to contain physiological stress responses, and that low predictability and control contribute to increases in physiological stress and worse health outcomes. Given the low control and predictability associated with family instability, its impact on physiological variables and health outcomes is of interest. Fifth, an experimental intervention approach, in which some children from unstable environments are randomly chosen to receive interventions that increase social stability, would help resolve the causality issue. For example, children in long-term foster care could be purposefully maintained in the same home, school, and neighborhood, so that they do not experience additional disruptions, or they could be provided a single case worker who would support them through any and all transitions. Studies of this nature could provide persuasive evidence that would bolster the argument for undertaking more widespread policy initiatives aimed at increasing the degree of stability in children's home lives.

In this review, I have suggested that in order to understand children's adjustment, researchers need to move beyond a focus on quality and also consider the degree of disruption or change children experience in their home environments. Although issues of causality remain to be clarified, family instability is a clear marker of risk for adjustment problems. In the past, developmental psychologists have encouraged practitioners and policymakers to ensure high quality in children's relationships and physical environments. If research continues to show that family instability is an important predictor of children's adjustment problems, ensuring high levels of stability in children's interpersonal relationships and physical environments will be an important additional policy recommendation, with implications for foster care, child custody, housing, and other child and family policies.

Recommended Reading

Ackerman, B.P., Kogos, J., Youngstrom, E., Schoff, K., & Izard, C. (1999). (See References)
Adam, E.K., & Chase-Lansdale, P.L. (2002). (See References)
Wood, D., Halfon, N., Scarlata, D., Newacheck, P., & Nessim, S. (1993). (See References)

Acknowledgments—This research was funded through support from the Carnegie Corporation of New York, the Ford Foundation, the Harrison Steans Foundation, the Social Sciences and Humanities Research Council of Canada, and the Alfred P. Sloan Foundation.

Notes

1. Address correspondence to Emma K. Adam, School of Education and Social Policy, Northwestern University, Evanston, IL 60208; e-mail: ek-adam@northwestern.edu.

2. Major separations are long-term separations that violate children's expectations for regular contact with their caregiver; they do not include short-term or predictable separations such as regular day-care experiences.

References

Ackerman, B.P., Kogos, J., Youngstrom, E., Schoff, K., & Izard, C. (1999). Family instability and the problem behaviors of children from economically disadvantaged families. *Developmental Psychology, 35*, 258–268.

Adam, E.K., & Chase-Lansdale, P.L. (2002). Home sweet home(s): Parental separations, residential moves and adjustment in low-income adolescent girls. *Developmental Psychology, 38*, 792–805.

Adam, K.S., Bouckoms, A., & Streiner, D. (1982). Parental loss and family stability in attempted suicide. *Archives of General Psychiatry, 39*, 1081–1085.

Capaldi, D.M., & Patterson, G.R. (1991). Relation of parent transitions to boys' adjustment problems: I. A linear hypothesis. II. Mothers at risk for transitions and unskilled parenting. *Developmental Psychology, 27*, 489–504.

Cherlin, A.J., Chase-Lansdale, P.L., & McRae, C. (1998). Effect of divorce on mental health through the life course. *American Sociological Review, 63*, 239–249.

Collins, W.A., Maccoby, E.E., Steinberg, L., Hetherington, E.M., & Bornstein, M.H. (2000). Contemporary research on parenting: The case of nature and nurture. *American Psychologist, 55*, 218–232.

Faber, C.S. (1998). *Geographic mobility: March 1996 to March 1997 (Update)* (Report No. P20-510). Washington, DC: U.S. Bureau of the Census.

Kaplan, J.R. (1983). Social stress and atherosclerosis in normocholesterolemic monkeys. *Science, 220*, 733–735.

Kobak, R. (1999). The emotional dynamics of disruptions in attachment relationships: Implications for theory, research, and clinical intervention. In J. Cassidy & P. Shaver (Eds.), *Handbook of attachment* (pp. 21–43). New York: Guilford.

Kochanska, G. (2002). Mutually responsive orientation between mothers and their young children: A context for the early development of conscience. *Current Directions in Psychological Science, 11*, 191–195.

Kurdek, L.A., Fine, M.A., & Sinclair, R.J. (1994). The relation between parenting transitions and adjustment in young adolescents: A multi-sample investigation. *Journal of Early Adolescence, 14*, 412–432.

Linver, M.R., Brooks-Gunn, J., & Kohen, D.E. (2002). Family processes as pathways from income to young children's development. *Developmental Psychology, 38*, 719–734.

Pribesh, S., & Downey, D.B. (1999). Why are residential and school moves associated with poor school performance? *Demography, 36*, 521–534.

Simmons, R.G., Burgeson, R., Carlton-Ford, S., & Blyth, D. (1987). The impact of cumulative change in early adolescence. *Child Development, 58*, 1220–1234.

Wood, D., Halfon, N., Scarlata, D., Newacheck, P., & Nessim, S. (1993). Impact of family relocation on children's growth, development, school function, and behavior. *Journal of the American Medical Association, 270*, 1334–1338.

This article has been reprinted as it originally appeared in *Current Directions in Psychological Science*. Citation information for this article as originally published appears above.

Siblings' Direct and Indirect Contributions to Child Development

Gene H. Brody[1]

Department of Child and Family Development and Center for Family Research, University of Georgia

Abstract

Since the early 1980s, a growing body of research has described the contributions of sibling relationships to child and adolescent development. Interactions with older siblings promote young children's language and cognitive development, their understanding of other people's emotions and perspectives, and, conversely, their development of antisocial behavior. Studies address the ways in which parents' experiences with older children contribute to their rearing of younger children, which in turn contributes to the younger children's development. Finally, by virtue of having a sibling, children may receive differential treatment from their parents. Under some conditions, differential treatment is associated with emotional and behavioral problems in children.

Keywords

siblings; interaction; development; differential treatment

The first studies of the contributions that older siblings make to their younger brothers' and sisters' development were conducted in Britain around the turn of the 20th century by Sir Francis Galton, a cousin of Charles Darwin. Sibling research, however, only recently has begun to address many of the issues that concern families. Parents, clinicians, and now researchers in developmental psychology recognize the significance of the sibling relationship as a contributor to family harmony or discord and to individual children's development. Since the early 1980s, a growing interest in the family has prompted research on those aspects of sibling relationships that contribute to children's cognitive, social, and emotional adjustment. These contributions can be direct, occurring as a result of siblings' encounters with one another, or indirect, occurring through a child's impact on parents that influences the care that other brothers and sisters receive. Differential treatment by parents is a third way in which having a sibling may contribute to child development. Children may be treated differently by their parents than their siblings are, or at least believe that they are treated differently. The development of this belief has implications for children's and adolescents' mental health. In this article, I present an overview of the ways in which siblings' direct and indirect influences and parental differential treatment contribute to child development.

SIBLINGS' DIRECT CONTRIBUTIONS TO DEVELOPMENT

Currently, research suggests that naturally occurring teaching and caregiving experiences benefit cognitive, language, and psychosocial development in both older and younger siblings. Studies conducted in children's homes and in laboratories show that older siblings in middle childhood can teach new cognitive concepts and language skills to their younger siblings in early childhood. Across the middle childhood years, older siblings become better teachers as they learn how to simplify tasks for their younger siblings. The ability to adjust their teaching behaviors to their younger siblings' capacities increases as older siblings develop the ability to take other people's perspectives (Maynard, 2002). Older siblings who assume teaching and caregiving roles earn higher reading and language achievement scores, gain a greater sense of competence in the caregiving role, and learn more quickly to balance their self-concerns with others' needs than do older siblings who do not assume these roles with their younger siblings (Zukow-Goldring, 1995). When caregiving demands on the older sibling become excessive, however, they may interfere with the older child's time spent on homework or involvement in school activities. Caregiving responsibilities during middle childhood and adolescence can compromise older siblings' school performance and behavioral adjustment (Marshall et al., 1997).

Children who are nurtured by their older siblings become sensitive to other people's feelings and beliefs (Dunn, 1988). As in all relationships, though, nurturance does not occur in isolation from conflict. Sibling relationships that are characterized by a balance of nurturance and conflict can provide a unique opportunity for children to develop the ability to understand other people's emotions and viewpoints, to learn to manage anger and resolve conflict, and to provide nurturance themselves. Indeed, younger siblings who experience a balance of nurturance and conflict in their sibling relationships have been found to be more socially skilled and have more positive peer relationships compared with children who lack this experience (Hetherington, 1988).

Sibling relationships also have the potential to affect children's development negatively. Younger siblings growing up with aggressive older siblings are at considerable risk for developing conduct problems, performing poorly in school, and having few positive experiences in their relationships with their peers (Bank, Patterson, & Reid, 1996). The links between older siblings' antisocial behavior and younger siblings' conduct problems are stronger for children living in disadvantaged neighborhoods characterized by high unemployment rates and pervasive poverty than for children living in more advantaged neighborhoods (Brody, Ge, et al., 2003). Younger siblings who live in disadvantaged neighborhoods have more opportunities than do children living in more affluent areas to practice the problematic conduct that they learn during sibling interactions as they interact with peers who encourage antisocial behavior.

The importance of the sibling relationship is probably best demonstrated by older siblings' ability to buffer younger siblings from the negative effects of family turmoil. Younger siblings whose older siblings provide them with emotional support (caring, acceptance, and bolstering of self-esteem) during bouts of intense, angry interparental conflict show fewer signs of behavioral or emotional problems than do children whose older siblings are less supportive (Jenkins, 1992).

SIBLINGS' INDIRECT CONTRIBUTIONS

Conventional wisdom suggests that parents' experiences with older children influence their expectations of subsequent children and the child-rearing strategies that parents consider effective. Similarly, the experiences that other adults, particularly teachers, have with older siblings may influence their expectations and treatment of younger siblings. Research has confirmed the operation of these indirect effects on younger siblings' development. Whiteman and Buchanan (2002) found that experiences with earlier-born children contributed to parents' expectations about their younger children's likelihood of experiencing conduct problems, using drugs, displaying rebellious behavior, or being helpful and showing concern for others. Teachers are not immune from the predisposing effects of experiences with older siblings. As a result of having an older sibling in class or hearing about his or her accomplishments or escapades, teachers develop expectations regarding the younger sibling's academic ability and conduct even before the younger child becomes their student (Bronfenbrenner, 1977). Some parents and teachers translate these expectations into parenting and teaching practices they subsequently use with younger siblings that influence the younger children's beliefs about their academic abilities, interests, and choice of friends; children often choose friends whom they perceive to be similar to themselves.

Rather than viewing behavioral influence as flowing in one direction, from parents to children, developmental psychologists now recognize that these influences are reciprocal. The behaviors that children use during everyday interactions with their parents partially determine the behaviors that the parents direct toward their children. Children with active or emotionally intense personalities receive different, usually more negative, parenting than do children with calm and easygoing personalities. Some studies suggest that older siblings' individual characteristics may contribute indirectly to the quality of parenting that younger siblings receive. For example, East (1998) discovered that negative experiences with an earlier-born child lead parents to question their ability to provide good care for their younger children and to lower their expectations for their younger children's behavior.

In our research, my colleagues and I explored the specific ways in which older siblings' characteristics contribute to the quality of parenting that younger siblings receive, which in turn contributes to younger siblings' development of conduct problems and depressive symptoms. The premise of the study was simple. Rearing older siblings who are doing well in school and are well liked by other children provides parents with opportunities for basking in their children's achievements. (Basking is a phenomenon in which one's psychological well-being increases because of the accomplishments of persons to whom one is close.) Using a longitudinal research design in which we collected data from families for 4 years, we found that academically and socially competent older siblings contributed to an increase in their mothers' self-esteem and a decrease in their mothers' depressive symptoms. Positive changes in mothers' psychological functioning forecast their use of adjustment-promoting parenting practices with younger siblings. Over time, these practices forecast high levels of self-control and low levels of behavior problems and depressive symptoms in the younger siblings (Brody, Kim, Murry, & Brown, 2003). We expect future research to clarify further the indirect pathways through which siblings influence one another's development, including the processes by which children's negative characteristics affect their parents' child-rearing practices. A difficult-to-rear older sibling, for example, may contribute over time to decreases in his or her parents' psychological well-being, resulting in increased tension in the family. Under these circumstances, the parents' negativity and distraction decrease the likelihood that a younger sibling will experience parenting that promotes self-worth, academic achievement, and social skills.

PARENTAL DIFFERENTIAL TREATMENT

Any discussion of siblings' contributions to development would be incomplete without acknowledging parental differential treatment. Having a sibling creates a context in which parental behavior assumes symbolic value, as children use it as a barometer indicating the extent to which they are loved, rejected, included, or excluded by their parents. Children's and adolescents' beliefs that they receive less warmth and more negative treatment from their parents than do their siblings is associated with poor emotional and behavioral functioning (Reiss, Neiderhiser, Hetherington, & Plomin, 2000).

Not all children who perceive differential treatment develop these problems, however. Differential parental treatment is associated with poor adjustment in a child only when the quality of the child's individual relationship with his or her parents is distant and negative. The association between differential treatment and adjustment is weak for children whose parents treat them well, even when their siblings receive even warmer and more positive treatment (Feinberg & Hetherington, 2001). Children's perceptions of the legitimacy of differential treatment also help determine its contribution to their adjustment. Children who perceive their parents' differential behavior to be justified report fewer behavior problems than do children who consider it to be unjust, even under conditions of relatively high levels of differential treatment. Children and adolescents who perceive differential treatment as unfair experience low levels of self-worth and have high levels of behavior problems (Kowal, Kramer, Krull, & Crick, 2002). Children justify differential treatment by citing ways in which they and their siblings differ in age, personality, and special needs. Sensitive parenting entails treating children as their individual temperaments and developmental needs require. Nevertheless, it is important that children understand why parents treat siblings differently from one another so that they will be protected from interpreting the differences as evidence that they are not valued or worthy of love.

FUTURE DIRECTIONS

Considerable work is needed to provide a comprehensive understanding of the processes through which siblings influence one another's cognitive development, language development, psychological adjustment, and social skills. Current studies can best be considered "first generation" research. They describe associations between older and younger siblings' behaviors and characteristics. Some studies have demonstrated that the prediction of younger siblings' outcomes is more accurate if it is based on older siblings' characteristics plus parenting, rather than parenting alone (Brody, Kim, et al., 2003). More research is needed to isolate influences other than parenting, such as shared genetics, shared environments, and social learning, before siblings' unique contributions to development can be specified. The next generation of research will address the ways in which sibling relationships contribute to children's self-images and personal identities, emotion regulation and coping skills, explanations of positive and negative events that occur in family and peer relationships, use of aggression, and involvement in high-risk behaviors.

Recommended Reading

Brody, G.H. (1998). Sibling relationship quality: Its causes and consequences. *Annual Review of Psychology, 49,* 1–24.
Feinberg, M., & Hetherington, E.M. (2001). (See References)
Kowal, A., Kramer, L., Krull, J.L., & Crick, N.R. (2002). (See References)
Maynard, A.E. (2002). (See References)
Whiteman, S.D., & Buchanan, C.M. (2002). (See References)

Acknowledgments—I would like to thank Eileen Neubaum-Carlan for helpful comments. Preparation of this article was partly supported by grants from the National Institute of Child Health and Human Development, the National Institute of Mental Health, and the National Institute on Alcohol Abuse and Alcoholism.

Note

1. Address correspondence to Gene H. Brody, University of Georgia, Center for Family Research, 1095 College Station Rd., Athens, GA 30602-4527.

References

Bank, L., Patterson, G.R., & Reid, J.B. (1996). Negative sibling interaction patterns as predictors of later adjustment problems in adolescent and young adult males. In G.H. Brody (Ed.), *Sibling relationships: Their causes and consequences* (pp. 197–229). Norwood, NJ: Ablex.
Brody, G.H., Ge, X., Kim, S.Y., Murry, V.M., Simons, R.L., Gibbons, F.X., Gerrard, M., & Conger, R. (2003). Neighborhood disadvantage moderates associations of parenting and older sibling problem attitudes and behavior with conduct disorders in African American children. *Journal of Consulting and Clinical Psychology, 71,* 211–222.
Brody, G.H., Kim, S., Murry, V.M., & Brown, A.C. (2003). Longitudinal direct and indirect pathways linking older sibling competence to the development of younger sibling competence. *Developmental Psychology, 39,* 618–628.
Bronfenbrenner, U. (1977). Toward an experimental ecology of human development. *American Psychologist, 32,* 513–531.
Dunn, J. (1988). Connections between relationships: Implications of research on mothers and siblings. In R.A. Hinde & J. Stevenson-Hinde (Eds.), *Relationships within families: Mutual influences* (pp. 168–180). New York: Oxford University Press.
East, P.L. (1998). Impact of adolescent childbearing on families and younger siblings: Effects that increase younger siblings' risk for early pregnancy. *Applied Developmental Science, 2,* 62–74.
Feinberg, M., & Hetherington, E.M. (2001). Differential parenting as a within-family variable. *Journal of Family Psychology, 15,* 22–37.
Hetherington, E.M. (1988). Parents, children, and siblings: Six years after divorce. In R.A. Hinde & J. Stevenson-Hinde (Eds.), *Relationships within families: Mutual influences* (pp. 311–331). New York: Oxford University Press.
Jenkins, J. (1992). Sibling relationships in disharmonious homes: Potential difficulties and protective effects. In F. Boer & J. Dunn (Eds.), *Children's sibling relationships: Developmental and clinical issues* (pp. 125–138). Hillsdale, NJ: Erlbaum.

33

Kowal, A., Kramer, L., Krull, J.L., & Crick, N.R. (2002). Children's perceptions of the fairness of parental preferential treatment and their socioemotional well-being. *Journal of Family Psychology, 16,* 297–306.

Marshall, N.L., Garcia-Coll, C., Marx, F., McCartney, K., Keefe, N., & Ruh, J. (1997). After-school time and children's behavioral adjustment. *Merrill-Palmer Quarterly, 43,* 497–514.

Maynard, A.E. (2002). Cultural teaching: The development of teaching skills in Maya sibling interactions. *Child Development, 73,* 969–982.

Reiss, D., Neiderhiser, J.M., Hetherington, E.M., & Plomin, R. (2000). *The relationship code: Deciphering genetic and social influences on adolescent development.* Cambridge, MA: Harvard University Press.

Whiteman, S.D., & Buchanan, C.M. (2002). Mothers' and children's expectations for adolescence: The impact of perceptions of an older sibling's experience. *Journal of Family Psychology, 16,* 157–171.

Zukow-Goldring, P.G. (1995). Sibling caregiving. In M.H. Bornstein (Ed.), *Handbook of parenting: Vol. 3. Status and social conditions of parenting* (pp. 177–208). Mahwah, NJ: Erlbaum.

Section 1: Critical Thinking Questions

1. The studies reviewed here indicate that environmental effects can be acute or gradual, and immediate or delayed. What does this characteristic of environments imply about the time lag that should be employed as a unit of measurement and analysis in longitudinal studies of the effects of environmental factors?

2. These reports suggest that the interpretation and meaning of the environment to the child may be more important in predicting its impact than any physical characteristic. How should researchers group disparate environmental variables such as divorce, parental death, and birth of a new sibling in designing empirical analyses of the impact of environments on child psychopathology outcomes?

3. A methodological concern with correlational studies of environmental factors is that the conclusions are subject to alternate interpretations, such as the disorder causing the environmental factor or a third variable causing both the environmental factor and the disorder. Discuss how well these articles address the possibility of alternate interpretations of findings.

This article has been reprinted as it originally appeared in *Current Directions in Psychological Science.* Citation information for this article as originally published appears above.

Section 2: How Environments "Get Under the Skin" to Lead to Psychopathology

This section addresses the question of how environmental variables "get under the skin" of the child to affect child psychopathology outcomes. A general model suggests that environmental stressors have their effect by altering internal processes that, in turn, lead to behaviors that are characteristic of child psychopathology.

Studies with rats suggest that environmental adversity leads to parent-offspring interactions that result in enhanced stress reactivity in brain regions known to regulate responses to stress. One specific mechanism is the release of corticotropin-releasing factor in response to childhood trauma, which then leads to mood and anxiety disorders. Some environmental factors operate in utero, but their mechanisms remain unclear. Prenatal maternal stress empirically predicts child psychopathology, but the mechanisms need better articulation. Maternal drug and alcohol use and smoking during pregnancy also are risk factors for psychopathology in offspring, but the mechanisms of this effect are complicated by correlated factors in the mother's life, such as socioeconomic disadvantage, nutrition, and selection factors into maternal substance abuse.

These concepts can be integrated with a model of how exposure to stressors enhances biological sensitivity to context, which sets up a child to respond to later challenges in ways that characterize child psychopathology. However, similar exposure does not lead to the same outcomes in all children, and so the interaction between genes and the environment must be added to a comprehensive model of how the environment gets under the skin.

Maternal Care and Individual Differences in Defensive Responses

Carine Parent, Tie-Yuan Zhang, Christian Caldji, Rose Bagot, Frances A. Champagne, Jens Pruessner, and Michael J. Meaney[1]

McGill Program for the Study of Behavior, Genes and Environment, Douglas Hospital Research Centre, Departments of Psychiatry and Neurology & Neurosurgery, McGill University, Montreal, Quebec, Canada

Abstract

Familial transmission of mental illness is common. Recent studies in behavioral neuroscience and biological psychiatry reveal the importance of epigenetic mechanisms of transmission that center on the developmental consequences of variations in parental care. Studies with rats suggest that environmental adversity results in patterns of parent–offspring interactions that increase stress reactivity through sustained effects on gene expression in brain regions known to regulate behavioral, endocrine, and autonomic responses to stress. While such effects might be adaptive, the associated cost involves an increased risk for stress-related illness.

Keywords

maternal care; stress responses; epigenesis; stress hormones; individual differences

To explain the relation between family function and health in adulthood, researchers have proposed *stress-diathesis* models (Repetti, Taylor, & Seeman, 2002). These models suggest that a decreased quality of parental care alters the development of neural and endocrine systems, increasing the magnitude of emotional, autonomic, and endocrine responses to stress (collectively referred to here as defensive responses) and thus pre-disposing individuals to illness. The term diathesis refers to the interaction between development—including the potential influence of genetic variations—and the prevailing level of stress experienced by an individual in predicting health outcomes. Such models have considerable appeal, and could identify both the origins of illness and the nature of underlying vulnerabilities.

A critical assumption of stress-diathesis models is that the increased expression of defensive responses endangers health. In response to neural signals associated with the perception of a stressor, there is an increased release into the bloodstream of stress hormones, including glucocorticoids from the adrenal gland and catecholamines, particularly norepinephrine, from the sympathetic nervous system. These hormones increase the availability of energy (such as derived from fat and glucose metabolism) to maintain the normal cellular output and organ efficiency and protect against catastrophies such as hypotensive shock (a crash in blood pressure). These stress hormones, along with the release of catecholamines in the brain, increase vigilance and fear and enhance adaptive processes such as avoidance learning and fear conditioning. However, there are costs associated with chronic activation of stress hormones: chronically enhanced emotional arousal, persistent increases in blood sugars and fats, and disruption of sleep and normal cognitive and emotional function. For this reason, chronic activation of defensive responses can predispose individuals to illnesses such as diabetes, heart disease, and mood disorders, and individuals with enhanced stress reactivity are at greater risk for chronic illness. However, insufficient activation of defensive responses under appropriate conditions also compromises health and is associated with chronic fatigue, chronic pain, and hyperinflammation. People walk a fine line.

THE ORIGINS OF INDIVIDUAL DIFFERENCES IN DEFENSIVE RESPONSES

In the late 1950s and early 1960s, psychologists Seymore Levine and Victor Denenberg reported that postnatal handling of infant rats or mice by researchers decreased the magnitude of both behavioral and hypothalamic-pituitary-adrenal (HPA) responses to stress in adulthood (see Fig. 1). These findings demonstrated

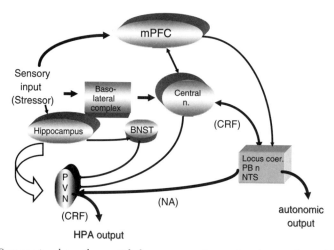

Fig. 1. Systems involving the peptide hormone corticotropin-releasing factor (CRF) that mediate defensive responses to stress in mammals. CRF is released from neurons in the paraventricular hypothalamus (PVN) into the blood supply of the pituitary, activating a hypothalamic–pituitary–adrenal (HPA) response that includes the release of pituitary adrenocorticotropin and glucocorticoids from the adrenal gland. CRF production and release is subsequently inhibited through a negative-feedback system involving the action of glucocorticoids in a number of brain regions including the hippocampus. CRF is also produced in the neurons of the central nucleus of the amygdala and the bed nucleus of the stria terminalis (BNST) that project directly to the locus coeruleus and nucleus tractus solitarius (NTS)/parabrachial nucleus (PBn), stimulating the increased release of noradrenaline (NA) throughout the forebrain, including the medial prefrontal cortex (mPFC) and the PVN.

the influence of the early environment on the development of rudimentary defensive responses to threat. Levine and others suggested that the effects of handling are actually mediated by changes in maternal care. Indeed handling by the researcher increases the licking and grooming of pups by the mother (e.g., Liu et al., 1997), a major source of tactile stimulation for newborn rats. Subsequent studies examining the consequences of naturally occurring variations in pup licking and grooming among lactating rats support the maternal-mediation hypothesis. Thus, the adult offspring of mothers that naturally exhibit increased levels of pup licking and grooming (high-LG mothers) resemble postnatally handled animals on measures of behavioral and endocrine responses to stress, while those of low-LG mothers are comparable to animals that weren't handled (Liu et al., 1997; Caldji et al., 1998). Specifically, the offspring of high-LG mothers show reduced fearfulness and more modest HPA responses to stress. Cross-fostering studies, in which pups born to high-LG mothers are raised by low-LG mothers (and vice versa), suggest a direct relationship between maternal care and the postnatal development of individual differences in behavioral and HPA responses to stress (Francis, Diorio, Liu, & Meaney, 1999).

It is important to note that, in these rodent studies, the experimental design is one that maximizes the chances of detecting maternal effects. Following weaning, animals are housed under very stable laboratory conditions. Although the maternal effects are certainly reliable, the environmental complexity of a real natural setting that would normally be experienced in the post-weaning period might obscure such effects. Nevertheless, these studies also suggest that rather subtle variations within a normal range of parental care can dramatically alter development. In large measure, this is likely due to the fact that natural selection has shaped offspring to respond to subtle variations in parental behaviors as a forecast of the environmental conditions they will ultimately face following independence from the parent (Hinde 1986).

The effects of maternal care on the development of defensive responses to stress in rats involve alterations in the production and activity of a hormone called corticotropin-releasing factor (CRF; Fig. 1) in brain regions that activate behavioral, emotional, autonomic, and endocrine responses to stressors. As adults, the offspring of high-LG mothers showed decreased CRF production in the hypothalamus, as well as reduced plasma adrenocorticotropin (ACTH) and glucocorticoid responses to acute stress, as compared with the adult offspring of low-LG mothers (Liu et al., 1997). The offspring of the high- and low-LG mothers also differed in behavioral responses to novelty (Caldji et al., 1998; Francis et al., 1999). As adults, the offspring of high-LG mothers showed decreased startle responses, substantially less fear in novel environments, and decreased defensive burying of an electrified probe placed into the home cage.

Increased pup licking and grooming is associated with enhanced sensitivity in systems that inhibit CRF expression, including the hippocampal glucocorticoid receptor and the receptor for the neurotransmitter $GABA_A$ in the amygdala. Both effects involve sustained alterations in gene expression (or activity) as a function of maternal care. The complexity of such maternal effects on gene expression is apparent in the alterations in $GABA_A$ receptor function. The adult offspring of high-LG mothers show significantly increased expression of specific proteins within this receptor that increase its function of inhibiting CRF expression; this effect is unique to the amygdala and is reversed with cross-fostering. Thus, for both the glucocorticoid-receptor feedback system and the $GABA_A$ receptor there is an increased capacity for the inhibition of stress responses as a function of maternal licking and grooming. These findings suggest that maternal care can "program" responses to stress in the offspring through effects on the expression of genes in brain regions that mediate responses to stress. These findings provide a potential mechanism for the influence of parental care on vulnerability or resistance to stress-induced illness over the lifespan.

TRANSGENERATIONAL EFFECTS

Maternal effects might serve as a possible nongenomic, or *epigenetic,* mechanism by which selected traits are transmitted across generations. Indeed, low-LG mothers are more fearful than high-LG mothers are: Fearful mothers beget more stress-reactive offspring. The question concerns the mode of inheritance. The results of cross-fostering studies cited above indicate that individual differences in stress reactivity or in the expression of relevant genes can be directly altered by maternal behavior. A critical finding of the cross-fostering studies is that individual differences in maternal behavior are also transmitted from mothers to female offspring. Hence, the female offspring of more fearful, low-LG mothers are, as adults, more fearful, low-LG mothers. The mechanism for the intergenerational transmission of such individual differences is the difference in pup licking and grooming.

Variations in pup licking and grooming involve individual differences in estrogen-receptor-gene expression in the medial preoptic area (MPOA) of the hypothalamus, a region that is critical for maternal behavior in the rat. Estrogen increases oxytocin-receptor levels in this region; oxytocin appears to act there to facilitate the release of dopamine from neurons in another region called the ventral tegmental nucleus. The increased dopamine release activates maternal licking and grooming (Champagne, Stevenson, Gratton, & Meaney, 2004). Infusing an oxytocin-receptor antagonist directly into the brain completely eliminates the differences in maternal behavior between high- and low-LG mothers. And again, differences in estrogen-receptor expression or in oxytocin-receptor levels are reversed with cross-fostering, suggesting that maternal care regulates the activity of the estrogen receptor, forming the basis for subsequent "inherited" differences in maternal behavior (Champagne, Weaver, Diorio, Sharma, & Meaney, 2003).

ADAPTIVE VALUE OF ENHANCED STRESS REACTIVITY IN MAMMALS

The interesting question is, why bother? Why would nature configure such a process? Why transmit individual differences in stress reactivity across generations?

Environmental adversity influences emotional well-being in parents, and these effects are reflected in alterations in parental care. In humans, parental depression and anxiety are associated with harsh, inconsistent discipline, neglect, and abuse, which can enhance stress reactivity of the offspring. In other words, the anxiety of parents is transmitted to their offspring. Since offspring usually inhabit an environment that is similar to their parents, the transmission of individual differences in traits from parent to offspring could be adaptive with respect to survival. Adversity over the adult life of the parent is likely to predict more of the same for the offspring. Under conditions of increased environmental demand, it is commonly in the animal's interest to enhance its behavioral (e.g., vigilance, fearfulness) and endocrine (HPA and metabolic/cardiovascular) responses to stress. These responses promote detection of potential threats, fear conditioning to stimuli associated with threats, and avoidance learning. Moreover, stress hormones mobilize energy reserves, essential for animals exposed to famine. Impoverished environments are also commonly associated with multiple sources of infection, and adrenal glucocorticoids are a potent defense against increased immunological activity that can lead to septic shock (organ failure). Rats with increased HPA responses to bacteria are at reduced risk for septic shock. These findings underscore the potentially adaptive value of increased HPA responses to threat.

THE EFFECTS OF STRESS ON MATERNAL BEHAVIOR IN MAMMALS

If parent–offspring interactions are to serve as a forecast for the young, then there must be a predictable relation between the quality of the environment and parental care. Perhaps the most compelling evidence for such a relation emerges from the studies of Rosenblum, Coplan, and colleagues with nonhuman primates (Coplan et al., 1996). In Bonnet macaque mother–infant pairs kept in conditions requiring extensive maternal effort to obtain food, there were severe disruptions in the quality of mother–infant interactions. Infants of mothers housed under these conditions were more timid and fearful and, even while in contact with their mothers, actually showed signs of depression commonly observed in infants who have been separated from their mothers. As adolescents, the infants reared in the more demanding conditions were more fearful and submissive and showed less social-play behavior. As expected, these conditions affected the development of neural systems that mediate behavioral and endocrine response to stress, increasing their CRF levels and their noradrenergic responses to stress. It will be fascinating to see if these traits are then transmitted to the next generation.

The critical issue is the effect of environmental adversity on maternal behavior. High-LG rat mothers exposed daily to stress during pregnancy showed a decrease in their licking and grooming to levels comparable to those of low-LG mothers. And the effects on maternal behavior were apparent in the offspring. As adults, the offspring of high-LG mothers who had been gestationally stressed were comparable to those of low-LG mothers on measures of behavioral responses to stress. These effects were due to a "prenatal stress" effect, as the decreased maternal licking and grooming and the same developmental scenario were apparent in a subsequent litter, even in the absence of any further experimental manipulation. The effects of gestational stress were also apparent in the

41

maternal behavior of the female offspring. The female offspring of high-LG mothers exposed to gestational stress, even in a previous pregnancy, behaved toward their pups in a manner consistent with the behavior of their mothers; as adults, these females were low-LG mothers with reduced levels of oxytocin-receptor binding in the MPOA. Hence the effects of environmental adversity are transmitted from parent to offspring.

IMPLICATIONS

The question of vulnerability lies very much at the heart of research on anxiety disorders such as posttraumatic stress disorder (PTSD). Surprisingly, only a minority (roughly 20–30%) of people subjected to profound trauma develop PTSD, and early family life serves as a highly significant predictor of vulnerability to PTSD following trauma. These findings suggest that early-life events might alter the development of neural systems in brain regions that mediate emotional and cognitive responses to adversity and thus contribute to individual differences in vulnerability to anxiety disorders. Childhood abuse significantly alters autonomic and HPA responses to stress (Heim et al., 2000); and there is evidence for more subtle effects that do not involve stressors as extreme as persistent neglect or abuse. For example, Maternal Care scores on the Parental Bonding Index predict trait anxiety, HPA responses to stress, and stress-induced activation of the brain catecholamine system (Pruessner, Champagne, Meaney & Dagher, 2004).

There is also evidence that vulnerability to anxiety disorders may be transmitted from generation to generation. Yehuda et al. (2000) found that the adult offspring of Holocaust survivors exhibited altered HPA function and were at increased risk for PTSD. More recent studies suggest that the intergenerational transmission of the risk for PTSD in this population is mediated by alterations in parental care. This finding is consistent with earlier studies revealing that anxiety is a strong, negative predictor of maternal responsiveness in humans.

Recent studies reflect the potential for the epigenetic transmission of individual differences in behavior and gene expression from parent to offspring. Studies with humans and nonhuman primates show that variants of the serotonin-transporter gene (which metabolizes serotonin) are associated with forms of temperament that predispose individuals to depression and alcoholism (Bennett et al., 2002; Caspi et al., 2003). However, this effect is modified by environmental conditions, especially the availability of parent–offspring interactions, prevailing during early development. In macaques, normal mother–infant relations reduced the risk for impaired serotonin metabolism and impulse control that is otherwise associated with the serotonin-transporter variant. These findings remind us that measures of heritability, by definition, reflect both variation in the genome and interactions between genes and the environment.

Traits that render individuals vulnerable for psychopathology emerge as a function of the constant interaction of genes and environment over the course of development. Indeed, there is currently considerable confusion in distinguishing the characteristics of pathology from those of developmentally determined vulnerabilities. In a study involving Vietnam veterans and their twins, Gilbertson et al. (2002) found that individuals who experienced combat service in Vietnam and developed PTSD showed reduced hippocampal volume by comparison to those with a similar military history but no PTSD; importantly, the twins who never served in Vietnam or showed PTSD showed the same difference, suggesting that the reduced hippocampal volume is a trait that preceded the PTSD. These and other studies focus researchers on the developmental origins of psychopathology and on critical questions, such as how reduced hippocampal volume or other neurobiological aspects of phenotypes might render individuals vulnerable to psychopathology.

Nowhere is the interplay between genes and environment more evident than in the relationships that exist between family environment and vulnerability or resistance to chronic illness. Vulnerability for mental illness is increased by a wide range of risk factors that are common in families living in conditions of adversity, such as low socioeconomic status. These risk factors include genetic variations, complications of pregnancy and birth, familial dysfunction, child abuse and neglect, and maternal depression. Such factors define "risky" families (Repetti, Taylor, & Seeman, 2002). All forms of mental disorders are "familial"—they run in families—and the mechanisms by which vulnerability is transmitted from parent to offspring involve both genomic and epigenetic processes of transmission. The challenge is to clearly define the mechanisms of transmission; the reward would be the ability to identify remarkably effective targets for prevention. Of particular interest are the parent–child relations that define family life and the mechanisms by which the effects of family life become "biologically embedded," thereby influencing vulnerability and resistance. We (Weaver et al., 2004) recently described the effect of maternal care on the structure (not sequence) of the DNA that regulates the activity of the gene encoding for the glucocorticoid receptor in the hippocampus. These epigenetic modifications of the DNA regulate glucocorticoid-receptor expression and thus HPA responses to stress. Such findings might illustrate the processes by which a dynamic environment interacts with a fixed genome to produce a phenotype. Understanding such processes requires not only the relevant biological tools but a clear understanding of the relevant environmental signals. Obviously, such studies will require a commitment to research at the biological, psychological, and social levels of analysis.

Recommended Reading

McEwen, B.S. (1998). Protective and damaging effects of stress mediators. *New England Journal of Medicine, 338,* 171–179.

Meaney, M.J. (2001). The development of individual differences in behavioral and endocrine responses to stress. *Annual Reviews of Neuroscience, 24,* 1161–1192.

Repetti, R.L., Taylor, S.E., Seeman, T.E. (2002). (See References)

Acknowledgments—The authors' research is supported by grants from the Canadian Institutes for Health Research, the Natural Sciences and Engineering Research Council of Canada, and the National Institutes of Health, and by career awards from the Canadian Institutes for Health Research and the National Alliance for Research on Schizophrenia and Related Disorders.

Note

1. Address correspondence to Michael J. Meaney, McGill Program for the Study of Behaviour, Genes and Environment, Douglas Hospital Research Centre, 6875 boul. LaSalle, Montréal, Québec, Canada H4H 1R3; e-mail: michael.meaney@mcgill.ca.

References

Bennett, A.J., Lesch, K.P., Heils, A., Long, J.C., Lorenz, J.G., Shoaf, S.E., Champoux, M., Suomi, S.J., Linnoila, M.V., & Higley, J.D. (2002). Early experience and serotonin transporter gene variation interact to influence primate CNS function. *Molecular Psychiatry, 7,* 118–122.

Caldji, C., Tannenbaum, B., Sharma, S., Francis, D., Plotsky, P.M., & Meaney, M.J. (1998). Maternal care during infancy regulates the development of neural systems mediating the expression of behavioral fearfulness in adulthood in the rat. *Proceedings of the National Academy of Sciences USA, 95,* 5335–5340.

Caspi, A., Sugden, K., Moffitt, T.E., Taylor, A., Caraig, I.W., Harrington, H., McClay, J., Mill, J., Martin, J., Braithwaite, A., & Poulton, R. (2003). Influence of life stress on depression: Moderation by a polymorphism in the 5-HTT gene. *Science, 301,* 386–390.

Champagne, F.A., Stevenson, C., Gratton, A., & Meaney, M.J. (2004). Individual differences in maternal behavior are mediated by dopamine release in the nucleus accumbens. *Journal of Neuroscience, 24,* 4113–4123.

Champagne, F.A., Weaver, I.C.G., Diorio, J., Sharma, S., & Meaney, M.J. (2003). Natural Variations in Maternal Care are associated with Estrogen Receptor Alpha Expression and Estrogen Sensitivity in the MPOA. *Endocrinology, 144,* 4720–4724.

Coplan, J.D., Andrews, M.W., Rosenblum, L.A., Owens, M.J., Friedman, S., Gorman, J.M., & Nemeroff, C.B. (1996). Persistent elevations of cerebrospinal fluid concentrations of corticotropin-releasing factor in adult nonhuman primates exposed to early-life stressors: Implications for the pathophysiology of mood and anxiety disorders. *Proceedings of the National Academy of Sciences USA, 93,* 1619–1623.

Francis, D.D., Diorio, J., Liu, D., & Meaney, M.J. (1999). Nongenomic transmission across generations in maternal behavior and stress responses in the rat. *Science, 286,* 1155–1158.

Gilbertson, M.W., Shenton, M.E., Ciszewski, A., Kasai, K., Lasko, N.B., Orr, S.P., & Pitman, R.K. (2002). Smaller hippocampal volume predicts pathologic vulnerability to psychological trauma. *Nature Neuroscience, 5,* 1242–1247.

Heim, C., Newport, D.J., Heit, S., Graham, Y.P., Wilcox, M., Bonsall, R., Miller, A.H., & Nemeroff, C.B. (2000). Pituitary-adrenal and autonomic responses to stress in women after sexual and physical abuse in childhood. *Journal of the American Medical Association, 284,* 592–597.

Hinde, R.A. (1986). Some implications of evolutionary theory and comparative data for the study of human prosocial and aggressive behaviour. In D. Olweus, J. Block, & M. Radke-Yarrow (Eds.), *Development of anti-social and prosocial behaviour* (pp. 13–32). Orlando: Academic Press.

Liu, D., Tannenbaum, B., Caldji, C., Francis, D., Freedman, A., Sharma, S., Pearson, D., Plotsky, P.M., & Meaney, M.J. (1997). Maternal care, hippocampal glucocorticoid receptor gene expression and hypothalamic-pituitary-adrenal responses to stress. *Science, 277,* 1659–1662.

Pruessner, J.L., Champagne, F.A., Meaney, M.J., & Dagher, A. (2004). Parental care and neuroendocrine and dopamine responses to stress in humans: A PET imaging study. *Journal of Neuroscience, 24,* 2825–2831.

Repetti, R.L., Taylor, S.E., & Seeman, T.E. (2002). Risky families: Family social environments and the mental and physical health of offspring. *Psychological Bulletin, 128,* 330–366.

Weaver, I.C.G., Cervoni, N., D'Alessio, A.C., Champagne, F.A., Seckl, J.R., Szyf, M., & Meaney, M.J. (2004). Epigenetic programming through maternal behavior. *Nature Neuroscience, 7,* 847–854.

Yehuda, R., Bierer, L.M., Schmeidler, J., Aferiat, D.H., Breslau, I., & Dolan, S. (2000). Low cortisol and risk for PTSD in adult offspring of Holocaust survivors. *American Journal of Psychiatry, 157,* 1252–1259.

This article has been reprinted as it originally appeared in *Current Directions in Psychological Science*. Citation information for this article as originally published appears above.

Corticotropin-Releasing Factor and the Psychobiology of Early-Life Stress

Charles F. Gillespie and Charles B. Nemeroff[1]
Department of Psychiatry & Behavioral Sciences
Emory University School of Medicine

Abstract

Trauma and neglect during childhood are increasingly appreciated as factors in the etiology of adult mood and anxiety disorders. Much has been learned about the role of stress biology in the persisting effects of early adverse experience on adult psychopathology. Here we present an overview of developmental trauma in the psychobiology of depression and anxiety. We emphasize the role of corticotropin-releasing factor in the patho-physiology of these disorders, focusing on the transduction of early life trauma into adult psychopathology.

Keywords

trauma; neglect; depression; stress; corticotropin-releasing factor

An epidemic of child abuse exists in the United States (reviewed in Gillespie & Nemeroff, 2005a). Conservative estimates suggest that every year more than 1,000,000 children experience sexual or physical abuse or severe neglect. Individuals abused in childhood are at elevated risk of depression during adulthood. Women abused in childhood attempt suicide at greater frequency and report greater numbers of depression, anxiety, somatic, and substance-abuse symptoms than do women who have not experienced such abuse. Further, child abuse and neglect also independently elevate risk for stress-related illnesses including cardiac disease, peptic ulcer, autoimmune disease, diabetes mellitus, and lung disease. While it is clear that many people abused or neglected as children will develop psychiatric and other forms of medical illness as adults, the variables that determine the form and magnitude of adult psychiatric and medical disease in these individuals remain uncertain.

The hypothesis that traumatic experiences during childhood result in adult mood and anxiety disorders was first disseminated in psychoanalytic theories of critical periods or phases disrupted by adverse experience during psychological development. Indeed, William Wordsworth's statement that "The child is father of the man" encapsulates this idea succinctly. More recently, the concept of the critical period as a temporal window through which environmental experience impacts brain development by effects on the timing and extent of gene expression has gained ascendance in clinical neuroscience.

The quest to understand the causes of depression has led to the development of numerous hypotheses regarding chemical or hormonal imbalances to explain the biological foundations of psychiatric illness. Over 40 years ago, a number of patients with depression were found to secrete excessive amounts of the steroid stress hormone cortisol (Gibbons & McHugh, 1962). The observation that

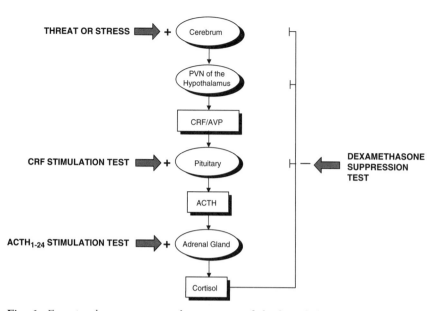

Fig. 1. Functional organization and assessment of the hypothalamic-pituitary-adrenal (HPA) axis. Information about threat or stress is relayed from the cerebrum to the paraventricular nucleus (PVN) of the hypothalamus. Neurons of the PVN secrete corticotropin-releasing factor (CRF) and arginine vasopressin (AVP) into blood vessels that transport these chemicals to the pituitary gland. Activation of CRF and AVP receptors on pituitary cells results in secretion of adrenocorticotrophic hormone (ACTH). ACTH released from the pituitary into the systemic circulatory system stimulates the production and release of cortisol from the adrenal gland. Cortisol provides feedback inhibition to the hypothalamus, pituitary gland, and other brain areas to inhibit further release of CRF and ACTH. Certain medical and psychiatric illnesses involve dysregulation of the HPA axis and result in insufficient or excessive secretion of CRF, ACTH, or cortisol; several endocrine challenge tests exist for functional assessment of the HPA axis to localize the site of pathology. The CRF stimulation test assesses pituitary function by measuring the secretion of ACTH into the bloodstream following standardized intravenous administration of CRF. The ACTH$_{1-24}$ stimulation test assesses adrenal secretion of cortisol following intravenous administration of ACTH$_{1-24}$. The dexamethasone suppression test assesses the adequacy of feedback inhibition to the pituitary, hypothalamus, and other brain areas such as the hippocampus that participate in the regulation of the HPA axis.

patients with Cushing's disease or syndrome, endocrine diseases characterized by excessive secretion of cortisol, often also experience severe depression and anxiety, in conjunction with the finding of increased production and secretion of cortisol in healthy individuals exposed to stress, contributed to the modern *stress-diathesis* hypothesis of depression. In this model of illness, individual predisposition to excess reactivity of the neural and endocrine stress-response systems following exposure to environmental stressors is believed to play a significant role in both the initiation and relapse of certain forms of depression (reviewed in Gillespie & Nemeroff, 2005b).

Research with animals in the laboratory and clinical research with humans has yielded insight into the relationship between the neurobiology of stress and the physiology of depressive illness. Much of this work has focused on corticotropin-releasing factor (CRF) and other elements of the hypothalamic-pituitary-adrenal (HPA) axis, a collection of neural and endocrine structures that facilitate the response to stress, as mediating variables in this relationship between stress and depression (Fig. 1).

EARLY-LIFE STRESS AND DEPRESSION

A number of alterations of CRF and HPA-axis function have been observed in depressed patients (reviewed in Gillespie & Nemeroff, 2005a, 2005b). Elevated concentrations of CRF are found in the cerebrospinal fluid (CSF) of depressed patients and postmortem studies of individuals who have committed suicide have demonstrated decreased density of CRF receptors in the frontal cortex of the brain, decreased activity of the CRF receptor gene, and increased CRF concentrations in the frontal cortex as compared with control subjects. Effective treatment of depression normalizes the concentration of CSF CRF and other indices of HPA-axis activity measured by HPA-challenge tests (which assess normality of function within the HPA axis). This suggests that increased CSF CRF and enhanced activity of the HPA axis may be "state," rather than "trait," markers of depression. In this context, state refers to phenomena related to a particular phase of illness (e.g., depressed or in remission) as opposed to being present throughout all phases of illness as a trait of the illness or a marker for susceptibility to the development of illness. Clinically asymptomatic patients retaining elevated CSF CRF levels following treatment of depression are at increased risk for early relapse of depression, indicating perhaps that persistently elevated CSF CRF is a marker for vulnerability to early recurrence of depression.

Child abuse, neglect, or the loss of a parent during childhood are the most salient forms of early-life stress, although other forms of early-life stress, including accidents, surgeries, protracted illness, war- or terrorism-related events, natural disasters, and chaotic or unstable family environments, are also equally significant traumatic events. Trauma and/or neglect are common features in the history of many patients with depression, particularly those whose depression has been chronic. Certain types of depression may be the outcome of gene–environment interactions—that is, interaction between "nature," in the form of latent genetic vulnerability, and "nurture," in the form of stressful experiences early in life. Exposure to stress, particularly on a chronic basis, during early development is one way that the environment influences susceptibility to depression in vulnerable individuals. As such, the biology of depression may also include the biology of early-life stress.

Animal models have provided insight into the consequences of early-life stress in adult humans. A consistent finding in animals exposed to early-life stress has been both short- and long-term adverse neurobiological and endocrine effects, as well as cognitive dysfunction and abnormal behavior associated with alterations of the physiology and genetic regulation of the CRF system (reviewed in Gutman & Nemeroff, 2003). For example, repeated brief separation of rat pups from their mothers is associated in adult animals with enhanced reactivity of the HPA axis to stress and increased activity of the CRF gene within areas of the brain that facilitate adaptation to stress or threat. Similar studies showed that infant bonnet macaques whose mothers faced variable and unpredictable foraging conditions for food later demonstrated chronically elevated concentrations of CRF in the CSF as adults. Thus, in two different species, the effects of early-life stress continue into adulthood in the form of persistent hyper-responsiveness of the HPA axis to environmental stress.

A limitation of the comparative approach to investigations of early-life stress is that much of the present animal literature models reduced, inconsistent, or absent interaction between parent and offspring during development but does not model abuse. Experimental deprivation paradigms are presumably stressful because they subtract care from the social environment during development. As such, they are more likely informative of the effects of "deficit states" such as neglect, instability of living environment, or parental loss on human physiology and behavior and complement the clinical literature on the consequences of child neglect. In contrast, much of what is known about the role of CRF in depression and the psychobiological consequences of child abuse has been derived from clinical research in humans.

To evaluate the relationship between childhood trauma, reactivity of the HPA axis, and adult psychopathology, Heim and colleagues (Heim et al., 2000) conducted a series of studies with adult women. The four groups of women in this study included women without psychiatric illness or history of early-life stress serving as a control group, depressed women without early-life stress, depressed women who did experience early-life stress, and nondepressed women who experienced early-life stress. Subjects participated in the Trier Social Stress Test (TSST), a laboratory psychosocial stress test that reliably activates the HPA axis. This test consists of a 10-minute speech and performance of mental arithmetic under the gaze of three members of the investigative team. Variables measured include heart rate, plasma adrenocorticotrophic hormone (ACTH), and cortisol concentrations at several intervals before, during, and after the test.

Abnormal ACTH responses during the TSST were observed exclusively in women who experienced early-life stress. The most striking results were found in the group of women with current major depression and a history of early-life stress. These women also more frequently held an additional diagnosis of post-traumatic stress disorder (PTSD) and demonstrated the largest ACTH and cortisol responses, as well as the largest increases in heart rate. In fact, the ACTH response of this group was nearly three times greater than that observed in the control group. In contrast, depressed women who had not been stressed in early life exhibited ACTH and cortisol responses comparable to healthy controls. Interestingly, elevated ACTH responses were also observed in women without current depression but with a history of early-life stress. Unlike depressed women with such a history, these women retained normal levels of cortisol release during the TSST despite an abnormal ACTH response. This suggests that, over time, the adrenal cortex has adapted to the excess release of ACTH during stress by reducing its secretion of cortisol in response to ACTH. More generally, these data indicate that childhood trauma exerts long-term effects on the responsiveness of the HPA axis to stress, effects that continue into adulthood. Functionally, these effects are likely to be a consequence of altered regulation between the brain and different components of the HPA axis.

The hypothesis that early-life stress alters the response of different components of the HPA axis to chemical signals was evaluated in a subsequent study (Heim, Newport, Bonsall, Miller, & Nemeroff, 2001). As in the Heim et al. (2000) study, the subjects in this study were women with and without early-life stress and depression. The HPA axis was assessed using two standardized endocrine challenge tests, the CRF stimulation test and the $ACTH_{1-24}$ stimulation test (Fig. 1). Unlike the TSST, which uses psychosocial stress to elicit a response of the HPA axis, endocrine challenge tests allow for very specific assessment of function within the different components of the HPA axis.

Women who had experienced early-life stress but who were not currently depressed exhibited an increased ACTH response following infusion of CRF. In contrast, depressed women with and without early-life stress both exhibited a blunted ACTH response to intravenous infusion of CRF. With respect to the $ACTH_{1-24}$ stimulation test, women who had experienced early-life stress but were not currently depressed had lower plasma cortisol levels at baseline and after administration of $ACTH_{1-24}$ compared to depressed women with and without early-life stress. Similar to the findings of our previous study (Heim et al., 2000), women with major depressive disorder and a history of early-life stress were more likely to report current life stress and to fulfill diagnostic criteria for concurrent PTSD than were women who had experienced early-life stress but who were not currently depressed.

The data from the CRF stimulation test suggest that the pituitary gland is sensitized to CRF in abused women without depression. Conversely, the blunted ACTH response to CRF found in depressed women both with and without early-life stress may reflect adaptation by the pituitary, possibly through a reduction in the number of CRF receptors, to chronic hyper-secretion of CRF in response to current depression or life stress. While this particular finding may initially appear to conflict with data from our previous study (Heim et al., 2000) using the TSST (i.e., depressed women with early-life stress have an exaggerated ACTH response to the TSST but a blunted response to CRF infusion), it is important to appreciate that stress exposure and the CRF stimulation test are different ways of activating the HPA axis and are not directly comparable. The increased ACTH response to psychosocial stress observed in women with depression and early-life stress likely reflects involvement of multiple levels of neural systems and neurotransmitters mediating cognitive and emotional information that converge on the pituitary. The combined effects of such input may be able to override limitations on ACTH response imposed by reductions in the number of pituitary CRF receptors. Such reductions in the number of CRF receptors would limit the ACTH response to CRF infusion. Finally, and consistent with our previous study (Heim et al., 2000), we found reduced activity of the adrenal cortex, as evidenced by reduced secretion of cortisol, in response to ACTH infusion. This suggests that adaptation by the adrenal cortex to chronic hypersecretion of ACTH has taken place.

More recently, Carpenter and colleagues (Carpenter et al., 2004) evaluated the relationship between the perception of early-life stress and the CSF CRF concentration of drug-free patients with depression in comparison to matched healthy control subjects. The developmental timing of stress exposure was predictive of either relatively increased or decreased CSF CRF. Early-life stress before the age of 6 years was associated with elevated CSF CRF, whereas exposure to stressful events around the time of birth or in the preteen years was associated with decreased CSF CRF. Further, the individual's perception of trauma intensity was predictive of CSF CRF concentration (relative increase or decrease) independent of the presence or absence of depression. A limitation of this study was its retrospective design, which relies on participants' recall of past experiences not subject to independent confirmation. Additional studies using experimentally validated stress paradigms controlling for patient perception of trauma intensity may provide insight into the complex relationship between the subjective perception of trauma by an individual, the objective qualities of the trauma (duration, intensity, and frequency of neglect or abuse), and the individual's objective response to experimentally validated stressors.

These three clinical studies support the hypothesis that early-life stress results in an enduring sensitization of the HPA axis and the autonomic nervous system response to stress. That sensitization to stress in turn may elevate risk to develop depression or experience relapse of depression. Further, these data suggest that the developmental timing of early-life stress may have specific directional consequences with respect to the regulation of the HPA axis. However, a number of questions remain. For example, it is not clear whether individuals exposed to early-life stress that have PTSD but not depression differ from individuals with depression but not PTSD on the neuroendocrine profile generated by the TSST or HPA-axis challenge tests. In our sample of depressed women who experienced early-life stress, nearly 85% also had PTSD. From an experimental perspective, the presence of concurrent diagnoses of depression and PTSD makes recruitment of adequate sample sizes of discrete "depression only" and "PTSD only" subject groups in traumatized populations to perform these types of studies very difficult and the topic awaits further investigation. Clinically, patients with a history of early-life stress rarely have purely depressive or anxious symptoms, and both need to be addressed. Consequently, our appreciation of what constitutes the best standard of care is still evolving.

TREATMENT ISSUES

Evidence suggesting that depressed patients with early-life stress may be unique in their response to treatment continues to mount (reviewed in Craighead & Nemeroff, 2005). Early-life stress affects the response of patients with either dysthymia or depression to drug therapy. Compared to subjects without a history of early-life stress, depressed patients who experienced such stress exhibit increased rates of relapse following treatment of their depression. The course of depression in individuals with a history of early-life stress is often characterized by chronicity.

What is known about the treatment of depression in patients who experienced early-life stress? Keller and colleagues (Keller et al., 2000) conducted a large multicenter trial designed to compare the relative efficacy of pharmacotherapy (treatment with the antidepressant nefazodone) to psychotherapy or their combination in the treatment of chronic depression. Psychotherapy and pharmacotherapy were both comparible in efficacy but were less effective than the combination of the two in treating patients with chronic depression. However, a striking demographic feature of the study population was the widespread prevalence of early-life stress. Nearly one third of the subjects had experienced loss of a parent before age 15 years, 45% experienced childhood physical abuse, 16% experienced childhood sexual abuse, and 10% experienced neglect.

As a consequence of the results from the Keller et al. (2000) trial and the broad prevalence of early-life stress in that study population, Nemeroff and colleagues (Nemeroff et al., 2003) reanalyzed the data from this trial to determine whether a history of early-life stress in patients with chronic depression altered their response to pharmacotherapy or psychotherapy. Patients were stratified into groups based on the presence or absence of early-life stress and their response to treatment with psychotherapy or pharmacotherapy was reassessed. Patients with a history of early-life stress had a better response to psychotherapy alone compared to treatment with an antidepressant alone, using remission, the most stringent measure of treatment response, as the endpoint. Further, the combination of the antidepressant and psychotherapy was only slightly more effective than psychotherapy alone in the group of patients with early-life stress. These data suggest that a history of early-life stress is both common in the population of patients with chronic depression and that psychotherapy is a crucial component of treatment for depressed patients with such a history.

FUTURE DIRECTIONS

Thomas Edison once said "The doctor of the future will give no medicine, but will interest his patients in the care of the human body, in diet, and in the cause and prevention of disease." While we are not yet at the point predicted by Edison, we have gained considerable insight into the roots of depression at the intersection between the biology of CRF and early-life stress. This work has resulted in the discovery of candidate compounds for new pharmacological treatments for depression and anxiety in the form of CRF and glucocorticoid receptor antagonists. As social relationships are often the context of early life stress, it has also refined our appreciation of their importance in the cause, treatment, and prevention of psychiatric illness. Future research using the tools of psychiatric genetics may allow greater understanding of the gene–gene and gene–environment interactions during development that confer vulnerability or resilience to environmental stress and facilitate intervention with children or young adults at risk for developing trauma-related psychopathology.

Recommended Reading

Craighead, W.E., & Nemeroff, C.B. (2005). (See References)
Gillespie, C.F., & Nemeroff, C.B. (2005a). (See References)
Gutman, D.A., & Nemeroff, C.B. (2003). (See References)

Acknowledgments—Charles Gillespie was supported as a postdoctoral trainee on National Institutes of Health (NIH) Grant DA-015040. This research was supported by NIH Grants MH-42088 and MH-52899 to Charles Nemeroff and NIH Grant NCRRM01-RR00039 to Emory University. Dr. Gillespie has received funding from APIRE/Wyeth and NIDA. Dr. Nemeroff consults to, serves on the Speakers' Bureau and/or Board of Directors of, has been a grant recipient of, and/or owns equity in one or more of the following: Abbott Laboratories, Acadia Pharmaceuticals, AFSP, APIRE, AstraZeneca, BMC-JR LLC, Bristol-Myers-Squibb, CeNeRx, Corcept, Cypress Biosciences, Cyberonics, Eli Lilly, Entrepreneur's Fund, Forest Laboratories, George West Mental Health Foundation, GlaxoSmithKline, i3 DLN, Janssen Pharmaceutica, Lundbeck, NARSAD, Neuronetics, NIMH, NFMH, NovaDel Pharma, Otsuka, Pfizer Pharmaceuticals, Quintiles, Reevax, UCB Pharma, Wyeth-Ayerst.

Note

1. Address correspondence to Charles B. Nemeroff, Emory University School of Medicine, Department of Psychiatry & Behavioral Sciences, 101 Woodruff Circle, Suite 4000, Atlanta, GA 30322; e-mail: cnemero@emory.edu.

References

Carpenter, L.L., Tyrka, A.R., McDougle, C.J., Malison, R.T., Owens, M.J., Nemeroff, C.B., & Price, L.H. (2004). Cerebrospinal fluid corticotropin-releasing factor and perceived early-life stress in depressed patients and healthy control subjects. *Neuropsycho-pharmacology, 29*, 777–784.

Craighead, W.E., & Nemeroff, C.B. (2005). The impact of early trauma on response to psychotherapy. *Clinical Neuroscience Research, 4*, 405–411.

Gibbons, J.L., & McHugh, P.R. (1962). Plasma cortisol in depressive illness. *Journal of Psychiatric Research, 1*, 162–171.

Gillespie, C.F., & Nemeroff, C.B. (2005a). Early life stress and depression. *Current Psychiatry, 4*, 15–30.

Gillespie, C.F., & Nemeroff, C.B. (2005b). Hypercortisolemia and depression. *Psychosomatic Medicine, 67*(S1), 26–28.

Gutman, D.A., & Nemeroff, C.B. (2003). Persistent central nervous system effects of an adverse early environment: Clinical and preclinical studies. *Physiology and Behavior, 79*, 471–478.

Heim, C., Newport, D.J., Bonsall, R., Miller, A.H., & Nemeroff, C.B. (2001). Altered pituitary-adrenal axis responses to provocative challenge tests in adult survivors of childhood abuse. *American Journal of Psychiatry, 158*, 575–581.

Heim, C., Newport, D.J., Heit, S., Graham, Y.P., Wilcox, M., Bonsall, R., et al. (2000). Pituitary-adrenal and autonomic responses to stress in women after sexual and physical abuse in childhood. *JAMA: The Journal of the American Medical Association, 284*, 592–597.

Keller, M.B., McCullough, J.P., Klein, D.N., Arnow, B., Dunner, D.L., Gelenberg, A.J., et al. (2000). A comparison of nefazodone, the cognitive behavioral-analysis system of psychotherapy, and their combination for the treatment of chronic depression. *New England Journal of Medicine, 342*, 1462–1470.

Nemeroff, C.B., Heim, C.M., Thase, M.E., Klein, D.N., Rush, A.J., Schatzberg, A.F., et al. (2003). Differential responses to psychotherapy versus pharmacotherapy in patients with chronic forms of major depression and childhood trauma. *Proceedings of the National Academy of Sciences, USA, 100*, 14293–14296.

This article has been reprinted as it originally appeared in *Current Directions in Psychological Science*. Citation information for this article as originally published appears above.

Drug Addiction During Pregnancy: Advances in Maternal Treatment and Understanding Child Outcomes

Hendree E. Jones[1]

Department of Psychiatry, Johns Hopkins University

Abstract

Drug use during pregnancy is a significant risk factor for compromised child develop-ment. National statistics reveal that many pregnant women smoke tobacco (18%), drink alcohol (9.8%), and use illicit drugs (4%). Animal and clinical data show that prenatal alcohol and tobacco exposure have direct deleterious consequences on child development. Recent large multicenter studies have failed to show that prena-tal cocaine or heroin exposure causes devastating child consequences when environ-mental variables are controlled. However, prenatal exposure to both licit and illicit drug use mostly occurs in the presence of environmental and contextual risk factors that together can impede healthy outcomes. Thus, treating these addiction disorders while addressing other lifestyle factors in a comprehensive way is critical.

Keywords

contingency management; substance abuse; neonatal; methadone; buprenorphine

Drug use during pregnancy is a critical health concern. Among pregnant women, 18% report smoking tobacco, 9.8% report drinking alcohol, and 4% report using at least one illicit drug in the past month (Substance Abuse and Mental Health Services Administration, 2005). Both animal and clinical data show that prena-tal alcohol and tobacco exposure have deleterious consequences. Alcohol causes compromised physical growth and development and morphological and psycho-logical impairments. Tobacco smoking may have multiple effects including low birth weight, intrauterine growth restriction, and sudden-infant-death syndrome (Lester, Andreozzi, & Appiah, 2004). It is also commonly assumed that prenatal exposure to cocaine or heroin is worse than exposure to licit drugs, directly causing obstetrical complications, low birth weight, and fetal morbidity and mortality. This assumption may be partially based on early research using small retrospective samples. This research characterized the effects on mothers and infants of a selected drug abused during pregnancy and applied a simple linear cause-and-effect model to this complex medical illness. Research now shows that the effects of alcohol or nicotine exposure are often worse than those of illicit-drug exposure (Lester et al., 2004).

The early reports of adverse effects of prenatal heroin or cocaine exposure resulted in the development of treatments for this special population. Although recent data controlling for environmental factors fails to show that prenatal expo-sure to heroin or cocaine causes severe deleterious child consequences, treating maternal drug addiction is still critical. Since drug addition often occurs in the context of violence, poverty, and medical and psychosocial impairment, treating this complex illness can provide a context for improving multiple areas of life that are impacted by illicit drug use and may thereby improve maternal and child outcomes.

Early treatment research with pregnant women addicted to illicit drugs examined long-term residential or outpatient treatment. To date, no empirical data support the superiority of either of these treatment modalities over the other. However, there is consensus that treatment of pregnant drug-addicted women is best provided in a single-gender, comprehensive approach (e.g., medical care, life-skills training, trauma treatment). While rich descriptive data support this treatment philosophy, well controlled studies examining different treatment models are lacking. Recently, treatment advances in this population are based upon theoretically grounded behavioral and pharmacotherapy principles and processes.

One important insight is that an accumulation of numerous risk factors appears to have a greater negative impact on child development than any single risk factor by itself (Sameroff & Chandler, 1975). The underlying complex issues associated with drug use—including poor nutrition, domestic violence, poverty, environmental toxins, disease, and inadequate housing and health care—can overshadow the effects of illicit drugs and cause more harm to a fetus than drugs alone (Robins & Mills, 1993). Current research is investigating the complex relationship between children's developmental outcomes and variations in the type, timing, and amount of exposure to multiple substances during pregnancy in the context of various contextual and environmental factors. The strong methodological designs being used involve large samples, multiple sites, and experimental designs that follow participants over time.

This article focuses on two areas of current research on drug addiction during pregnancy: the examination of outcomes of prenatally drug-exposed children and advances in treating pregnant drug-addicted women with behavioral interventions and with medications. Both parts of this article draw on the relevant underlying theories to provide an overview of recent advances and to suggest directions for future research.

CHILD OUTCOME

Only recently have researchers recognized that trying to isolate the specific effect of a single drug used during pregnancy is almost impossible. Prenatal drug exposure is best characterized as one of many risk factors that place the mother and newborn at risk for adverse outcomes. The Maternal Lifestyle Study provides empirical data showing that drug use during pregnancy often occurs in the context of poly-drug use (i.e., combined use of multiple substances), lack of prenatal care, high rates of violence exposure, co-occurrence of other psychiatric problems, inadequate nutrition, and poverty (Bauer et al., 2002). Before this study, knowledge about the prenatal effects of abused drugs was largely based on retrospective studies lacking appropriate controls.

In contrast to previous reports, the Maternal Lifestyle Study found that drug-addicted pregnant women used more prenatal-care services than expected (77% received some prenatal care) although at a lower rate than non-exposed women

(97%). It also found that (a) most (93%) pregnant women using cocaine or opioids (e.g., heroin) also used other drugs—mostly alcohol and nicotine—that are known to negatively affect the fetus; (b) cocaine and opioid users are at higher risk than non-exposed women for hepatitis and HIV; and (c) although there is an increased risk of abruptio placenta (tearing of the placenta from the uterus before delivery), it occurs in less than 5% of the drug-exposed groups (Bauer et al., 2002). Later follow-up data controlling for factors including birth weight and environmental risks showed that infant prenatal exposure to cocaine or opioid was not associated with mental, motor, or behavioral deficits (Messinger et al., 2004). These well controlled data refute the early uncontrolled reports of significant damage as a direct result of cocaine or opioid exposure (cf. Bauer et al., 2002).

Recently, prenatal-methamphetamine-exposure studies reported cleft palates, cardiac abnormalities, fetal growth restriction, and cranial abnormalities. Unfortunately, these studies are confounded by small sample sizes, use of other drugs, and unreliable methamphetamine-exposure status (c.f. Arria et al., 2006). In response to the concerns over the effects of prenatal exposure, a large, multi-center, prospective, matched-comparison cohort design study is systematically investigating the interaction between poly-drug use and psychological and demographic factors on the possible short- and long-term maternal and child consequences of methamphetamine use. The results from this study may provide needed information about the effects of methamphetamine exposure and prevent the sensationalized coverage of "methamphetamine babies" that occurred in the 1980s with "crack babies."

Since prenatal cocaine and/or heroin exposure occurs in the presence of many environmental and contextual factors that together can impede healthy outcomes, treating these addiction disorders while addressing other lifestyle factors in a comprehensive way is critical.

The second part of this article highlights underlying theories and advancements in the development of behavioral and pharmacotherapy treatments for pregnant women.

TREATMENTS

Behavioral Interventions

The recent behavioral interventions for drug-addiction treatment are theoretically rooted in Skinner's operant-conditioning theory (i.e., behaviors positively reinforced are more likely to be exhibited again). Extending Skinner's theory to drug addiction suggests that drug use occurs in the absence of other positive reinforcers. Thus, drug use can be eliminated by increasing the density of non-drug positive reinforcers and decreasing the positive reinforcement attained from substance use. One example of a behavioral intervention based on the operant-conditioning theory is contingency management. Contingency management systematically delivers reinforcing (e.g., rewards redeemable for goods or services) or punishing consequences contingent on a target behavior (e.g., providing a drug-negative urine sample) and withholding the consequences in the absence of the target behavior (Higgins, Heil, & Lussier, 2004). Higgins and colleagues developed a voucher incentive system to establish and maintain both cocaine abstinence and treatment retention. This intervention has been subsequently used in a variety of addicted populations including nicotine, heroin, and poly-drug users. In 85% of reports published, this type of intervention produced significant changes in target behaviors (Higgins, Heil, & Lussier, 2004).

Given the efficacy of contingency management, it has been examined in drug-addicted pregnant women. The method successfully reduced relapse to cocaine or heroin use and increased treatment attendance (e.g., Jones, Haug, Silverman, Stitzer, & Svikis, 2001). It also reduced prenatal smoke exposure. A combination of contingency management (i.e., monetary reward for verified smoking abstinence) with social support (a supportive peer receives a monetary reward based on the patient's smoking abstinence) for eliminating smoking in pregnant women was compared to a usual-care group receiving verbal and written smoking-cessation messages. The randomized trial showed a confirmed smoking-abstinence rate of 32% in the intervention group relative to 9% in the usual-care group (Donatelle, Prows, Champeau, & Hudson, 2000). Contingency management dependent on smoking abstinence has also been examined against a non-contingent condition in which vouchers were earned independent of smoking status. From delivery to 24 weeks after giving birth, the contingency-management group had significantly greater verified rates of smoking abstinence than did the noncontingent controls (27% vs. 0%; Higgins et al., 2004). This is a powerful demonstration that the benefits gained with contingency management can be sustained even after the intervention is discontinued.

Another successful use of contingency management to treat pregnant and postpartum drug-addicted women is the therapeutic workplace (in which drug-negative patients earn monetary rewards for work and work-related behaviors). Forty participants were randomly assigned to a therapeutic-workplace or usual-care control group. Participants in the therapeutic-workplace condition gained access to the workplace contingent upon providing daily drug-negative urine samples. Within the therapeutic workplace, participants were reinforced for many work-related behaviors including attendance, performance, and professional demeanor. The control group had no access to the therapeutic workplace; they only left urine samples and completed follow-up interviews. Over 3 years, therapeutic-workplace participants significantly increased cocaine abstinence relative to controls (54% vs. 28%) and opioid abstinence relative to controls (60% vs. 37%; Silverman et al., 2002).

The importance of these results cannot be overstated. The therapeutic workplace translates the idea of contingency management into a practical application and demonstrates its sustainability. Although contingency management is the most powerful behavioral intervention available for drug-addiction treatment, there are barriers preventing its widespread adoption. First, many participants do not respond to it. This problem may be overcome by better matching rewards to patient desires or using procedures to ensure that patients receive the rewards early in treatment. Second, contingency management is costly to providers. However, the incentive costs are miniscule compared to the health-care costs associated with no treatment. Third, the burden on clinical staff to implement contingency management must be considered. Staff experiencing positive experiences with this efficacious treatment may be willing to allocate more time to it and reduce time spent using less effective traditional approaches.

Pharmacotherapy

In the past decade, tremendous progress has been made in developing and approving medications to treat addiction disorders. Currently there are several medications approved to treat opioid, alcohol, or nicotine dependence in nonpregnant patients. The focus on the use of medications to treat addictive disorders is based on two central premises: (a) that drug addiction is a disease with biological changes that can have psychological, spiritual, and social consequences; and (b) that brain cells are modified due to repeated drug exposure and these cellular changes interfere with a person's ability to control his or her behavior (Hyman, 1996). Thus, compulsive use and alterations in brain cells can be countered through medications that reduce the subjective or rewarding effects of drug use.

Unfortunately, pregnant women are largely left out of these addiction-medication advances. Clinical trials exclude pregnant women for fear of ethical concerns and legal prosecution if a negative birth outcome occurs. Yet it may be unethical to continue to avoid testing these medications in limited samples of pregnant women. In practice, once a drug is released, it will be prescribed to thousands of women. Many will be pregnant or become pregnant, resulting in potential mass exposure and harm if no information is known about the fetal effects of these medications.

Although neither methadone nor buprenorphine—the latest medication approved for treating opioid dependence—are approved in pregnancy, the safety and efficacy of these medications in pregnancy is being examined. Specifically, a randomized, double-blind controlled trial was conducted in a comprehensive drug-treatment facility that also included contingency management in the form of rewards based on drug-negative urine samples. Participants were opioid-dependent pregnant women who were given daily flexible doses of either buprenorphine (4–24 mg) or methadone (20–100 mg). Hospitalization was significantly shorter for buprenorphine-exposed newborns than it was for methadone-exposed newborns, and the amount of morphine administered to treat neonatal abstinence syndrome (NAS) in methadone-exposed newborns was three times greater than for buprenorphine-exposed newborns. No significant differences were observed in either the number of NAS-treated newborns (20% of buprenorphine-exposed vs. 45.5% of methadone-exposed) or the Peak NAS total scores. These clinical-trial results, in combination with uncontrolled case reports and prospective studies, show that buprenorphine is as safe as methadone for treating pregnant women (Jones et al., 2005). A current multi-center trial using similar methodology may replicate the above results and provide critical data for the U.S. Food and Drug Administration to make labeling changes for pregnancy indications for both drugs.

Another area of medication advancement is the field of smoking cessation. Cigarette smoking results in the intake of thousands of reproductive toxins. These cigarette-smoke toxins, and not nicotine, may be responsible for multiple adverse outcomes associated with smoking (cf. Oncken & Kranzler, 2003). Although several small studies of the safety of nicotine medication in pregnant women have shown somewhat promising results, trials of nicotine medication's effectiveness for smoking cessation during pregnancy and the postpartum period (i.e., in breast-fed infants) are needed (Oncken & Kranzler, 2003). Finally, other medications like bupropion that are used for depression and smoking-cessation and a recently developed nicotine vaccine may hold promise for treating pregnant smokers.

FUTURE DIRECTIONS

Although the effects of prenatal exposure to cocaine and heroin appear minimal after controlling for multiple other factors, treating drug addiction during pregnancy remains important, both for minimizing fetal exposure to drugs and for creating the environment to address the other factors that place mother and infant at risk for adverse outcomes. Current research on treatments for drug addiction during pregnancy shows that pregnant women can successfully be treated using the same reinforcement principles used for nonpregnant patients. However, not all patients respond in the same way to the same reinforcers. Future research should focus on refining reinforcers to maximize patient response. This could be accomplished by progressively rewarding greater decreases in drug use until abstinence is reached, tailoring rewards to patient desires, or both. Rewards that address basic needs (e.g., housing and employment) may be more suited to sustaining drug abstinence following treatment completion. Research–practice partnerships are needed to move contingency management into community substance-abuse clinics. Recently, medication research has begun to focus on pregnant women. Including pregnant women in medication research is critical for avoiding mass uncontrolled exposure and minimizing medication-related harm to infants and mothers. Further, the next generation of maternal-addiction treatment research should focus on examining the use of combinations of pharmacological and behavioral treatments. This combination approach may more effectively address the multicomponent nature of the disorder than single-modality approaches do.

Finally, prenatal-drug-exposure studies are based on low-socioeconomic-status populations who face multiple risk factors inextricably linked with chronic poverty. To tease apart the relationships among prenatal drug exposure and other co-occurring risk and protective factors in predicting children's outcomes, future research will require more heterogeneous samples for whom such factors vary. Tools are needed that can evaluate both short- and long-term aspects of children's development and the environments in which this development occurs. Future studies of prenatal exposure also need to conceptualize the environment in which the mother and child live as more than just a set of confounding variables in their research designs. Reliance on statistical control of selected environmental variables overlooks the dynamic relations among parent–child interactions, parental stress, violence exposure, drug use, psychiatric status, and child development.

Recommended Reading

Lester, B.M., Andreozzi, L., & Appiah, L. (2004). (See References)
Robins, L., & Mills, J.L. (1993). (See References)
Sameroff, A.J., & Chandler, M.J. (1975). (See References)

Note

1. Address correspondence to Hendree E. Jones, JHBMC, 4940 Eastern Ave, Mason F. Lord Building, East Tower, 3rd Floor, Baltimore, MD 21224; e-mail: hejones@jhmi.edu.

References

Arria, A.M., Derauf, C., Lagasse, L.L., Grant, P., Shah, R., Smith, L., Haning, W., Huestis, M., Strauss, A., Grotta, S.D., Liu, J., & Lester, B. (2006). Methamphetamine and other substance use during pregnancy: Preliminary estimates from the infant development, environment, and lifestyle (IDEAL) study. *Maternal and Child Health Journal, 5,* 1–10.

Bauer, C.R., Shankaran, S., Bada, H.S., Lester, B., Wright, L.L., Krause-Steinrauf, H., Smeriglio, V.L., Finnegan, L.P., Maza, P.L., & Verter, J. (2002). The maternal lifestyle study: Drug exposure during pregnancy and short-term maternal outcomes. *American Journal of Obstetrics and Gynecology, 186,* 487–495.

Donatelle, R.J., Prows, S.L., Champeau, D., & Hudson, D. (2000). Randomized controlled trial using social support and financial incentives for high risk pregnant smokers: Significant other supporter (SOS) program. *Tobacco Control, 9*(Suppl. 3), 67–69.

Higgins, S.T., Heil, S.H., & Lussier, J.P. (2004). Clinical implications of reinforcement as a determinant of substance use disorders. *Annual Review of Psychology, 55,* 431–461.

Higgins, S.T., Heil, S.H., Solomon, L.J., Bernstein, I.M., Lussier, J.P., Abel, R.L., Lynch, M.E., & Badger, G.J. (2004). A pilot study on voucher-based incentives to promote abstinence from cigarette smoking during pregnancy and postpartum. *Nicotine and Tobacco Research, 6,* 1015–1020.

Hyman, S.E. (1996). Addiction to cocaine and amphetamine. *Neuron, 16,* 901–904.

Jones, H.E., Haug, N., Silverman, K., Stitzer, M., & Svikis, D. (2001). The effectiveness of incentives in enhancing treatment attendance and drug abstinence in methadone-maintained pregnant women. *Drug and Alcohol Dependence, 61,* 297–306.

Jones, H.E., Johnson, R.E., Jasinski, D.R., O'Grady, K.E., Chisholm, C.A., Choo, R.E., Crocetti, M., Dudas, R., Harrow, C., Huestis, M.A., Jansson, L.M., Lantz, M., Lester, B.M., & Milio, L. (2005). Buprenorphine versus methadone in the treatment of pregnant opioid-dependent patients: effects on the neonatal abstinence syndrome. *Drug and Alcohol Dependence, 79,* 1–10.

Lester, B.M., Andreozzi, L., & Appiah, L. (2004). Substance use during pregnancy: Time for policy to catch up with research. *Harm Reduction Journal, 1,* 5–49.

Messinger, D.S., Bauer, C.R., Das, A., Seifer, R., Lester, B.M., Lagasse, L.L., Wright, L.L., Shankaran, S., Bada, H.S., Smeriglio, V.L., Langer, J.C., Beeghly, M., & Poole, W.K. (2004). The maternal lifestyle study: Cognitive, motor, and behavioral outcomes of cocaine-exposed and opiate-exposed infants through three years of age. *Journal of Pediatrics, 113,* 1677–1685.

Oncken, C.A., & Kranzler, H.R. (2003). Pharmacotherapies to enhance smoking cessation during pregnancy. *Drug and Alcohol Review, 22,* 191–202.

Robins, L., & Mills, J.L. (1993). Effects of in utero exposure to street drugs. *American Journal of Public Health, 83,* 1–32.

Sameroff, A.J., & Chandler, M.J. (1975). Reproductive risk and the continuum of caretaking causality. In F.D. Horowitz (Ed), *Review of child development research: Vol. 3* (pp. 187–244). Chicago: The University of Chicago Press.

Silverman, K., Svikis, D., Wong, C.J., Hampton, J., Stitzer, M.L., & Bigelow, G.E. (2002). Reinforcement-based therapeutic workplace for the treatment of drug abuse: Three-year abstinence outcomes. *Experimental and Clinical Psychopharmacology, 10,* 228–240.

Substance Abuse and Mental Health Services Administration (2005). *Substance use during pregnancy: 2002 and 2003 update.* Rockville, MD.

This article has been reprinted as it originally appeared in *Current Directions in Psychological Science*. Citation information for this article as originally published appears above.

The Role of Prenatal Maternal Stress in Child Development

Janet A. DiPietro[1]

Johns Hopkins University

Abstract

The notion that a woman's psychological state during pregnancy affects the fetus is a persistent cultural belief in many parts of the world. Recent results indicate that prenatal maternal distress in rodents and nonhuman primates negatively influences long-term learning, motor development, and behavior in their offspring. The applicability of these findings to human pregnancy and child development is considered in this article. Potential mechanisms through which maternal psychological functioning may alter development of the fetal nervous system are being identified by current research, but it is premature to conclude that maternal prenatal stress has negative consequences for child development. Mild stress may be a necessary condition for optimal development.

Keywords

pregnancy; fetus; fetal development; stress

"Ay ay, for this I draw in many a tear,
And stop the rising of blood-sucking sighs,
Lest with my sighs or tears I blast or drown
King Edward's fruit, true heir to the English Crown"

— Queen Elizabeth's response upon learning of her husband's imprisonment in Shakespeare's *King Henry VI* (Part 3), Act IV, Scene IV

Since antiquity, people have thought that the emotions and experiences of a pregnant woman impinge on her developing fetus. Some of these notions, such as the idea that a severe fright marks a child with a prominent birthmark, no longer persist. However, the premise that maternal psychological distress has deleterious effects on the fetus is the focus of active scientific inquiry today. A resurgence of interest in the prenatal period as a staging period for later diseases, including psychiatric ones, has been fostered by the enormous attention devoted to the hypothesis of fetal programming advanced by D.J. Barker and his colleagues. Fetal programming implies that maternal and fetal factors that affect growth impart an indelible impression on adult organ function, including functioning of the brain and nervous system. That earlier circumstances, including those during the prenatal period, might affect later development is hardly newsworthy to developmentalists. In the 1930s, the Fels Research Institute initiated a longitudinal study of child development that commenced with intensive investigation of the fetal period.

Possible effects of maternal psychological distress during pregnancy range along a continuum from the immediate and disastrous (e.g., miscarriage) to the more subtle and long term (e.g., developmental disorders). Most existing research has focused on the effects of maternal distress on pregnancy itself. For example, there are numerous comprehensive reviews of research indicating that women who express greater distress during pregnancy give birth somewhat earlier to somewhat lighter babies than do women who are less distressed. The focus of this report is on the potential for maternal stress to generate more far-reaching effects on behavioral and cognitive development in childhood.

MECHANISMS AND EVIDENCE FROM ANIMAL STUDIES

There are no direct neural connections between the mother and the fetus. To have impact on the fetus, maternal psychological functioning must be translated into physiological effects. Three mechanisms by which this might occur are considered most frequently: alteration in maternal behaviors (e.g., substance abuse), reduction in blood flow such that the fetus is deprived of oxygen and nutrients, and transport of stress-related neurohormones to the fetus through the placenta. Stress-related neurohormones, such as cortisol, are necessary for normal fetal maturation and the birth process. However, relatively slight variations in these hormones, particularly early in pregnancy, have the potential to generate a cascade of effects that may result in changes to the fetus's own stress response system.

The most compelling evidence of a link between maternal psychological functioning and later development in offspring is found in animal studies. Stress responses in rodents can be reliably induced by a variety of experimental methods. Deliberate exposure of pregnant laboratory animals to stressful events (e.g., restraint) produces effects on offspring. These include deficits in motor development, learning behavior, and the ability to cope effectively in stressful situations. There is a tendency for the effects to be greater in female than in male offspring. Changes in brain structure and function of prenatally stressed animals have also been documented (Welberg & Seckl, 2001). Yet not all documented effects of prenatal stress are negative; mild stress has been observed to benefit, not damage, later learning in rats (Fujioka et al., 2001).

In a series of studies, pregnant rhesus monkeys that were exposed to repeated periods of loud noise were shown to bear offspring with delayed motor development and reduced attention in infancy. A constellation of negative behaviors, including enhanced responsiveness to stress and dysfunctional social behavior with peers, persisted through adolescence (Schneider & Moore, 2000). In general, studies of stress in nonhuman primates find males to be more affected than females. However, although a study comparing offspring of pregnant pigtailed macaques that were repeatedly stressed with offspring of nonstressed mothers did find that the behavior of prenatally stressed males was less mature than the behavior of non-prenatally stressed males, for females the results were reversed. The females born to the stressed mothers displayed more mature behavior than non-prenatally stressed females (Novak & Sackett, 1996). Thus, although most studies have reported detrimental consequences, reports of either no effects or beneficial ones make it clear that much is left to be learned about the specific characteristics of stressors that either accelerate or retard development.

DOES MATERNAL STRESS AFFECT DEVELOPMENT IN HUMANS?

Several important factors make it difficult to generalize results based on animal studies to humans. First, there are substantial physiological differences inherent to pregnancies in different species. Second, researchers are unable to control the events that transpire after birth in humans. Women who are psychologically stressed before pregnancy are also likely to be stressed after pregnancy, so it is critical that the role of social influences after birth be carefully distinguished from pregnancy effects that are transmitted biologically. Finally, the nature of the prenatal stress studied in animals and humans is very different, and this may pose the greatest barrier to the ability to generalize. In animal research, stressors are external events that are controlled in terms of duration, frequency, and intensity. The closest parallel in human studies is found in the few studies that have taken advantage of specific events, including an earthquake and the World Trade Center disaster, to study the effects on pregnancy in women residing in physical proximity. No such study has examined children's cognitive or behavioral outcomes. However, what is measured in virtually all human studies of "stress" during pregnancy is women's affect, mood, and emotional responses to daily circumstances in their lives. Maternal anxiety and, to a lesser extent, depression are prominent foci of research. Both may reflect emotional responses to stressful circumstances, but they also represent more persistent features of personality. Thus, not only are the physiological consequences and nature of prenatal stress different between animal and human studies, but when human studies detect an association between mothers' prenatal anxiety, for example, and their children's later behavior, it may be the result of shared genes or child-rearing practices related to maternal temperament.

Despite these concerns, there is a small but growing literature indicating that there is a relation between pregnant women's psychological distress and their children's behavioral outcomes. In one study, the ability of 8-month-old infants to pay attention during a developmental assessment was negatively correlated with the amount of anxiety their mothers reported about their pregnancy (Huizink, Robles de Medina, Mulder, Visser, & Buitelaar, 2002). This study is one of the few in which infants' behavior was rated by an independent observer and not a parent. Two separate studies with large numbers of participants found positive associations between maternal distress (primarily anxiety) in the first half of pregnancy and behavioral disorders or negative emotionality at preschool age (Martin, Noyes, Wisenbaker, & Huttunen, 2000; O'Connor, Heron, Golding, Beveridge, & Glover, 2002). Unfortunately, both relied on mothers' reports of their children's problems, so it is impossible to know whether the results simply indicate that anxious mothers perceive their children to be more difficult than nonanxious mothers do. However, new information about potential mechanisms whereby maternal stress might affect fetal development gives plausibility to these results. Maternal anxiety is associated with reduced blood flow to the fetus (Sjostrom, Valentin, Thelin, & Marsal, 1997), and fetal levels of stress hormones reflect those of their mothers (Gitau, Cameron, Fisk, & Glover, 1998).

Remarkably, this handful of published studies represents most of what we know about the effects of maternal distress on child development. There are several additional reports in the literature, but because of problems in methods or analysis, their results are not compelling. As the field matures, methodological, analytical, and interpretational standards will emerge over time.

THE NEXT LEVEL OF INVESTIGATION

The implicit assumption has been that prenatal stress and emotions have consequences for child development after birth because they have more immediate effects on the development of the nervous system before birth. Until recently, the fetal period of development was a black box. Although fetuses remain one of the few categories of research participants who can be neither directly viewed nor heard, opportunities to measure fetal development now exist. As pregnancy advances, the behavioral capabilities of the fetus become similar to those of a newborn infant, although the fetus is limited by the constraints of the uterus. Nonetheless, measurement of fetal motor activity, heart rate, and their relation to each other provides a fairly complete portrait of fetal development. New techniques present an opportunity to examine the manner in which the psychological state of the pregnant woman may affect development prior to birth, and perhaps permanently change the offspring's course of development.

In our first efforts to examine the link between fetal behavior and maternal stress, my colleagues and I relied on commonly used paper-and-pencil questionnaires to measure maternal psychological attributes. In a small study, we found that mothers' perception of experiencing daily hassles in everyday life was inversely related to the degree to which their fetuses' movement and heart rate were in synchrony. Such synchrony is an indicator of developing neural integration (DiPietro, Hodgson, Costigan, Hilton, & Johnson, 1996). In a second study, we found that mothers' emotional intensity, perception of their lives as stressful, and, in particular, feelings that they were more hassled than uplifted by their pregnancy were positively related to the activity level of their fetuses (DiPietro, Hilton, Hawkins, Costigan, & Pressman, 2002). We had previously reported that active fetuses tend to be active 1-year-olds, so fetal associations portend postnatal ones.

Measures of maternal stress and emotions that are based on mothers' self-reports are important only to the extent that they correspond to physiological signals that can be transmitted to the fetus; thus, they provide limited information. We turned to investigating the degree to which maternal physiological arousal, as measured by heart rate and electrical conductance of the skin, a measure of emotionality, is associated with fetal behavior. The results were unexpected in that fetal motor activity, even when it was imperceptible to women, stimulated transient increases in their heart rate and skin conductance.

It became apparent to us that the only way to truly examine the effect of stress on the fetus was to subject women to a standard, noninvasive stressor and measure the fetal response. The stressor we selected was a common cognitive challenge known as the Stroop Color-Word Test. In this test, subjects are asked to read color names that are printed in various colors and so must dissociate the color of the words from their meaning. The test is not aversive but reliably induces physiological arousal. In general, when pregnant women engaged in this task, fetal motor activity was suppressed, although individual responses varied. The degree to which individual women and fetuses responded to the Stroop test was similar from the middle to the end of pregnancy. These results lead us to propose three hypotheses. First, women respond to stress in characteristic ways that fetuses are repeatedly exposed to over the course of pregnancy. This experience serves to sensitize the developing nervous system. Second, there are both short-term and longer-term adaptive responses to stress by the fetus, depending on the intensity and repetitiveness of the stimulation. Finally, the immediacy of the fetal response to the Stroop, as well as to maternal viewing of graphic scenes from a movie on labor and delivery, suggest an additional mechanism whereby maternal stress might affect the fetus. We propose that the fetus responds to changes in the sensory environment of the uterus that occur when maternal heart rate, blood pressure, and other internal functions are abruptly altered. This proposal cannot be readily tested, but hearing is among the first perceptual systems to develop prenatally, and it is well documented that the fetus can perceive sounds that emanate from both within and outside the uterus.

Our final foray into this area of inquiry has been to follow children who participated in our studies as fetuses. Recently, we completed developmental testing on approximately one hundred 2-year-old children. The results, as is often the case in fetal research, surprised us. Higher maternal anxiety midway through pregnancy was strongly associated with better motor and mental development scores on the Bayley Scales of Infant Development, a standard developmental assessment. These associations remained even after controlling statistically for other possible contributing factors, including level of maternal education and both anxiety and stress after giving birth. This finding is in the direction opposite to that which would be predicted on the basis of most, but not all, of the animal research. Yet it is consistent with what is known about the class of neurohormones known as glucocorticoids, which are produced during the stress response and also play a role in the maturation of body organs. Our results are also consistent with findings from a series of studies on physical stress. The newborns of pregnant women who exercised regularly were somewhat smaller than the newborns of women who did not exercise much, but showed better ability to remain alert and track stimuli; the children of the regular exercisers also had higher cognitive ability at age 5 (Clapp, 1996). Exercise and psychological distress do not necessarily have the same physiological consequences to the fetus, but the parallel is intriguing.

CONCLUSIONS

At this time, there is too little scientific evidence to establish that a woman's psychological state during pregnancy affects her child's developmental outcomes. It is premature to extend findings from animal studies to women and children, particularly given the disparity in the way the animal and human studies are designed. The question of whether maternal stress and affect serve to accelerate or inhibit maturation of the fetal nervous system, and postnatal development in turn, remains open. It has been proposed that a certain degree of stress during early childhood is required for optimal organization of the brain, because stress provokes periods of disruption to existing structures (Huether, 1998), and this may be true for the prenatal period as well.

The relation between maternal stress and children's development may ultimately be found to mirror the relation between arousal and performance, which is characterized by an inverted U-shaped curve. This function, often called the Yerkes-Dodson law, posits that both low and high levels of arousal are associated with performance decrements, whereas a moderate level is associated with enhanced performance. This model has been applied to a spectrum of psychological observations, and a parallel with prenatal maternal stress may exist as well. In other words, too much or too little stress may impede development, but a moderate level may be formative or optimal. The current intensive investigation in this research area should provide better understanding of the importance of the prenatal period for postnatal life as investigators direct their efforts toward determining how maternal psychological signals are received by the fetus.

Recommended Reading

Kofman, O. (2002). The role of prenatal stress in the etiology of developmental behavioral disorders. *Neuroscience and Biobehavioral Reviews, 26,* 457–470.

Mulder, E., Robles de Medina, P., Huizink, A., Van den Bergh, B., Buitelaar, J., & Visser, G. (2002). Prenatal maternal stress: Effects on pregnancy and the (unborn) child. *Early Human Development, 70,* 3–14.

Paarlberg, K.M., Vingerhoets, A., Passchier, J., Dekker, G., & van Geijn, H. (1995). Psychosocial factors and pregnancy outcome: A review with emphasis on methodological issues. *Journal of Psychosomatic Research, 39,* 563–595.

Wadhwa, P., Sandman, C., & Garite, T. (2001). The neurobiology of stress in human pregnancy: Implications for prematurity and development of the fetal central nervous system. *Progress in Brain Research, 133,* 131–142.

Acknowledgments—This work has been supported by Grant R01 HD5792 from the National Institute of Child Health and Development.

Note

1. Address correspondence to Janet DiPietro, Department of Population and Family Health Sciences, 624 N. Broadway, Johns Hopkins University, Baltimore, MD 21205; e-mail: jdipietr@jhsph.edu.

References

Clapp, J. (1996). Morphometric and neurodevelopmental outcome at age five years of the offspring of women who continued to exercise regularly throughout pregnancy. *Journal of Pediatrics, 129,* 856–863.

DiPietro, J., Hilton, S., Hawkins, M., Costigan, K., & Pressman, E. (2002). Maternal stress and affect influence fetal neurobehavioral development. *Developmental Psychology, 38,* 659–668.

DiPietro, J.A., Hodgson, D.M., Costigan, K.A., Hilton, S.C., & Johnson, T.R.B. (1996). Development of fetal movement-fetal heart rate coupling from 20 weeks through term. *Early Human Development, 44,* 139–151.

Fujioka, T., Fujioka, A., Tan, N., Chowdhury, G., Mouri, H., Sakata, Y., & Nakamura, S. (2001). Mild prenatal stress enhances learning performance in the non-adopted rat offspring. *Neuroscience, 103,* 301–307.

65

Gitau, R., Cameron, A., Fisk, N., & Glover, V. (1998). Fetal exposure to maternal cortisol. *Lancet, 352,* 707–708.

Huether, G. (1998). Stress and the adaptive self-organization of neuronal connectivity during early childhood. *International Journal of Neuroscience, 16,* 297–306.

Huizink, A., Robles de Medina, P., Mulder, E., Visser, G., & Buitelaar, J. (2002). Psychological measures of prenatal stress as predictors of infant temperament. *Journal of the American Academy of Child & Adolescent Psychiatry, 41,* 1078–1085.

Martin, R., Noyes, J., Wisenbaker, J., & Huttunen, M. (2000). Prediction of early childhood negative emotionality and inhibition from maternal distress during pregnancy. *Merrill-Palmer Quarterly, 45,* 370–391.

Novak, M., & Sackett, G. (1996). Reflexive and early neonatal development in offspring of pigtailed macaques exposed to prenatal psychosocial stress. *Developmental Psychobiology, 29,* 294.

O'Connor, T., Heron, J., Golding, J., Beveridge, M., & Glover, V. (2002). Maternal antenatal anxiety and children's behavioural/emotional problems at 4 years. *British Journal of Psychiatry, 180,* 502–508.

Schneider, M., & Moore, C. (2000). Effects of prenatal stress on development: A non-human primate model. In C. Nelson (Ed.), *Minnesota Symposium on Child Psychology: Vol. 31. The effects of early adversity on neurobehavioral development* (pp. 201–244). Mahwah, NJ: Erlbaum.

Sjostrom, K., Valentin, L., Thelin, T., & Marsal, K. (1997). Maternal anxiety in late pregnancy and fetal hemodynamics. *European Journal of Obstetrics and Gynecology, 74,* 149–155.

Welberg, L., & Seckl, J. (2001). Prenatal stress, glucocorticoids and the programming of the brain. *Journal of Neuroendocrinology, 13,* 113–128.

This article has been reprinted as it originally appeared in *Current Directions in Psychological Science*. Citation information for this article as originally published appears above.

Biological Sensitivity to Context

Bruce J. Ellis[1]
John and Doris Norton School of Family and Consumer Science,
University of Arizona

W. Thomas Boyce
College for Interdisciplinary Studies and Faculty of Medicine,
University of British Columbia

Abstract

Conventional views suggest that exaggerated biological reactivity to stress is a harmful vestige of an evolutionary past in which threats to survival were more prevalent and severe. Recent evidence, however, indicates that effects of high reactivity on behavior and health are bivalent rather than univalent in character, exerting both risk-augmenting and risk-protective effects depending on the context. These observations suggest that heightened stress reactivity may reflect increased biological sensitivity to context, with potential for negative health effects under conditions of adversity and for positive effects under conditions of support. From an evolutionary perspective, the developmental plasticity of the stress-response systems, along with their structured, context-dependent effects, suggests that variation in these systems has been adaptively patterned to increase the capacity of children to match their stress-response profiles to anticipated developmental environments. Taken together, these theoretical perspectives generate a novel hypothesis: that there is a curvilinear, U-shaped relation between early exposures to adversity and the development of stress-reactive profiles, with high-reactivity phenotypes disproportionately emerging within both highly stressful and highly protected early social environments.

Keywords

stress reactivity; evolutionary psychology; developmental psychobiology

Developmental psychologists frequently consider the effects of life experience on development but rarely consider how these effects have been structured by natural selection. Despite this oversight, the burgeoning field of evolutionary-developmental biology has exciting and profound implications for the study of human development (see especially West-Eberhard, 2003). Over the last two decades, theory and research in the field has come to acknowledge that, in most species, single "best" strategies for survival and reproduction are unlikely to evolve. This is because the optimal strategy varies as a function of the physical, economic, and socioemotional parameters of one's specific environment (Crawford & Anderson, 1989), and thus a strategy that promotes success in some environmental contexts may lead to failure in others. Selection pressures therefore tend to favor *adaptive phenotypic plasticity*, the capacity of a single genotype to support a range of phenotypes in response to particular ecological conditions that recurrently influenced fitness during a species' evolutionary history. Importantly, the development of alternative phenotypes is a nonrandom process; that is, it is the outcome of structured transactions between genes and environments that were shaped by natural selection to increase the capacity and tendency of individuals to track their developmental environments and adjust their phenotypes accordingly.

We have recently proposed a developmental model of adaptive phenotypic plasticity in the human stress-response systems (see Boyce & Ellis, 2005). The model articulates the precepts and rationale for a new claim about the nature of relations between early life experience and stress reactivity, a claim that we have also explored empirically (Ellis, Essex, & Boyce, 2005). We contend that heightened stress reactivity may reflect not simply exaggerated arousal under challenge but, rather, a form of enhanced, neurobiologically mediated sensitivity to context, or *biological sensitivity to context* (BSC).

The logic of our argument can be summarized in the following way. Biological reactivity to psychological stressors comprises a complex, integrated system of central neural and peripheral neuroendocrine responses designed to prepare the organism for challenge or threat. Developmental experience plays a role, along with heritable variation, in calibrating the response dynamics of this system. Individual differences in such stress reactivity are thought to underlie broad variability in associations between stress and illness and to reflect constitutional variation in susceptibility to stressful challenge. Highly reactive phenotypes, in which affected individuals mount vigorous or sustained autonomic, adrenocortical (cortisol), or other biological responses to stressors, have been viewed as an atavistic health risk factor, a legacy of physiological responses more commensurate with the perils of prehistoric human environments. Often overlooked in such accounts is a body of anomalous observations revealing oppositional, counter-regulatory processes within the stress-response circuitry itself and, even more compellingly, bidirectional effects of reactivity on biomedical and psychiatric outcomes. Highly reactive children sustain disproportionate rates of morbidity when raised in adverse environments but unusually low rates when raised in low-stress, highly supportive settings (Boyce & Ellis, 2005).

Such bidirectional, environment-contingent health effects suggest that BSC is the core, defining feature of highly reactive phenotypes. These observations call into question the presumably unitary pathogenic effects of high reactivity and suggest that its protective effects within specific developmental ecologies might explain the conservation of such phenotypic variation over evolutionary history. BSC reflects sensitivity to both harmful and protective contextual effects. Indeed, the subset of children with highly reactive biological profiles reveals a unique sensitivity or "permeability" to the influence of environmental conditions (Boyce & Ellis, 2005). Further, although a substantial literature documents the capacity of early developmental trauma to predispose individuals toward high biological reactivity, an evolutionary formulation of recent findings suggests a different and novel hypothesis: that the association between early adversity and reactivity is curvilinear in character, with both highly stressful and highly protective environments yielding disproportionate numbers of highly reactive children (Boyce & Ellis, 2005).

THE DANDELION AND THE ORCHID

A Swedish idiomatic expression, *maskrosbarn* or "dandelion child," refers to the capacity of some children—not unlike those with low-reactive phenotypes—to survive and even thrive in whatever circumstances they encounter, in much the same way that dandelions seem to prosper irrespective of soil, sun, drought, or rain. Observations of such children have generated, for example, an extensive developmental literature on the phenomenon of resilience, the capacity for positive adaptation despite experiences of significant adversity (e.g., Luthar, 2006; Masten, 2007). A contrasting Swedish neologism, *orkidebarn* or "orchid child," might better describe the context-sensitive individual, whose survival and flourishing is intimately tied, like that of the orchid, to the nurturant or neglectful character of the environment. In conditions of neglect, the orchid promptly declines, while in conditions of support and nurture, it is a flower of unusual beauty.

The metaphorical invocation of highly reactive children as *orkidebarn* is consistent with a growing number of studies revealing that high-reactivity phenotypes under specific environmental conditions may be associated with protective, rather than harmful, effects and generate normative or improved health outcomes. Such bivalent effects of BSC on human and primate morbidities have thematically characterized a series of studies reported by Boyce and colleagues. In examining cardiovascular and immunologic reactivity in two samples of 3- to 5-year-old children, for example, significant interactions with environmental stressors were detected (Fig. 1A) in the prediction of respiratory illness incidence over the ensuing several months (Boyce et al., 1995). Specifically, the noted interactions suggested bidirectional effects of reactivity on illness incidence: Highly reactive children in high-stress families or childcare centers sustained significantly higher rates of respiratory illness than their low-reactive peers did, but equally reactive children in low-stress settings were the healthiest of all children in the samples. By contrast, the respiratory-illness incidence of low-reactivity children was unresponsive to environmental stress levels, showing approximately the same, mid-level illness rates in both low- and high-stress conditions. Similarly significant interactions were found for injury incidence (Boyce, 1996).

Even though they were prospective in design, both of these studies were observational in nature and lacked experimental data on the incidence of illnesses or injuries among the same group of highly reactive children in both low- and high-stress conditions. In a subsequent study of semi-free-ranging rhesus macaques, however, such quasiexperimental conditions were satisfied (Boyce, O'Neill-Wagner, Price, Haines, & Suomi, 1998). The troop of macaques, which had been previously assessed for levels of BSC (degree of biobehavioral reactivity to novel or challenging stimuli), lived in a 6-acre wooded habitat in rural Maryland. In 1993, the troop encountered a 6-month period of protective confinement to a small, 1,000-square-foot building, during a construction project on the habitat grounds. The confinement proved highly stressful, and the incidence of violent injuries increased fivefold during the 6-month period. Blinded ascertainment of medically attended injury rates from veterinary records produced evidence for a significant interaction between reactivity status and confinement stress, plotted in Fig. 1B. As with the prior studies of children, low-reactivity individuals showed little effect of the confinement, while those with high reactivity showed dramatically higher rates of violent injuries in the high-stress situation but lower rates in the low-stress condition.

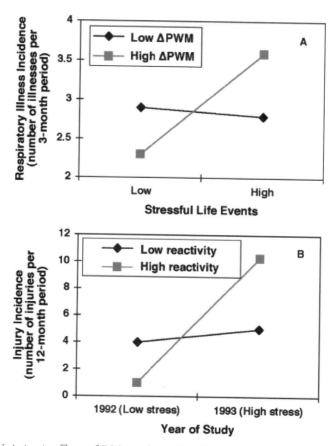

Fig. 1. Variation in effects of BSC on physical health across socioecological conditions. The top graph (A) shows a cross-over interaction between immune reactivity (changes in pokeweed mitogen response [ΔPWM]) and family stressful events in prediction of respiratory illness incidence in kindergartners (N = 99; redrawn from Boyce et al., 1995). The bottom graph (B) shows a cross-over interaction between biobehavioral reactivity and confinement stress in prediction of injury rates in a troop of semi-free-ranging rhesus monkeys (N = 36; redrawn from Boyce, O'Neill-Wagner, Price, Haines, & Suomi, 1998).

These findings complement research on the bidirectional, context-dependent effects of high intelligence (or high ego development): Whereas highly intelligent, introspective people tend to flourish under relatively benign life conditions, they also tend to be more reactive than others to distress (see Luthar, 2006). Thus, just as high reactivity to stress has generally been considered pathogenic but can be protective in supportive environmental contexts, high intelligence/introspection has generally been thought of as beneficial, but can be harmful if surrounding forces are negative.

DEVELOPMENT OF BSC: AN EVOLUTIONARY APPROACH

Adaptive phenotypic plasticity enables children to match their biological and behavioral systems to the parameters of their early (and predicted future)

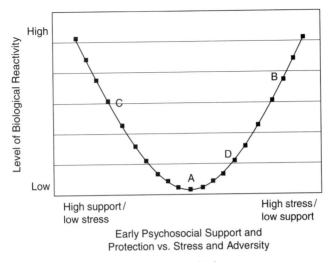

Fig. 2. Hypothesized curvilinear relation between biologic reactivity to stress and experiences of support and protection versus stress and adversity in early environments. Comparisons of subjects at points A and B would lead to the conclusion that low support/high stress results in heightened stress reactivity. Comparisons at points C and D, on the other hand, would generate the inference that low support/high stress produces diminished reactivity (adapted from Boyce & Ellis, 2005).

developmental environments. Given past evidence that early trauma can increase stress reactivity and new evidence that high reactivity can be protective in highly supportive settings, we (Boyce & Ellis, 2005) postulated a curvilinear, U-shaped relation (shown in Fig. 2) between levels of early adversity and the magnitude of biological response dispositions. Specifically, we hypothesized (a) that exposure to acutely stressful childhood environments up-regulates stress reactivity, increasing the capacity and tendency of individuals to detect and respond to environmental dangers and threats; and (b) that exposure to exceptionally supportive childhood environments also up-regulates stress reactivity, increasing susceptibility to social resources and ambient support. Both of these proposed functions of BSC converge with theory and data indicating that temporary, moderate increases in stress hormones and associated neurotransmitters enhance mental activities in localized domains, focus attention, and prime memory storage and thus improve cognitive processes for dealing with environmental opportunities and threats (Flinn, 2006). By contrast, and typically for the large majority of children, (c) exposure to childhood environments that are not extreme in either direction down-regulates stress reactivity, buffering individuals against the chronic stressors encountered in a world that is neither highly threatening nor consistently safe. Although the cellular mechanisms that calibrate such response dispositions are currently unknown in humans, recent work in animal models suggests that epigenetic modifications resulting in differential gene expression may well play an important role (Meaney, Szyf, & Seckl, 2007).

Although the theory predicts up-regulation of stress-response systems in both highly supportive and stressful environments (the U-shaped curve), high stress reactivity may translate into different behavioral phenotypes in support-ive versus stressful contexts. Reactive, sensitive children have been found to be more reflective and perhaps more conscious of self and environment; to be more able to delay gratification in pursuit of goals; and to perform better on neuropsy-chological measures of inhibitory control, executive function, and self-regulation (e.g., Aron & Aron, 1997; Blair, Granger, & Razza, 2005). Up-regulated stress-response systems in children may therefore interact with protective, beneficial developmental environments to produce relatively high levels of cognitive and social competence. Conversely, interactions between high stress reactivity and risky, threatening developmental environments may result in lower thresholds for anticipating threat in ambiguous or unfamiliar situations (e.g., elevated sensitiv-ity to threat cues such as angry faces) and support greater vigilance and wariness in children.

Although the U-shaped curve depicted in Figure 2 specifies environmental sources of variation in BSC, genetic sources of variation and gene–environment interactions are also important and need to be addressed in a comprehensive the-ory of BSC (see Ellis, Jackson, & Boyce, 2006). Reaction norms are genetically based "bookends" that constrain the range of phenotypes that can develop within varying environmental contexts. Importantly, children differ in the location of these bookends along phenotypic dimensions. For example, children whose reac-tion norms are located on the upper end of the BSC spectrum have higher start-ing points for stress reactivity than do children whose reaction norms are on the lower end. These differences can generally be expected to maintain variation in BSC, even if children have equivalent life experiences. In addition, children dif-fer in how widely their bookends are placed. That is, some children have broad reaction norms and display high levels of plasticity in response to developmental experience, whereas others have more narrow reaction norms and display more fixed developmental trajectories (see Belsky, 2005). The current theory should be more successful in accounting for developmental variation in BSC among chil-dren with wider reaction norms.

EMPIRICAL EXPLORATIONS OF BSC THEORY

We have initially investigated our curvilinear, U-shaped model of the develop-ment of BSC in two studies comprising 249 children and their families (Ellis et al., 2005). In the first study, 3- to 5-year-old children were concurrently assessed on levels of support and adversity in home and preschool environments and on cardiovascular reactivity to laboratory challenges. Because the early environ-ments of these children ranged from exceptionally stable and supportive to mod-erately stressful, the sample only provided a window into a portion of the proposed U-shaped association between support/adversity and BSC (i.e., the left half of the curve shown in Fig. 2). Within this range, the theory posits that higher stress will be associated with reduced biological responsivity to stressors. In the second study, children were prospectively assessed on family stress in both infancy and preschool and on autonomic and adrenocortical reactivity to labora-tory challenges at age 7. This second study sampled the broad range of variation in early childhood environments that is needed to fully explore the curvilinearity hypothesis. Within this range, both highly protected and highly stressful environments should promote heightened BSC.

We found in both studies that a disproportionate number of children in supportive, low-stress environments displayed high autonomic reactivity. Conversely, in the second study a relatively high proportion of children in very stressful environments showed evidence of heightened sympathetic and adrenocortical reactivity. Consistent with our evolutionary-developmental theory, these exploratory analyses also suggested that relations between levels of childhood support/adversity and the magnitude of stress reactivity are curvilinear, with children from moderately stressful environments displaying the lowest reactivity levels in both studies.

CONCLUSIONS AND FUTURE DIRECTIONS

The proposed U-shaped curve can potentially reconcile important contradictions in the existing literature on the origins and consequences of stress reactivity in children. Investigators comparing individuals from points A and B in Figure 2, for example, would conclude, as many researchers in this area have (e.g., De Bellis et al., 1999), that experiences of family and environmental stress are associated with up-regulatory calibrations in biological reactivity systems. Yet studies comparing individuals from points C and D would find, as those reviewed by Gunnar and Vazquez (2001) have, that early stressors are rather associated with down-regulatory changes in salient biological responses. The current theory, which posits two oppositionally distinctive ontogenies for BSC, explains both of these regulatory effects.

A guiding assumption of our work on stress reactivity is that developmental mechanisms have been organized by natural selection to produce enhanced BSC when it is advantageous to the developing person—in both acutely stressful and exceptionally supportive childhood environments. In shaping intervention strategies to prevent developmental psychopathology and other early morbidities, we may do well to consider this conceptualization of individual differences in stress reactivity. Under some circumstances, highly sensitive children may be usefully targeted for interventions involving the provision of ancillary supportive services, while in other circumstances, the needs of highly sensitive children might define the minimum standards of provision for an entire population of children. In still other settings, ascertainment of reactivity status might simply prevent the adoption of a "one size fits all" approach, facilitating the design of strategies and policies specifically tailored to the needs of children with different biological response phenotypes. Whatever the future direct utility of the theory and research described here, it is our hope that this work will advance collective understanding of the sources of individual differences and their implications for the rearing and well-being of children.

Recommended Reading

Aron, E.N., & Aron, A. (1997). (See References). An insightful empirical paper on sensory-processing sensitivity, which has interesting parallels with BSC.

Belsky (2005). (See References). A very thoughtful presentation of a complementary evolutionary theory of differential susceptibility to environmental influence.

Boyce, W.T., & Ellis, B.J. (2005). (See References). The original, thorough, and more far-reaching theoretical analysis of BSC.

Ellis, B.J., Jackson, J.J., & Boyce, W.T. (2006). (See References). A detailed analysis of the evolutionary bases of individual differences in activity of the stress response systems.

Note

1. Address correspondence to Bruce J. Ellis, Division of Family Studies and Human Development, University of Arizona, P.O. Box 210078, Tucson, AZ 85721-0078; e-mail: bjellis@email.arizona.edu.

References

Aron, E.N., & Aron, A. (1997). Sensory-processing sensitivity and its relation to introversion and emotionality. *Journal of Personality and Social Psychology, 73,* 345–368.

Belsky, J. (2005). Differential susceptibility to rearing influence. In B.J. Ellis & D.F. Bjorklund (Eds.), *Origins of the social mind: Evolutionary psychology and child development* (pp. 139–163). New York: Guilford Press.

Blair, C., Granger, D., & Razza, R.P. (2005). Cortisol reactivity is positively related to executive function in preschool children attending Head Start. *Child Development, 76,* 554–567.

Boyce, W.T. (1996). Biobehavioral reactivity and injuries in children and adolescents. In M.H. Bornstein & J. Genevro (Eds.), *Child development and behavioral pediatrics: Toward understanding children and health.* Mahwah, NJ: Erlbaum.

Boyce, W.T., Chesney, M., Alkon-Leonard, A., Tschann, J., Adams, S., Chesterman, B., et al. (1995). Psychobiologic reactivity to stress and childhood respiratory illnesses: Results of two prospective studies. *Psychosomatic Medicine, 57,* 411–422.

Boyce, W.T., & Ellis, B.J. (2005). Biological sensitivity to context: I. An evolutionary-developmental theory of the origins and functions of stress reactivity. *Development & Psychopathology, 17,* 271–301.

Boyce, W.T., O'Neill-Wagner, P., Price, C.S., Haines, M., & Suomi, S.J. (1998). Crowding stress and violent injuries among behaviorally inhibited rhesus macaques. *Health Psychology, 17,* 285–289.

Crawford, C.B., & Anderson, J.L. (1989). Sociobiology: An environmentalist discipline? *American Psychologist, 44,* 1449–1459.

De Bellis, M.D., Baum, A.S., Birmaher, B., Keshavan, M.S., Eccard, C.H., Boring, A.M., et al. (1999). Developmental traumatology. Part I: Biological stress systems. *Biological Psychiatry, 45,* 1259–1270.

Ellis, B.J., Essex, M.J., & Boyce, W.T. (2005). Biological sensitivity to context: II. Empirical explorations of an evolutionary-developmental theory. *Development & Psychopathology, 17,* 303–328.

Ellis, B.J., Jackson, J.J., & Boyce, W.T. (2006). The stress response systems: Universality and adaptive individual differences. *Developmental Review, 26,* 175–212.

Flinn, M.V. (2006). Evolution and ontogeny of stress response to social challenges in the human child. *Developmental Review, 26,* 138–174.

Gunnar, M.R., & Vazquez, D.M. (2001). Low cortisol and a flattening of expected daytime rhythm: Potential indices of risk in human development. *Development and Psychopathology, 13,* 515–538.

Luthar, S.S. (2006). Resilience in development: A synthesis of research across five decades. In D. Cicchetti & D.J. Cohen (Eds.), *Developmental psychopathology, Vol. 3: Risk, disorder, and adaptation* (pp. 739–795). Hoboken, NJ: John Wiley & Sons.

Masten, A.S. (2007). Resilience in developing systems: Progress and promise as the fourth wave rises. *Development and Psychopathology, 19,* 921–930.

Meaney, M.J., Szyf, M., & Seckl, J.R. (2007). Epigenetic mechanisms of perinatal programming of hypothalamic-pituitary-adrenal function and health. *Trends in Molecular Medicine, 13,* 269–277.

West-Eberhard, M.J. (2003). *Developmental plasticity and evolution.* New York: Oxford University Press.

Section 2: Critical Thinking Questions

1. How does an understanding of biological mechanisms through which environmental factors operate on child psychopathology help the design of preventive interventions?

2. Does the discovery of biological mechanisms in environmental effects enhance or detract from the importance of the environmental variables in children's development?

3. Under what conditions do animal studies provide important contribution to our understanding of child psychopathology? When are animal studies poor models for human behavior? What are unique advantages of animal studies that are not usually possible in human studies?

This article has been reprinted as it originally appeared in *Current Directions in Psychological Science*. Citation information for this article as originally published appears above.

Section 3: Models of Gene-Environment Interaction Processes

This section provides theoretical and empirical treatises of *how* the gene-environment interaction effect operates on children's behavior. It is not sufficient to discover that genes and environments interact. The shape of the interaction effect and the processes through which it exerts an impact on child psychopathology must be discovered in order to identify interventions that can treat or prevent childhood disorders.

Reiss provides a very readable discussion of the multiple ways that genes and family environments relate to each other, in "interplay" as he calls it. Fox, Hane, and Pine report the implications of their empirical discovery of an interaction effect between the serotonin transporter gene 5HTTLPR and maternal social support in predicting children's fearful behavior. They integrate their understanding in a model of plasticity for affective neurocircuitry. Belsky, Bakermans-Kranenburg, and van IJzendoorn propose that the fundamental nature of genetic effects in child psychopathology is to alter the child's susceptibility to the impact of the environment. That is, some children's genes may render them especially responsive to environmental impacts, both for positive effects as well as negative impacts. This prospect is exciting because it suggests that children who are otherwise regarded as high-risk may be especially ready to benefit from positive environments in the form of preventive intervention and treatment.

Raine provides a more specific understanding of how genetic effects, environmental effects, and their interaction lead to neural, psychophysiological, and hormonal changes that in turn lead to children's aggressive behavior.

Together, these articles provide a blueprint for the upcoming decade of research in how gene-by-environment interaction effects operate on children's development of psychopathology.

The Interplay Between Genotypes and Family Relationships: Reframing Concepts of Development and Prevention

David Reiss[1]

Center for Family Research, Department of Psychiatry and Behavioral Sciences, George Washington University

Abstract

Children's genotypes and their social relationships are correlated throughout their development. Heritable characteristics of children evoke strong and specific responses from their parents; frequently, these same heritable characteristics also influence the children's adjustment. Moreover, parental heritable traits that influence their parenting are also transmitted to children and influence their children's adjustment. Thus, genetically influenced evocative processes from children and parental-transmission mechanisms influence the covariances between measures of family relationships and child development. These findings suggest new targets for preventing adverse development: altering parental responses to heritable characteristics of children and influencing the genetically influenced ontogeny of parenting.

Keywords

genotype; relationships; parenting; prevention

Conventional models of psychological development acknowledge that genetic and social factors both play a role. Older models assumed that these two influences were independent from each other and that differences among individuals in personality development, cognitive development and psychological development could be explained by adding their effects together. More recently, it has become clear that, in many cases, the social environment interacts with genetic influences. For example, the genetic risk for schizophrenia seems to be fully expressed only when children at genetic risk grow up in families with high conflict, emotional restriction, and chaotic intergenerational boundaries (Tienari et al., 2004). Such a perspective still allows social and genetic variables to be thought of as relatively distinct: Genetic factors render individuals susceptible to adverse social environments; then, at some point—perhaps in early childhood or much later in development—unfavorable social factors elicit behavioral difficulties.

Recent data suggest that genetic and social influences are even more intertwined, however. From early development through adulthood, genetic and social factors are *correlated*; that is, individuals' genotypes are associated with many specific characteristics of their environment. This association occurs in two ways. First, as can be inferred from twin, sibling, and adoption studies, heritable characteristics of children can evoke highly specific responses from the social environment. For example, certain heritable characteristics of children evoke warmth and involvement from their parents. More importantly, the same genetic factors that evoke parental warmth also contribute to a child's social responsibility, including adherence to community norms and helping and sharing behaviors. In the research of my colleagues and I, almost all of the covariance between maternal warmth and child social responsibility is due to these genetic influences common to both parenting and child development (Reiss, Neiderhiser, Hetherington, & Plomin, 2000).

The second way such associations may occur is that heritable traits that influence a mother's or father's parenting may be genetically transmitted to their children. Those same traits in children may make them vulnerable to psychopathology. For example, a recent twin study suggests that heritable factors influence maternal smoking during pregnancy and, when transmitted to children, increase the childrens' likelihood of having conduct problems. These data raise questions about whether fetal exposure to tobacco products is the main cause of their postnatal conduct problems (Maughan, Taylor, Caspi, & Moffitt, 2004).

In behavioral genetics, associations between individuals' genotypes and their environment are called *genotype–environment correlations*. When a correlation is due to the effects of heritable features stimulating responses from the environment, it is called an *evocative* genotype–environment correlation. When it is due to genes transmitted by parents to their children, the term is *passive* genotype–environment correlation. Use of the word *genotype* in this type of research signifies the cumulative effect of all genetic influences on a particular trait, as examined in studies that usually use twin, sibling, or adoption designs.

GENOTYPE–ENVIRONMENT CORRELATIONS AND MECHANISMS OF DEVELOPMENT

Parent–Child Relationships May Amplify Genetic Influences

Rowe (1981) first reported data suggesting evocative genotype–parenting correlations. Monozygotic (i.e. derived from a single egg and genetically identical) twins' reports of how accepted they were by their parents were correlated more than twice as highly as the reports of dizygotic (i.e. from different eggs and 50% genetically related) twins. Figure 1 illustrates how monozygotic–dizygotic comparisons are used to make inferences about such correlations. Rowe's finding was subsequently replicated many times using different methods of assessing parent–child relationships: interviews of parents (Goodman & Stevenson, 1991), parental self-reports, and direct observation of parent–child relationships (O'Connor, Hetherington, Reiss, & Plomin, 1995). These findings do not reflect parental bias due to their knowledge of whether their twins were monozygotic or dizygotic, since the findings also hold where monozygotic twins have been misdiagnosed as dizygotic (Goodman & Stevenson, 1991).

Adoption studies have confirmed the importance of evocative genotype–parenting correlations: The behavior of an adoptive parent toward his or her child can be predicted from patterns of behavior in the birth parent. For example, two separate studies predicted adoptive parents' degree of harsh discipline and hostility toward their children from the level of aggressive behavior in the birth parents. These studies suggest that inherited externalizing (including aggressive and

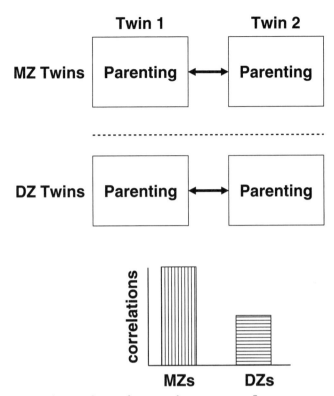

Fig. 1. Diagram showing how inferences about genetic influences on variation of a measured variable, in this case parenting, may be drawn from twin data. Boxes represent measured variable in a comparison of monozygotic (MZ) and dizygotic (DZ) child twins; the arrows represent correlations. The bar graph at the bottom of the figure represents example findings. The example finding shows MZ child twins correlate much more strongly than DZ child twins, enabling the inference that heritable characteristics of the child influence parenting (Reiss, Neiderhiser, Hetherington, & Plomin, 2000).

delinquent) behavior in the children evoked the response in the adoptive parents (Ge et al., 1996; O'Connor, Deater-Deckard, Fulker, Rutter, & Plomin, 1998).

Heritable evoked parental responses have been reported from age 1 through late adolescence. For example, one study compared nonadoptive siblings, who share 50% of their individual-differences genes, with siblings adopted from different birth parents. Data gathered at age 1 and again at age 2 suggested that children's genotypes greatly influenced how much intellectual stimulation their parents provided to them: Parental behavior correlated much higher toward the nonadoptive siblings than toward the adoptive siblings (Braungart, Plomin, Fulker, & DeFries, 1992). Other studies have reported on genetic influences on parenting at age 3, in middle childhood, and in adolescence. One longitudinal twin study suggested that heritable evocative effects increase across adolescence; this increase across age was particularly marked for fathers (Elkins, McGue, & Iacono, 1997).

To study heritable evocative effects, the Nonshared Environment in Adolescent Development study (NEAD; Reiss et al., 2000) combined a twin design with a stepfamily design. We drew genetic inferences from comparisons among monozygotic twins, dizygotic twins, full siblings, half siblings (e.g., a mother brings a child from a previous marriage and has a child with her new husband) and unrelated siblings (i.e., each parent brings a child from a previous marriage). NEAD showed that heritable evocative effects may be quite specific. For example, genetic factors that evoke maternal warmth are distinct from those that evoke paternal warmth.

Additional findings reveal that heritable effects go beyond evocative effects on parents. The same genetic factors in a child that evoke particular parenting responses also influence many dimensions of their own adjustment during childhood and adolescence. Inferences about these influences are drawn by comparing *cross correlations* across sibling types (see Fig. 2). For example, a mother's harsh parenting towards sibling A can be correlated with the level of antisocial behavior of sibling B. Genetic influences on covariance are inferred when these cross correlations decline systematically from monozygotic twins at the highest to dizygotic twins and full siblings in the middle to unrelated siblings at the lowest.

NEAD found that over 70% of the covariance between a mother's hostile parenting and her adolescents' antisocial behavior was accounted for by genetic influences common to both. These findings have been confirmed by several subsequent studies (e.g., Burt, Krueger, McGue, & Iacono, 2003). NEAD found sizable genetic contributions to many other covariances including mothers' hostile parenting with impairment in adolescents' cognitive performance, fathers' warmth with adolescents' social responsibility, and fathers' hostility with adolescents' depression. NEAD, using longitudinal data collected from earlier and later adolescence, found that, in many cases, the child's heritable impact on parental response preceded the development of the behavior in question. For example, genetic influence on hostile parenting preceded the evolution of antisocial behavior.

Evocative genotype–parenting correlations may amplify more direct genetic influences on the child's problem behavior. Indeed, it is possible that parental responses to their children's heritable characteristics—responses to which the parents themselves are insensible—are critical for transforming heritable influences on children's temperaments into problems requiring clinical attention. To verify this hypothesis and test its significance for preventive intervention, my colleagues and I are currently conducting a prospective adoption study. We are following birth- and adoptive parents and adopted toddlers from age 9 months. This Early Growth and Development Study (EGADS) will allow us to pinpoint exactly what heritable noxious behaviors in the child evoke adverse parental responses and the consequence of these parental responses for subsequent child development.

The Heritable Development of Parenting

Evidence for passive genotype–parenting correlation requires evidence that (a) the parents' genes influence their parenting and (b) genetic factors that influence parenting are transmitted to their children and influence important dimensions of the

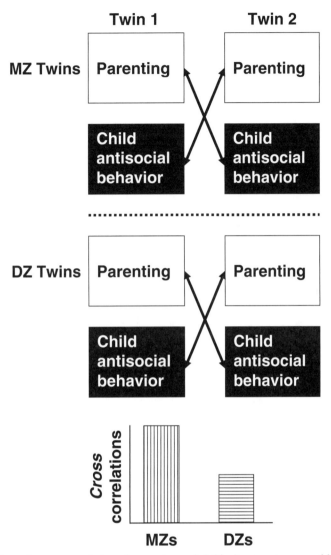

Fig. 2. Example cross correlation of parenting and child adjustment across sibling types. Parenting in one twin cross correlates with antisocial behavior in the other, more highly for monozygotic (MZ) twins than for dizygotic (DZ) twins. This suggests that the covariation between parenting and child antisocial behavior can be attributed to genetic influences common to both variables (Reiss et al., 2000).

children's adjustment. Evidence of this kind provides clues to childhood origins of parenting styles. For example, suppose it is observed that the same genetic factors that influence lack of warmth in mothers also influence depressive symptoms in their children. This would suggest that genetic factors link childhood internalizing with reduced maternal warmth, thereby offering clues about how genetically influenced parenting patterns unfold over the long term. Evidence for these passive effects comes from two sources.

First, studies using twins who are parents have shown genetic influences on dimensions of parenting. Our Twin Mom study investigated a sample of monozygotic and dizygotic twins who were mothers of adolescents. It showed that mothers' reports of their own warmth, hostility, and monitoring of the whereabouts of their children were more highly correlated for monozygotic than for dizygotic twins. A similar pattern of findings was shown using observer ratings for mothers' warmth and for children's ratings of their mothers' monitoring (Neiderhiser et al., 2004).

Second, adoption studies have found evidence for passive genetic links between parenting and the adjustment of children both in early childhood and in later adolescence. The correlation between parenting and child adjustment in birth families reflects evocative genotype–parenting correlations, environmental mechanisms, and passive genotype–parenting correlations. The last type are missing in adoptive families. Thus, by comparing correlations between parenting and child adjustment between the two groups it is possible to estimate—by elimination—the strength of passive genotype–parenting correlations. For example, one adoption study assessed parents' ratings of cohesiveness, lack of conflict, and open expression of feelings in their family during the time their children were 1 to 5 years old. For boys but not for girls, these ratings predicted teacher ratings of child delinquency and aggression at age 7, but only for boys raised by their own birth parents (Braungart-Rieker, Rende, Plomin, & DeFries, 1995). The correlations between parenting and teacher-rated aggression were insignificant in adoptive families. The correlations between adolescent problems and ratings of the quality of family relationships by their mothers were higher in families in which parents reared their own children than in adoptive families (McGue, Sharma, & Benson, 1996).

Taken together, these finding suggest that genotypic differences among parents influence their parenting and that these genotypic differences are transmitted to children, in whom they are manifested by psychiatric symptoms. We are currently investigating whether there are specific genetic links between childhood behavioral characteristics and patterns of parenting. For example, might internalizing problems in childhood be genetically linked to parental withdrawal and lack of support? Might childhood externalizing be genetically linked to aggressive and hostile parenting styles?

Highlighting Relationship Influences

Genetically informed studies highlight two sorts of family relationships that are linked with child psychological development independently of children's genotypes. Parent–child relationships are the first sort of such relationships identified by behavioral genetic data. For example, NEAD found that maternal rapport and affection was linked to adolescent autonomy and sociability. This is the case no matter what the child's genotype. Moreover, siblings within the same family are similar in their autonomy and sociability whether they are dizygotic or monozygotic twins or unrelated siblings. In contrast to parent hostility, the amount of maternal warmth received is also similar across both types of twins and unrelated siblings. Thus, taken together, our data suggest that mothers are relatively consistent in the positive feelings they show to children in their family and that all children benefit, no matter their genotype (Reiss et al., 2000).

Second, behavioral genetic data have highlighted nonparental family relationships that appear to influence childrens' development independently of their genotype. For example, NEAD showed that hostility and conflict in sibling relationships was strongly associated with adolescent antisocial behavior and depression. Conflict and hostility were highly reciprocal in adolescent siblings and put both siblings at equal risk for psychiatric symptoms independently of their genotypes. Moreover, NEAD showed a strong association between marital conflict and parent–child conflict on the one hand and sibling hostility on the other. More importantly, these links across family subsystems were independent of child genotype. Thus, in adolescence, hostility between siblings may be an indirect route through which family discord increases the vulnerability of children regardless of their genotype (Reiss et al., 2000).

Because it included the partners of the sisters who were the biological parents of the adolescent children, the Twin Mom study was able to yield valuable data on the role of adult genotypes in marital relationships. The study found that although genetic factors had a substantial influence on marital quality, as reported by both the twin siblings and their husbands, genetic factors explained little of the covariance between marital satisfaction and levels of wives' depressive symptoms. Rather, in this association, the dynamics of the marital relationships may play a central role (Spotts et al., 2004). These findings extend nongenetic studies of adult development that appeared to show that good marriages protect against depression and other behavior difficulties. However, nongenetic studies may miss heritable features of individuals that lead to both sustained, high-quality marriages and invulnerability to depression. Yet if the Twin Moms data is replicated, heritable features will seem unlikely to play a significant role in how marriages protect the marital partners.

IMPLICATIONS: NEW TARGETS FOR PREVENTION

Data on genotypes and family relationships offer three novel opportunities to design preventive interventions to forestall the development of serious problem behaviors and psychopathology.

First, findings suggesting that parent–child relationships amplify maladaptive genetic influences offer some of the most promising leads in preventing the expression of unfavorable genetic influences on many domains of child and adolescent adjustment. EGADS is designed to specify particular targets for intervention: parents' responses to heritable difficulties in their children. Numerous studies show that highly focused interventions can produce sustained changes in how parents respond to challenging children (Bakermans-Kranenburg, van Ijzendoorn, & Juffer, 2003). EGADS is designed to ascertain whether such interventions might suppress the parental amplification process and thus diminish adverse genetic influences.

Second, findings on passive genotype correlations provide a new target for interventions: promoting favorable parenting. The discovery of genetic links between childhood behavior and parenting suggests some childhood and adolescent origins of parenting behavior that should be addressed in efforts to prevent risky parental behavior such as drug abuse during pregnancy or hostile and abusive parenting subsequently. For example, efforts to prevent the early emergence of conduct problems may prevent later serious antisocial behavior as well as abusive parenting.

Finally, studies of genotype–environment correlation suggest new psychosocial targets for preventing psychological and behavioral disorders: siblings and marriages. Techniques already developed for clinical interventions with maladaptive sibling relationships and with marriages might be refashioned for preventing psychological disorders in the siblings or marital partners.

Recommended Reading

Maughan, B., Taylor, A., Caspi, A., & Moffitt, T.E. (2004). (See References)

Reiss, D., Pedersen, N.L., Cederblad, M., Lichtenstein, P., Hansson, K., Neiderhiser, J. M., et al. (2001). Genetic probes of three theories of maternal adjustment: I. Recent evidence and a model. *Family Process, 40,* 247–259.

Rutter, M., Pickles, A., Murray, R., & Eaves, L. (2001). Testing hypotheses on specific environmental causal effects on behavior. *Psychological Bulletin, 127,* 291–324.

Note

1. Address correspondence to David Reiss, Center for Family Research, Department of Psychiatry and Behavioral Sciences, George Washington University, 2300 K Street, NW, Washington, DC 20037; e-mail: cfrdxr@gwumc.edu.

References

Bakermans-Kranenburg, M.J., van Ijzendoorn, M.H., & Juffer, F. (2003). Less is more: Meta-analyses of sensitivity and attachment interventions in early childhood. *Psychological Bulletin, 129,* 195–215.

Braungart, J.M., Plomin, R., Fulker, D.W., & DeFries, J.C. (1992). Genetic mediation of the home environment during infancy: A sibling adoption study of the HOME. *Developmental Psychology, 28,* 1048–1055.

Braungart-Rieker, J., Rende, R.D., Plomin, R., & DeFries, J.C. (1995). Genetic mediation of longitudinal associations between family environment and childhood behavior problems. *Development & Psychopathology, 7,* 233–245.

Burt, S., Krueger, R.F., McGue, M., & Iacono, W. (2003). Parent–child conflict and the comorbidity among childhood externalizing disorders. *Archives of General Psychiatry, 60,* 505–513.

Elkins, I.J., McGue, M., & Iacono, W.G. (1997). Genetic and environmental influences on parent–son relationships: Evidence for increasing genetic influence during adolescence. *Developmental Psychology, 33,* 351–363.

Ge, X., Conger, R.D., Cadoret, R.J., Neiderhiser, J.M., Yates, W., Troughton, E., & Stewart, M.A. (1996). The developmental interface between nature and nurture: A mutual influence model of child antisocial behavior and parent behaviors. *Developmental Psychology, 32,* 574–589.

Goodman, R., & Stevenson, J. (1991). Parental criticism and warmth towards unrecognized monozygotic twins. *Behavior and Brain Sciences, 14,* 394–395.

Maughan, B., Taylor, A., Caspi, A., & Moffitt, T.E. (2004). Prenatal smoking and early childhood conduct problems: Testing genetic and environmental explanations of the association. *Archives of General Psychiatry, 61,* 836–843.

McGue, M., Sharma, A., & Benson, P. (1996). The effect of common rearing on adolescent adjustment: Evidence from a U.S. adoption cohort. *Developmental Psychology, 32,* 604–613.

Neiderhiser, J.M., Reiss, D., Pedersen, N.L., Lichtenstein, P., Spotts, E.L., Hansson, K., Cederblad, M., & Elthammar, O. (2004). Genetic and environmental influences on mothering of adolescents: A comparison of two samples. *Developmental Psychology, 40,* 335–351.

O'Connor, T.G., Deater-Deckard, K., Fulker, D., Rutter, M., & Plomin, R. (1998). Genotype-environment correlations in late childhood and early adolescence: Antisocial behavioral problems and coercive parenting. *Developmental Psychology, 34,* 970–981.

O'Connor, T.G., Hetherington, E.M., Reiss, D., & Plomin, R. (1995). A twin-sibling study of observed parent–adolescent interactions. *Child Development, 66,* 812–829.

Reiss, D., Neiderhiser, J., Hetherington, E.M., & Plomin, R. (2000). *The relationship code: Deciphering genetic and social patterns in adolescent development.* Cambridge, MA: Harvard University Press.

Rowe, D.C. (1981). Environmental and genetic influences on dimensions of perceived parenting: A twin study. *Developmental Psychology, 17,* 203–208.

Spotts, E.L., Neiderhiser, J.M., Ganiban, J., Reiss, D., Lichtenstein, P., Hansson, K., Cederblad, M., & Pedersen, N. (2004). Accounting for depressive symptoms in women: A twin study of associations with interpersonal relationships. *Journal of Affective Disorders, 82,* 101–111.

Tienari, P., Wynne, L.C., Sorri, A., Lahti, I., Laksy, K., Moring, J., Naarala, M., Nieminen, P., & Wahlberg, K. (2004). Genotype-environment interaction in schizophrenia spectrum disorder. *British Journal of Psychiatry, 184,* 216–222.

This article has been reprinted as it originally appeared in *Current Directions in Psychological Science*. Citation information for this article as originally published appears above.

Plasticity for Affective Neurocircuitry: How the Environment Affects Gene Expression

Nathan A. Fox[1]
University of Maryland, College Park

Amie A. Hane
Williams College

Daniel S. Pine
The National Institutes of Health

Abstract

We (Fox et al., 2005) recently described a gene-by-environment interaction involving child temperament and maternal social support, finding heightened behavioral inhibition in children homozygous or heterozygous for the serotonin transporter (5HTTLPR) gene short allele whose mothers reported low social support. Here, we propose a model, Plasticity for Affective Neurocircuitry, that describes the manner in which genetic disposition and environmental circumstances may interact. Children with a persistently fearful temperament (and the 5HTTLPR short allele) are more likely to experience caregiving environments in which threat is highlighted. This in turn will exacerbate an attention bias that alters critical affective neurocircuitry to threat and enhances and maintains anxious behavior in the child.

Keywords

temperament; gene × environment interaction; attention bias to threat; parenting

Individual differences in the stress response represent stable aspects of behavior that emerge early in life and reflect aspects of brain function. While behavioral-genetic studies implicate genes and the environment in these differences, the manner in which specific genes and environmental events shape specific aspects of brain function remains poorly specified. Recent work provides important clues, however, concerning these specific pathways. In particular, emerging findings suggest that specific genes associated with the function of the neurotransmitter serotonin (5-HT) interact with social stressors during development to shape function in a neural circuit implicated in the stress response.

RESEARCH ON GENE × ENVIRONMENT INTERACTIONS

A series of recent research reports provides evidence for gene-by-environment (denoted gene × environment) interactions with a protein crucially involved in the effects of 5-HT on behavior. This protein regulates the fate of 5-HT released from neurons. Each of the genetically derived variants in this protein is known as an expression of a serotonin transporter protein polymorphism (5HTTLPR; Caspi et al., 2003; Kaufman et al., 2004). The 5HTTLPR gene has two major functional alleles: a long and a short, as well as another long-variant allele that behaves, functionally, like the short allele. Individuals who are homozygous have two copies of either the long or the short. Individuals who are heterozygous have one copy of each. In general, studies of gene × environment interaction with this particular gene suggest that individuals who are homozygous for the short allele of the 5HTTLPR and who are exposed to significant stress are more likely to exhibit significant maladaptive behavior than are individuals who are homozygous for the long allele and are exposed to similar levels of stress. Individuals who are heterozygous, having one copy of the long and one of the short allele, usually fall somewhere in the middle, exhibiting more maladaptive outcomes compared to individuals homozygous for the long, and somewhat fewer than individuals who are homozygous for the short allele.

For example, Caspi et al. (2003) found that individuals homozygous for the short allele of 5-HTTLPR and exposed to five or more stressful life events were more likely to experience a major depressive episode, compared to individuals homozygous for the long allele exposed to such stress. Kaufman et al. (2004) reported that children carrying the short allele who had a history of abuse were more likely to evidence depression if their caregivers reported that they themselves were under high stress. Both of these studies reported psychiatric outcomes as a result of this particular gene × environment interaction. Caspi et al. (2003) examined the probability of major depression. Kaufman et al. (2004) reported on depressive symptoms in the subjects.

In a recent paper, we (Fox et al., 2005) reported on a similar gene × environment interaction in young children who were selected for the temperamental characteristic of behavioral inhibition. Signs of behavioral inhibition are detectable within the first months of life. For example, infants displaying high motor reactivity and negative affect when presented with novel auditory and visual stimuli are more likely to display behavioral inhibition as toddlers and preschoolers (Fox, Henderson, Rubin, Calkins, & Schmidt, 2001). Behaviorally inhibited children cease their ongoing activity and withdraw to their caregiver's proximity when confronted with novel events. They are also likely to isolate themselves when confronted with unfamiliar peers or adults. This behavioral style appears early in life, is associated with physiological markers of stress, social reticence with unfamiliar peers, low self-concept in childhood, and may be a risk factor for later psychopathology (Perez-Edgar & Fox, 2005).

We examined the relationship between childhood behavior and two variants of the 5-HTTLPR. As noted above, this protein mediates 5-HT influences on behavior by regulating the fate of 5-HT released from neurons into the synaptic cleft, the space that separates two communicating neurons. We found that children with lower-activity variants of the 5-HTTLPR whose mothers reported experiencing low social support were more likely to display behavioral inhibition at age 7, relative to children with similar 5-HT genetics but whose mothers reported more social support. The gene × environment interaction suggested that children with high-activity forms of the gene were "protected" from manifesting inhibition, even if their mothers reported experiencing low social support. Moreover, while child 5HTTLPR strongly related to inhibition in children with low levels of social support, for children with high levels of social support, no such relationship with 5HTTLPR emerged.

These data extend the findings of previous work, reporting the interaction of environmental stress and genes in predicting behavioral outcomes. Unlike other studies, though, the Fox et al. (2005) study presents data on a sample of typically developing children with nonpsychiatric outcomes. But like the other papers it does not address the mechanisms or processes by which the environmental stressor(s) affect variations in genotype to create the particular phenotypic outcome.

NEUROBIOLOGY OF 5HTTLPR

The short and long forms of the 5HTTLPR produce proteins known as reuptake transporters. These proteins lie within the synapse, the space separating two communicating neurons, and they function to remove serotonin from the synapse after it has been released. 5-HT neurons removed from the brain and studied in the laboratory revealed that the different forms of 5-HT reuptake transporters associated with distinct genotypes act differently. This early work clearly demonstrated functional consequences of the 5HTTLPR. More recent work has begun to describe possible influences of the different polymorphisms or variations in the 5HTTLPR in the neural-system function of living primates and humans.

5-HT neurons, like neurons for other modulatory neurotransmitters, make connections with broadly distributed networks in the brain. 5-HT influences on behavior are thought to emerge through the neurotransmitter's effects on information processing. The neural architecture engaged in the service of processing dangerous stimuli has been mapped in particularly precise detail, and 5-HT is thought to modulate functioning in this circuit (Gross & Hen, 2004). The circuit encompasses the ventral prefrontal cortex (vPFC), an area involved in decision making, and the amygdala, a structure involved in the detection of salient events such as those that are novel or threatening. Both structures receive strong 5-HT innervations. Thus, the amygdala, vPFC, and connections between them constitute a neural circuit that has been labeled "vPFC–amygdala circuitry." Consistent with the laboratory evidence of its effects on serotonin reuptake, the 5HTTLPR also predicts functional aspects of this ventral prefrontal–amygdala circuitry (Pezawas et al., 2005).

One of the most important issues to resolve concerns the mapping of these 5-HT influences across development. Neuroimaging studies in humans demonstrate robust developmental influences on prefrontal–amygdala circuitry (Monk et al., 2003). Studies in animal models suggest that these influences result from developmental changes in 5-HT function (Gross & Hen, 2004). This suggests that the relationship between the 5HTTLPR and prefrontal–amygdala function is likely to change across development. Neuroimaging studies have yet to examine this issue.

Interestingly, animal models suggest that 5-HT effects on neural development emerge through interactions with the environment (Gross & Hen, 2004). Given these data, how then precisely does the action of the environment interact with the 5HTTLPR to shape brain function and behavior? In the specific case of behavioral inhibition, how does the mother's report of her social support influence the expression of her child's 5-HTT gene in a way that ultimately impacts the child's tendency to display inhibited behavior? We propose a model, called Plasticity for Affective Neurocircuitry, and suggest two possible complementary mechanisms, based upon work in the area of anxiety and our own developmental studies. The first deals with the manner in which caregivers interact with behaviorally inhibited children; the second, with the attention bias that may develop as a result of temperamental disposition, caregiver influence, or their interaction.

CAREGIVER BEHAVIOR AND SOCIAL SUPPORT

Research suggests that reported level of social support correlates with quality of caregiver behavior. Mothers who report high levels of social support tend to be more sensitive toward their infants (Crockenberg & McCluskey, 1986) and more satisfied with their role as a parent (Thompson & Walker, 2004). Additional evidence indicates that level of social support may be particularly important for mothers of temperamentally distress-prone infants. Crockenberg and her colleagues found that the positive association between social support and maternal sensitivity was only significant for irritable infants (Crockenberg & McCluskey, 1986). Pauli-Pott, Mertesacker, and Beckmann (2004) found that maternal insensitivity was predicted by the joint effect of infant negative emotionality and low social support. Hence, social support is a factor contributing to the quality of maternal caregiving behavior, particularly for inhibited children who have a history of negative reactivity in infancy and early childhood.

An emergent body of research indicates that the quality of the mother–child relationship mitigates the relation between early and later forms of behavioral inhibition, such that some parents of behaviorally inhibited children interact with their children in a manner that appears to exacerbate or maintain their child's temperament. In our own research, we have identified a unique group of children who consistently withdraw from novelty at age 4 months and who receive insensitive maternal caregiving due to this proneness to distress. For instance, Ghera, Hane, Malesa, and Fox (2006) found that infants who responded negatively to novel stimuli at age 4 months and who were viewed by their mothers as difficult to soothe received low levels of maternal sensitivity. Hane, Fox, Henderson, and Marshall (2006) found that 9-month-old infants who showed high levels of behavioral avoidance to ominous stimuli and a corresponding pattern of right frontal electroencephalogram (EEG) asymmetry (itself a determinant of continued inhibition across early childhood; see Fox et al., 2001), received low levels of maternal sensitivity. Hane and Fox (2006) reported that infants who received low-quality maternal caregiving behavior showed more fearfulness and less sociability in the laboratory, more negative affect while interacting in the home with their mothers, and a pattern of right frontal EEG asymmetry. Taken together, this research suggests that quality of maternal caregiving behavior shapes the development of behavioral inhibition, perhaps by altering the neural systems that underlie reactivity to stress and novelty (see a review by Parent et al., 2005, for parallels in research with rodents).

ATTENTION BIAS TO THREAT

A second mechanism through which experience may affect the neural systems underlying behavioral inhibition involves the development of attention bias to threat. A variety of data using a number of different experimental paradigms suggests that individuals who self-report a high degree of anxious symptoms or who are diagnosed with a number of different anxiety disorders display an attention bias to threat. When presented with visual stimuli reflecting threat, anxious individuals are more vigilant toward these stimuli and take longer to disengage from visual attention to them (Mogg, Millar, & Bradley, 2000). In humans, as in other species, the ability to detect threatening stimuli in the environment appears to provide an important adaptive advantage for safety and survival. The neural systems that are involved in threat detection have been well described in nonhuman primates, rats, and, through the use of functional neuroimaging, in humans (Monk et al., 2006). These systems encompass prefrontal–amygdala circuitry previously tied to threat responses and 5HTTLPR in humans.

An enhanced sensitivity to threat has been suggested as an underlying mechanism in anxiety disorders (MacLeod, Rutherford, Campbell, Ebsworthy, & Holker, 2002). A recent meta-analysis (Bar-Haim, Lamy, Pergamin, Bakermans-Kraneburg, & van IJzendoorn, 2007) suggests that the distribution of attention in anxious individuals may be part of a resource-allocation system that biases the individual to pay close attention to threat. Such biases may develop over time and be the result of a person's ongoing transaction with threatening or aversive stimuli. Moreover, studies using experimental approaches, at least in adults, suggest that these attention biases are causally implicated in the genesis of anxiety following exposure to stress (MacLeod et al., 2002). From this perspective, children born with a disposition to react intensively and with negative affect to stress or novelty may go on to show different patterns of behavior, depending on the degree to which they are exposed to overzealous, intrusive maternal behavior as opposed to a more sensitive, nurturing style.

The Plasticity for Affective Neurocircuitry model that we propose suggests that early temperament influences quality of the caregiving environment and quality of the environment in turn shapes attention bias to threat and mediates the relation between early temperament and later inhibition (see Fig. 1). Rubin, Burgess, and Hastings (2002) showed that the relation between behavioral inhibition as a toddler and reticence at age 4 was significant and positive only for those children whose mothers were psychologically overcontrolling and derisive. Thus it appears that caregivers who highlight or identify negative events in their child's environment (often in an effort to control their child's behavior) may in fact be inadvertently promoting attention bias in the child. Evidence from studies of interactions between mothers and children with anxiety disorders supports this position. For example, Barrett, Rapee, and Dadds (1996) found that parental discussion of ambiguous situations was associated with increased perception of threat and the creation of avoidant plans of action in anxious children. Thus, from within the caregiving environment, children disposed to respond with negative affect to novelty or uncertainty may be further reinforced to bias their attention toward threat during the course of interactions with caregivers.

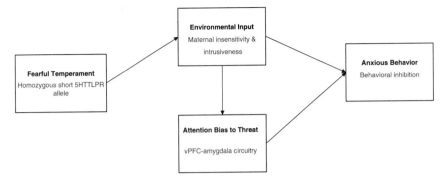

Fig. 1. Plasticity for Affective Neurocircuitry model. A child's genetically disposed fearful temperament (due to homozygosity for the short allele of the serotonin transporter, 5HTTLPR, gene) elicits and is elicited by caregiver behavior (maternal insensitivity and intrusiveness) to shape attention bias to threat and the underlying neural circuitry (in the ventral prefrontal cortex, vPFC, and amygdala) supporting this bias. Exaggerated attention bias contributes to the emergence and maintenance of anxious behaviors.

CONCLUSIONS

At the present time, there are preciously few data on the development of attention biases to evocative, threatening, or stressful stimuli. Research in this area is clearly needed in order to understand the development of these attention processes and their effects on social behavior.

Research in the area of behavioral inhibition already highlights the importance of both biological dispositions and caregiving environments in shaping the social responses of the young child. Evidence of gene × environment interactions in this group of children marks another important step toward understanding the developmental mechanisms involved in the emergence of important variations in social behavior. The next steps involve process-focused research. Studies that carefully model the development of gene × environment interactions and the factors that mitigate the relevance of such interactions to key social outcomes are warranted; such studies would elucidate the mechanisms by which the environment influences the phenotypic expression of critical genes such as the 5HTTLPR and the degree to which phenotypes change across development. Hane and Fox (in press) suggest that early environmental experiences not only change the phenotypic expression of stress reactivity, but also prime the child to respond with a similar behavioral repertoire upon encountering like environmental stressors in the future. Hence, the child who is genetically vulnerable to anxiety and who has also developed a tendency to focus on threat vis à vis interactions with his or her caregivers may develop a strong attention threat bias that maintains anxious behavior well into adulthood.

Recommended Reading

Fox, N.A., Henderson, H.A., Marshall, P.J., Nichols, K.E., & Ghera, M.M. (2005). Behavioral inhibition: Linking biology and behavior within a developmental framework. *Annual Reviews of Psychology,* 56, 235–262.

Perez-Edgar, K., & Fox, N.A. (2005). Temperament and anxiety disorders. *Child Adolescent Clinics of North America, 14,* 681–705.

Pine, D.S., Cohen, P., Gurley, D., Brook, J., & Ma, Y. (1998). The risk of early-adulthood anxiety disorders in adolescents with anxiety and depressive disorders. *Archives of General Psychiatry, 55,* 56–64.

Pine, D.S., Klein, R.G., Mannuzza, S., Moulton, J.L., Lissek, S., Guardino, M., & Woldehawariat, G. (2005). Face-emotion processing in offspring at-risk for panic disorder. *Journal of the American Academy of Child and Adolescent Psychiatry, 44,* 664–672.

Note

1. Address correspondence to Nathan A. Fox, Department of Human Development, University of Maryland, College Park, MD 20742; e-mail: fox@umd.edu.

References

Bar Haim, Y., Lamy, D., Pergamin, L., Bakermans-Kraneburg, M.J., & van IJzendoorn, M.H. (2007). Threat-related attentional bias in anxious and non-anxious individuals: A meta-analytic study. *Psychological Bulletin, 133,* 1–24.

Barrett, P.M., Rapee, R.M., & Dadds, M.M. (1996). Family enhancement of cognitive style in anxious and aggressive children. *Journal of Abnormal Child Psychology, 24,* 187–203.

Caspi, A., Snugden, K., Moffitt, T.E., Taylor, A., Craig, I.W., & Harrington, H., et al. (2003). Influence of life stress on depression: Moderation by a polymorphism in the 5-HTT gene. *Science, 301,* 386–389.

Crockenberg, S., & McCluskey, K. (1986). Change in maternal behavior during the baby's first year of life. *Child Development, 57,* 746–753.

Fox, N.A., Henderson, H.A., Rubin, K.H., Calkins, S.D., & Schmidt, L.A. (2001). Continuity and discontinuity of behavioral inhibition and exuberance: Psychophysiological and behavioral influences across the first four years of life. *Child Development, 72,* 1–21.

Fox, N.A., Nichols, K.E., Henderson, H.A., Rubin, K., Schmidt, L., Hamer, D., Ernst, M., & Pine, D.S. (2005). Evidence for a gene–environment interaction in predicting behavioral inhibition in middle childhood. *Psychological Science, 16,* 921–926.

Ghera, M.M., Hane, A.A., Malesa, E.M., & Fox, N.A. (2006). The role of infant soothability in the relation between infant negativity and maternal sensitivity. *Infant Behavior and Development, 29,* 289–293.

Gross, C., & Hen, R. (2004). The developmental origins of anxiety. *Nature Reviews Neuroscience, 5,* 545–552.

Hane, A.A., & Fox, N.A. (2006). Ordinary variations in maternal caregiving of human infants influence stress reactivity. *Psychological Science, 17,* 550–556.

Hane, A.A., & Fox, N.A. (in press). A closer look at the transactional nature of early social development: The relations among early caregiving environments, temperament, and early social development and the case for phenotypic plasticity. In F. Santoianni & C. Sabatano (Eds.), *Brain development in learning environments: Embodied and perceptual advancements.*

Hane, A.A., Fox, N.A., Henderson, H.A., & Marshall, P.J. (2006). *Setting the trajectories to social competence: The relations among temperamental reactivity, frontal EEG asymmetry and social behavior in infancy.* Unpublished manuscript.

Kaufman, J., Yang., B., Douglas-Palomberi, H., Houshyar, S., Lipschitz, D., Krystal, J.H., & Gerlernter, J. (2004). Social supports and serotonin transporter gene moderate depression in maltreated children. *Proceedings of the National Academy of Sciences, 101,* 17316–17321.

MacLeod, C., Rutherford, E., Campbell, L., Ebsworthy, G., & Holker, L. (2002). Selective attention and emotional vulnerability: Assessing the causal basis of their association through the experimental manipulation of attentional bias. *Journal of Abnormal Psychology, 111,* 107–123.

Mogg, K., Millar, N., & Bradley, B.P. (2000). Biases in eye movements to threatening facial expressions in generalized anxiety disorder and depressive disorder. *Journal of Abnormal Psychology, 109*, 695–704.

Monk, C., McClure, E.B., Nelson, E.B., Zarahn, E., Bilder, R.M., Leibenluft, E., Charney D, S., Ernst, M., & Pine, D.S. (2003). Adolescent immaturity in attention-related brain engagement to emotional facial expressions. *NeuroImage, 20*, 420–428.

Monk, C.S., Nelson, E.E., McClure, E.B., Mogg, K., Bradley, B.P., Leibenluft, E., Blair, R.J., Chen, G., Charney, D.S., Ernst, M., & Pine, D.S. (2006). Ventrolateral prefrontal cortex activation and attentional bias in response to angry faces in adolescents with generalized anxiety disorder. *American Journal of Psychiatry, 163*, 1091–1097.

Parent, C., Zhang, T., Caldji, C., Bagot, R., Champagne, F.A., Pruessner, J., Meaney, M.J. (2005). Maternal care and individual differences in defensive responses. *Current Directions in Psychological Science, 14*, 229–233.

Pauli-Pott, U., Mertesacker, B., & Beckmann, D. (2004). Predicting the development of infant emotionality from maternal characteristics. *Development and Psychopathology, 16*, 19–42.

Perez-Edgar, K., & Fox, N.A. (2005). A behavioral and electrophysiological study of children's selective attention under neutral and affective conditions. *Journal of Cognition and Development, 6*, 89–118.

Pezawas, L., Meyer-Lindenberg, A., Drabant, E.M., Verchinski, B.A., Munoz, K.E., Kolachana, B.S., Egan, M.F., Mattay, V.S., Hariri, A.R., & Weinberger, D.R. (2005). 5-HTTLPR polymorphism impacts human cingulated–amygdala interactions: A genetic susceptibility mechanism for depression. *Nature Neuroscience, 8*, 828–834.

Rubin, K.H., Burgess, K.B., & Hastings, P.D. (2002). Stability and social-behavioral consequences of toddlers' inhibited temperament and parenting behaviors. *Child Development, 73*, 483–495.

Thompson, S.D., & Walker, A.C. (2004). Satisfaction with parenting: A comparison between adolescent mothers and fathers. *Sex Roles, 50*, 677–687.

This article has been reprinted as it originally appeared in *Current Directions in Psychological Science*. Citation information for this article as originally published appears above.

For Better *and* For Worse: Differential Susceptibility to Environmental Influences

Jay Belsky[1]

Institute for the Study of Children, Families and Social Issues, Birkbeck University of London, London, United Kingdom

Marian J. Bakermans-Kranenburg and

Marinus H. van IJzendoorn

Centre for Child and Family Studies, Leiden University, the Netherlands

Abstract

Evidence that adverse rearing environments exert negative effects particularly on children presumed "vulnerable" for temperamental or genetic reasons may actually reflect something else: heightened susceptibility to the negative effects of risky environments *and* to the beneficial effects of supportive environments. Building on Belsky's (1997, 2005) evolutionary-inspired proposition that some children are more affected—both for better and for worse—by their rearing experiences than are others, we consider recent work on child vulnerability, including that involving measured genes, along with evidence showing that putatively vulnerable children are especially susceptible to both positive and negative rearing effects. We also consider methodological issues and unanswered questions in the differential-susceptibility equation.

Keywords

differential susceptibility; gene–environment interaction; parenting; temperament

Most students of child development probably do not presume that all children are equally susceptible to rearing effects; a long history of research on interactions between parenting and temperament, or *parenting-by-temperament interactions,* clearly suggests otherwise. Nevertheless, it remains the case that most work still focuses on parenting effects that apply equally to all children—so-called main effects of parenting—thus failing to consider interaction effects, which reflect the fact that whether, how, and how much parenting influences the child may depend on the child's temperament or some other characteristic of individuality.

Like classic work in educational and clinical psychology on interactions between learning aptitude and treatment, research on parenting-by-temperament interactions is based on the premise that what proves effective for some individuals in fostering the development of some valued outcome—or preventing some problematic one—may simply not do so for others. Commonly tested are hypotheses derived from multiple-risk/transactional frameworks in which individual characteristics that make children "vulnerable" to adverse experiences—placing them "at risk" of developing poorly—are mainly influential when there is at the same time some contributing risk from the environmental context.

After highlighting some research of just this kind, we raise questions—on the basis of other findings—about how the first set of data has been interpreted. We advance the evolutionary-inspired proposition that some children, for temperamental or genetic reasons, are actually more susceptible to *both* (a) the adverse effects of unsupportive parenting *and* (b) the beneficial effects of supportive rearing. The validity of this claim cannot be determined, however, so long as research focuses disproportionately on *vulnerable* (as opposed to merely *susceptible*) child characteristics and evaluates effects of *adverse* environments on *problematic* outcomes. What, then, would be required to distinguish vulnerability from susceptibility? We consider the answer after first reviewing research that meets the criteria for differential susceptibility. Finally, we draw conclusions and highlight some "unknowns in the differential-susceptibility equation."

DUAL-RISK CONDITIONS AND CONSEQUENCES

The view that infants and toddlers manifesting high levels of negative emotion are at special risk of problematic development when they experience poor-quality rearing is widespread. Evidence of this comes from Morrell and Murray (2003), who showed that it was only highly distressed and irritable 4-month-old boys who experienced coercive and rejecting mothering at this age who continued to show evidence, 5 months later, of emotional and behavioural dysregulation. Relatedly, Belsky, Hsieh, and Crnic (1998) observed that infants who scored high in negative emotionality at 12 months of age and who experienced the least supportive mothering and fathering across their second and third years of life scored highest on externalizing problems at 36 months of age. And Deater-Deckard and Dodge (1997) reported that children rated highest on externalizing-behavior problems by teachers across the primary-school years were those who experienced the most harsh discipline prior to kindergarten entry and who were characterized by mothers at age 5 as being negatively reactive infants.

The adverse consequences of the co-occurrence of a child risk factor (e.g., negative emotionality) and problematic parenting also is evident in Caspi and Moffitt's (2006) ground-breaking research on gene-by-environment interaction. Young men followed from early childhood were most likely to manifest high levels of antisocial behavior when they had both a history of child maltreatment and a particular variant of the *MAO-A* gene, a gene previously linked to aggressive behaviour. Such results led Rutter (2006), like others, to speak of "vulnerable individuals," a concept that also applies to children putatively at risk for compromised development due to their behavioral attributes. But is "vulnerability" the best way to conceptualize the kind of parenting-by-child interactions under consideration?

VULNERABILITY OR DIFFERENTIAL SUSCEPTIBILITY?

Working from an evolutionary perspective, Belsky (1997, 2005) theorized that children, especially within a family, should vary in their susceptibility to both adverse and beneficial effects of rearing influences: Because the future is uncertain, in ancestral times, just like today, parents could not know for certain (consciously or unconsciously) what rearing strategies would maximize reproductive fitness. To protect against all children being steered, inadvertently, in a parental direction that proved disastrous at some later point in time, developmental processes were selected to vary children's susceptibility to rearing.

Belsky (1997, 2005) further observed that children high in negative emotion, particularly in the early years, appeared to benefit disproportionately from supportive rearing environments (Boyce & Ellis, 2005). Crockenberg (1981) showed that social support predicted infant attachment security but only in the case of highly irritable infants. Denham et al. (2000) reported that the beneficial effects of proactive parenting (i.e., supportive presence, clear limit setting) at age 7 and/or age 9 were most pronounced in the case of children who scored high on externalizing problems (i.e., disobedient, aggressive, angry) at an earlier time of measurement (i.e., mean age 55 months), even after controlling for problem behavior at the initial measurement occasion.

Experimental studies designed to test Belsky's (1997) theory are even more suggestive of differential susceptibility than the longitudinal-correlational evidence. Blair (2002) discovered that it was highly negative infants who benefited most—in terms of both reduced levels of externalizing behavior problems and enhanced cognitive functioning—from a multifaceted infant-toddler intervention program whose data he reanalyzed. More recently, Klein Velderman, Bakermans-Kranenburg, Juffer, and Van IJzendoorn (2006) found that experimentally induced changes in maternal sensitivity exerted greater impact on the attachment security of highly negatively reactive infants than it did on other infants. In both experiments, environmental influences on "vulnerable" children were for better instead of for worse.

Better Evidence of Differential Susceptibility

Even though studies highlight the heightened susceptibility of temperamentally negative or genetically vulnerable offspring to either positive or negative rearing influences, more compelling would be data on a single sample substantiating the for-better-and-for-worse predictions of the differential-susceptibility hypothesis. Feldman, Greenbaum, and Yirmiya (1999) found that 9-month-olds scoring high on negativity who experienced low levels of synchrony in mother–infant interaction manifested more noncompliance during clean-up at age two than other children did. When such infants experienced mutually synchronous mother–infant interaction, however, they displayed greater self-control than did children manifesting much less negativity as infants. More recently, Kochanska, Aksan, and Joy (2007) observed that highly fearful 15-month-olds experiencing high levels of power-assertive paternal discipline were most likely to cheat in a game at 38 months, yet when cared for in a supportive manner such negatively emotional, fearful toddlers manifested the most rule-compatible conduct.

Recent studies involving measured genes and measured environments also document both-for-better-and-for-worse rearing effects in the case of susceptible infants, specifically those with a particular allele (variant) of a gene called *DRD4*, which codes for a type of dopamine receptor. Because the dopaminergic system is engaged in attentional, motivational, and reward mechanisms and the variant in question, the 7-repeat allele, has been linked to lower dopamine reception efficiency, Van IJzendoorn and Bakermans-Kranenburg (2006) predicted this allele would moderate the association between maternal unresolved loss or trauma and infant attachment disorganization. Having the 7-repeat DRD4 allele substantially increased risk for disorganization in children exposed to maternal unresolved loss/trauma, as expected; but when children with that allele were raised by mothers who had no unresolved loss, they displayed significantly less disorganization than agemates without the allele, regardless of mothers' unresolved-loss status (Bakermans-Kranenburg & Van IJzendoorn, in press).

Similar results emerged when the interplay between DRD4 and observed parental insensitivity in predicting externalizing problems was studied in a group of 47 twins (Bakermans-Kranenburg & Van IJzendoorn, 2007). Children with the 7-repeat DRD4 allele and insensitive mothers displayed more externalizing behaviors than children without that allele (irrespective of maternal sensitivity); and children with the 7-repeat DRD4 allele and sensitive mothers showed the lowest levels of externalizing problem behavior (Bakermans-Kranenburg & Van IJzendoorn, 2007). Such results suggest that conceptualizing the 7-repeat DRD4 allele exclusively in risk-factor terms is misguided, as this variant of the gene seems to heighten susceptibility to a wide variety of environments, with supportive and risky contexts promoting, respectively, positive and negative outcomes.

DETECTING DIFFERENTIAL SUSCEPTIBILITY

An environmental effect, be it involving parenting or something else, moderated by an organismic characteristic, be it temperamental negativity or genetic makeup, is a necessary condition for differential susceptibility but not a sufficient one. It would thus be a mistake to presume that all gene-by-environment (or temperament-by-parenting) interactions are examples of differential susceptibility. Differential susceptibility needs to be distinguished from other interaction effects, including that of "dual risk," which arises when the most "vulnerable" individuals (i.e., risk #1) are disproportionately affected in an adverse manner by a negative environment (i.e., risk #2) but do not also benefit disproportionately from positive environmental conditions). It is also important that there be no association between the moderator (i.e., the susceptibility factor) and the environment (i.e., the predictor). Belsky et al. (1998) tested the independence of negative emotionality and parenting as a step in their investigation of differential susceptibility. Had these factors been correlated, then the evidence would not have shown that the predictive power of parenting was greater for highly negative infants; it would instead have indicated either that high-negativity infants elicit negative parenting or that negative parenting fosters infant negativity. Similarly, Caspi and Moffitt (2006) determined that boys' MAO-A genotype did not elicit maltreatment.

The formal test of differential susceptibility consists of five steps (see Box 1). The first step concerns the application of conventional statistical criteria for evaluating genuine moderation (Dearing & Hamilton, 2006), with some emphasis on excluding interactions with regression lines that do not cross (sometimes referred

Box 1. *Stepwise testing for differential susceptibility*

Distinguishing true differential susceptibility from other types of interaction proceeds in five steps, as follows:

1. Statistical test for genuine (cross-over) interaction
2. Test of the independence of the susceptibility factor and the predictor
3. Test of the association between the susceptibility factor and the outcome; if the association is nonzero, there is no support for differential susceptibility
4. Comparison of the regression plot with the prototypical graphical displays shown in Figure 1; only the first model (a) represents differential susceptibility
5. Test of the specificity of the model by replacing susceptibility factors and outcomes

to as *removable* interactions). The next steps distinguish differential susceptibility from gene–environment correlations that may reflect rearing experiences evoked by genotypes (step 2) and from dual-risk models (steps 3 and 4), as defined above. If the susceptibility factor and the outcome are related, dual risk (or gain, when positive factors are involved) is suggested (Fig. 1, model d). For example, early negativity would itself lead to externalizing behavior, but even more so when combined with negative parenting. The specificity of the effect is demonstrated (step 5) if the model is not replicated when other susceptibility factors (i.e., moderators) and

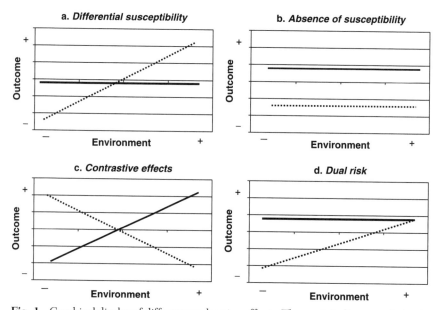

Fig. 1. Graphical display of different moderation effects. The x-axis indicates variation in the environmental factor from negative to positive; the y-axis indicates the outcome from negative to positive; and the lines depict the two groups differing on the susceptibility factor. Model a represents differential susceptibility. Model b depicts absence of susceptibility (fixed strategies)—that is, the two groups show different outcomes but variation in the environmental factor does not affect the outcome. In model c, the regression lines reflect contrastive effects. Model d represents a fan-shaped interaction, with the moderator affecting the outcome in just one direction.

outcomes are used (Caspi & Moffitt, 2006; Rutter, 2006). Differential susceptibility is demonstrated when the moderation reflects a cross-over interaction (Fig. 1, model a) that covers both the positive and the negative aspects of the environment (i.e., susceptibility instead of dual risk). The slope for the susceptible subgroup should be significantly different from zero and at the same time significantly steeper than the slope for the nonsusceptible subgroup (i.e., differential instead of general susceptibility). If both slopes are significantly different from zero but in opposite directions, contrastive effects are indicated (Fig. 1, model c), as in the case of positive and negative effects of harsh discipline on, respectively, African American and White children (Deater-Deckard & Dodge, 1997).

UNKNOWNS IN THE DIFFERENTIAL-SUSCEPTIBILITY EQUATION

The notion of differential susceptibility, derived as it is from evolutionary theorizing, has only recently been stated in a clear and testable form (Belsky, 1997, 2005). Although research summarized here suggests that the concept has utility, there are many "unknowns," four of which are highlighted.

Domain General or Domain Specific?

Is it the case that some children, perhaps those who begin life as highly negatively emotional, are more susceptible both to a wide variety of rearing influences and with respect to a wide variety of developmental outcomes—as is presumed in the use of concepts like "fixed" and "plastic" strategists (Belsky, 2005), with the latter being highly malleable and the former hardly at all? Boyce and Ellis (2005) contend that a general psychobiological reactivity makes some children especially vulnerable to stress and thus to general health problems. Or is it the case, as Belsky (2005) wonders and Kochanska et al. (2007) argue, that different children are susceptible to different environmental influences (e.g., nurturance, hostility) and with respect to different outcomes? Pertinent to this idea are findings of Caspi and Moffitt (2006) indicating that different genes differentially moderated the effect of child maltreatment on antisocial behavior (*MAO-A*) and depression (*5HTT*).

Also worth considering is the prospect that heritable (or experientially induced) variation in positive emotionality (e.g., exuberance) moderates effects of rearing experiences on positive developmental outcomes (e.g., empathic concern). Perhaps negative emotionality emerges as a differential-susceptibility marker due to the disproportionate focus upon negative developmental outcomes in so much research.

Continuous Versus Discrete Plasticity?

The central argument that children vary in their susceptibility to rearing influences raises the question of how to conceptualize differential susceptibility: categorically (some children highly plastic and others not so at all) or continuously (some children simply more malleable than others)? It may even be that plasticity is discrete for some environment–outcome relations, with some individuals affected and others not at all (e.g., gender-specific effects), but that plasticity is more continuous for other susceptibility factors (e.g., in the case of the increasing vulnerability to stress of parents with decreasing dopaminergic efficiency; Van IJzendoorn, Bakermans-Kranenburg, & Mesman, 2007).

Mechanisms

Susceptibility factors are the moderators of the relation between the environment and developmental outcome, but they do not elucidate the mechanism of differential influence. Several (non-mutually exclusive) explanations have been advanced for the heightened susceptibility of negatively emotional infants. Suomi (1997) posits that the timidity of "uptight" infants affords them extensive opportunity to learn by watching, a view perhaps consistent with Bakermans-Kranenburg and Van IJzendoorn's (2007) aforementioned findings pertaining to *DRD4*, given the link between the dopamine system and attention. Kochanska et al. (2007) contend that the ease with which anxiety is induced in fearful children makes them highly responsive to parental demands. And Belsky (2005) speculates that negativity actually reflects a highly sensitive nervous system on which experience registers powerfully—negatively when not regulated by the caregiver but positively when coregulation occurs—a point of view somewhat related to Boyce and Ellis' (2005) proposal that susceptibility may reflect prenatally programmed hyperreactivity to stress.

Within-Family Differences in Susceptibility

In light of evolutionary thinking about differential susceptibility (e.g., parental "bet hedging" or the trading off of costs and benefits), it is crucial to investigate within-family variation in susceptibility (Sulloway, 1996). Studies that include twins and other siblings from the same family might prove especially powerful, as they could distinguish genetically and environmentally induced variations in susceptibility. This will be especially the case if, in addition to measuring genes and environments, studies also measured hypothesized moderators, thereby enabling investigators to move beyond globally attributing variance to "nonshared" family environment (i.e., those experiences that make children in the same family different from each other).

At best, work on differential susceptibility has only just begun. Issues raised here remain to be addressed empirically. Doing so may shed further light on why environmental effects seem so much smaller than they are often presumed to be.

Recommended Reading

Belsky, J. (2005). (See References). A comprehensive presentation of theory and research on differential susceptibility that goes into more detail than the current article.
Boyce, W.T., & Ellis, B. (2005). (See References). A thoughtful evolutionary analysis of differential susceptibility, advancing the original claim that heightened susceptibility may itself be environmentally induced, not just genotypically determined.
Caspi, A., & Moffitt, T. (2006). (See References). A clearly written scholarly review of recent gene-by-environment interaction findings involving psychiatric disturbances in humans.

Rutter, M. (2006). (See References). A book-length treatment of "gene–environment interplay" for non-geneticists, highlighting work on genotypic vulnerability to adverse rearing environments (and much more).

Bakermans-Kranenburg, M.J., & Van IJzendoorn, M.H. (in press). (See References). The first experimental evidence of differential susceptibility in the case of attachment and externalizing behavior involving a genetic susceptibility factor.

Acknowledgments—The work of the second and third authors on this manuscript was supported by research grants from the Netherlands Organization for Scientific Research (MJBK: VIDI Grant 452-04-306; MHvIJ: NWO SPINOZA prize).

Note

1. Address correspondence to Jay Belsky, Institute for the Study of Children, Families and Social Issues, Birkbeck University of London, 7 Bedford Square, London WC1B 3RA, United Kingdom; e-mail: j.belsky@bbk.ac.uk.

References

Bakermans-Kranenburg, M.J., & Van IJzendoorn, M.H. (in press). Genetic vulnerability or differential susceptibility in child development: The case of attachment. *Journal of Child Psychology and Psychiatry*.

Belsky, J. (1997). Variation in susceptibility to rearing influence: An evolutionary argument. *Psychological Inquiry, 8*, 182–186.

Belsky, J. (2005). Differential susceptibility to rearing influence: An evolutionary hypothesis and some evidence. In B. Ellis & D. Bjorklund (Eds.), *Origins of the social mind: Evolutionary psychology and child development* (pp. 139–163). New York: Guilford.

Belsky, J., Hsieh, K., & Crnic, K. (1998). Mothering, fathering, and infant negativity as antecedents of boys' externalizing problems and inhibition at age 3: Differential susceptibility to rearing influence? *Development and Psychopathology, 10*, 301–319.

Blair, C. (2002). Early intervention for low birth weight preterm infants: The role of negative emotionality in the specification of effects. *Development and Psychopathology, 14*, 311–332.

Boyce, W.T., & Ellis, B. (2005). Biological sensitivity to context: I. An evolutionary-developmental theory of the origins and functions of stress reactivity. *Development and Psychopathology, 17*, 271–301.

Caspi, A., & Moffitt, T. (2006). Gene–environment interactions in psychiatry. *Nature Reviews Neuroscience, 7*, 583–590.

Crockenberg, S. (1981). Infant irritability, mother responsiveness, and social support influences on the security of infant-mother attachment. *Child Development, 52*, 857–865.

Dearing, E., & Hamilton, L.C. (2006). Contemporary advances and classic advice for analyzing mediating and moderating variables. *Monographs of the Society for Research in Child Development, 71*, 88–104.

Deater-Deckard, K., & Dodge, K. (1997). Spare the rod, spoil the authors: Emerging themes in research on parenting. *Psychological Inquiry, 8*, 230–235.

Denham, S., Workman, E., Cole, P., Weissbrod, C., Kendziora, K., & Zahn-Waxler, C. (2000). Prediction of externalizing behavior problems from early to middle childhood. *Development and Psychopathology, 12*, 23–45.

Feldman, R., Greenbaum, C., & Yirmiya, N. (1999). Mother-infant affect synchrony as an antecedent of the emergence of self-control. *Developmental Psychology, 35*, 223–231.

Klein Velderman, M., Bakermans-Kranenburg, M.J., Juffer, F., & van IJzendoorn, M.H. (2006). Effects of attachment-based interventions on maternal sensitivity and infant attachment: Differential susceptibility of highly reactive infants. *Journal of Family Psychology, 20*, 266–274.

Kochanska, G., Aksan, N., & Joy, M.E. (2007). Children's fearfulness as a moderator of aprenting in early socialization. *Developmental Psychology, 43*, 222–237.

Morrell, J., & Murray, L. (2003). Parenting and the development of conduct disorder and hyperactive symptoms in childhood. *Journal of Child Psychology and Psychiatry, 44,* 489–508.

Rutter, M. (2006). *Genes and behavior.* London: Blackwell.

Sulloway, F.J. (1996). *Born to rebel.* New York: Pantheon.

Suomi, S. (1997). Early determinants of behaviour. *British Medical Bulletin, 53,* 170–184.

Van IJzendoorn, M.H., & Bakermans-Kranenburg, M.J. (2006). *DRD4* 7-repeat polymorphism moderates the association between maternal unresolved loss or trauma and infant disorganization. *Attachment & Human Development, 8,* 291–307.

Van IJzendoorn, M.H., Bakermans-Kranenburg, M.J., & Mesman, J. (2007). Dopamine system genes associated with parenting in the context of daily hassles. *Genes, Brain & Behavior* (OnlineEarly Articles). doi: 10.1111/j.1601-183X.2007.00362.x

This article has been reprinted as it originally appeared in *Current Directions in Psychological Science*. Citation information for this article as originally published appears above.

From Genes to Brain to Antisocial Behavior

Adrian Raine[1]
Departments of Criminology, Psychiatry, and Psychology,
University of Pennsylvania

Abstract

This review summarizes recent brain-imaging and molecular-genetic findings on antisocial, violent, and psychopathic behavior. A "genes to brain to antisocial behavior" model hypothesizes that specific genes result in structural and functional brain alterations that, in turn, predispose to antisocial behavior. For instance, a common polymorphism in the monoamine oxidase A (*MAOA*) gene has been associated with both antisocial behavior and also reductions in the volume of the amygdala and orbitofrontal (ventral prefrontal) cortex—brain structures that are found to be compromised in antisocial individuals. Here I highlight key brain regions implicated in antisocial behavior, with an emphasis on the prefrontal cortex, along with ways these areas give expression to risk factors for antisocial behavior. Environmental influences may alter gene expression to trigger the cascade of events that translate genes into antisocial behavior. Neuroethical considerations include how responsibility and punishment should be determined given the hypothesis that neural circuits underlying morality are compromised in antisocial individuals.

Keywords

brain imaging; genetics; antisocial; moral; treatment

What specific genes predispose an individual to commit crime? How do they change brain processes to give rise to antisocial behavior? And what role does the environment play? While these questions may seem enigmatic, we are currently witnessing scientific advances that hold the promise of beginning to answer them and revolutionizing our understanding of antisocial, violent, and psychopathic behavior. The key concept highlighted in this review is that specific genes result in structural and functional brain alterations that, in turn, predispose to antisocial behavior. This article summarizes current research supporting this "genes to brain to antisocial behavior" hypothesis, places that knowledge into the context of the social environment, and explores wider neuroethical considerations for society and the criminal justice system. Antisocial behavior is here viewed as a dimension rather than as a category, and is defined as failure to conform to social norms for lawful behavior.

FROM GENES . . .

Despite strong resistance in many quarters, there is now little scientific doubt that genes play a significant role in antisocial behavior. The question of whether there is a genetic basis is no longer interesting, and it has been replaced by the second-generation question of "How much of antisocial behavior is influenced by genes?" While not all studies show significant effects, reviews of over 100 twin and adoption analyses provide clear evidence that about 50% of the variance in antisocial behavior is attributable to genetic influences (Moffitt, 2005).

From this strong basis, the field is now moving on to the more important, third-generation question: "*Which* genes predispose to which kinds of antisocial behavior?" Initial answers are starting to emerge from molecular genetic studies. If the monoamine oxidase A (*MAOA*) gene is knocked out (neutralized) in mice, they become highly aggressive, becoming "knock-out" fighters themselves. Knock the gene back in, and they return to their normal behavior patterns (Cases et al., 1995). Breakthrough family and community studies of humans have also implicated the *MAOA* gene in antisocial behavior (Caspi et al., 2002). One meta-analysis shows replicability of this interaction effect (Kim-Cohen et al., 2006), although inevitably there are environmental complexities that require further clarification.

The important challenge for this third generation of genetic work on antisocial behavior is to identify not just which genes are associated with antisocial behavior but also which among these genes code for the brain impairments found in antisocial groups. At least seven genes to date meet the criteria of being both associated with antisocial/aggressive behavior in humans or animals and of being thought to influence brain structure: *MAOA, 5HTT, BDNF, NOTCH4, NCAM, tlx,* and *Pet-1-ETS.* Taking *MAOA* as an example, the enzyme that this gene codes for breaks down serotonin, a neurotransmitter that is low in antisocial individuals. Males with a common polymorphism (variant) in the *MAOA* gene have an 8% reduction in the volume of the amygdala, anterior cingulate, and orbitofrontal (ventral prefrontal) cortex (Meyer-Lindenberg et al., 2006). These brain structures are involved in emotion and are found to be compromised in antisocial individuals. Thus, while these initial molecular-genetic findings still need to be replicated, it appears that one of the genes linked to antisocial behavior results in structural impairments to brain areas that are compromised in antisocial individuals—from genes, to brain, to antisocial behavior.

. . . TO BRAIN . . .

How does one progress from genes to antisocial behavior? One hypothesis is that gene abnormalities result in structural brain abnormalities that result in emotional, cognitive, or behavioral abnormalities, which in turn predispose to antisocial behavior. There is increasing evidence for brain impairments in antisocial groups, with particularly strong evidence for impairments in the prefrontal cortex (Raine & Yang, 2006). Neurological patients suffering damage to the ventral prefrontal cortex exhibit psychopathic-like disinhibited behavior, reduced autonomic and emotional functioning, and bad decision making (Damasio, 1994). Research using magnetic resonance imaging (MRI) has shown that those with antisocial personality disorder have an 11% reduction in prefrontal gray matter, together with reduced autonomic activity during a social stressor designed to elicit "secondary" emotions of shame, embarrassment, and guilt. (Raine, Lencz, Bihrle, LaCasse, & Colletti, 2000). The antisocial individuals with the least amount of gray matter also showed the least autonomic stress responsivity. Different clinical neuroscience paradigms are beginning to converge on the conclusion that there is a significant brain basis to antisocial behavior and that these neurobehavioral processes are relevant to understanding violence in everyday society.

Structural prefrontal impairments are paralleled by functional prefrontal impairments (i.e., reduced brain functioning) in a wide range of antisocial populations. Murderers have been found to show reduced glucose metabolism in the prefrontal cortex when this brain region is challenged by a task known to activate it, the continuous-performance task (Raine, Buchsbaum, & LaCasse, 1997). This impairment also specifically characterizes impulsively violent offenders, suggesting that the prefrontal cortex acts as an "emergency brake" on runaway emotions generated by limbic structures. Brain-imaging findings are supported by findings from neuropsychological, neurological, and psychophysiological studies, indicating that the findings are robust. However, the prefrontal cortex is not the only brain area compromised in antisocial populations. Reviews of imaging studies have documented impairments to the cingulate, temporal cortex, angular gyrus, amygdala, and hippocampus (Raine & Yang, 2006). Specific regions implicated to date are illustrated in Figure 1.

Are the brain impairments illustrated in Figure 1 caused by environmental factors or by genes? A significant role of genetics is hypothesized to operate for two reasons. First, the structural prefrontal impairment found in antisocial individuals was not accounted for by environmental risk factors for antisocial behavior (e.g., history of head injury, child abuse) or by drug or alcohol abuse (Raine et al., 2000). Second, an elegant methodological marriage of structural brain imaging with the behavioral-genetic twin design demonstrated that genes explain 90% of the variation in the volume of prefrontal gray matter in humans (Thompson et al., 2001). These two arguments, taken together, would strongly suggest that the structural impairments in antisocial individuals have a significant genetic basis, although future studies could still identify some role for the environment.

. . . TO ANTISOCIAL BEHAVIOR

The final step in the "from genes to brain to antisocial behavior" argument is to understand how brain structural and functional impairments give rise to the cognitive, emotional, and behavior risk factors predisposing to antisocial behavior. Table 1 outlines an initial model of brain areas found to be dysfunctional in antisocial individuals, the basic cognitive or affective processes that they give rise to, and how these risk factors translate into outcomes related to antisocial behavior. All of these linkages have an empirical basis, although some links (e.g., prefrontal impairments in antisocial populations) currently have stronger support than others (e.g., angular gyrus and responsibility for actions) and localizations of some elements are not agreed upon in the social science literature.

Table 1 shows that risk factors are not conceptualized as directly causing antisocial or aggressive behavior but that, instead, they bias social behavior in an antisocial direction. For example, the amygdala is centrally involved in fear conditioning. Poor fear conditioning may result in a failure to fully develop a conscience—a set of conditioned emotional responses that motivate individuals to desist from previously punished behavior. Poor conscience development is,

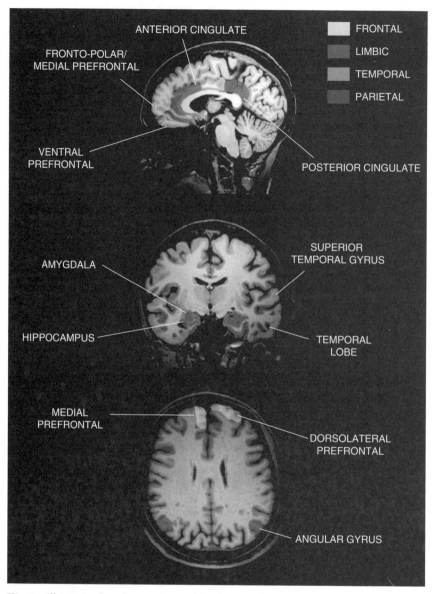

Fig. 1. Illustration based on midsagittal (top), coronal (middle), and axial (bottom) MRI slices of the brain regions found to be structurally or functionally impaired in antisocial, violent, and psychopathic populations (see Table 1).

in turn, viewed as a predisposition to antisocial behavior. Similarly, ventral prefrontal damage results in disinhibited behavior that predisposes to lawless behavior.

One pathway by which dysfunctional brain circuits can give rise to antisocial behavior is in breakdown of moral feeling. This neural moral theory of antisocial behavior (Raine & Yang, 2006) posits that antisocial individuals have a breakdown

Table 1. *The translation of brain impairments to risk factors for antisocial behavior*

Impaired brain region	Processes/risk factors	Outcome
Frontal cortex		
Dorsolateral	Response perseveration	Failure to desist from punished behavior
	Poor planning/organization	Occupational and social dysfunction, low income
	Theory of mind	Misperception of others intentions/behavior
Ventral–orbitofrontal	Decision making	Bad life judgments
	Emotion regulation	Poor anger control
	Mediation of emotional responses	Poor behavioral control
	guiding behavior	
	Empathy/concern for others	Callous disregard for others' feelings/situation
Medial-polar prefrontal	Moral judgment	Noncompliance with societal rules
	Self-reflection	Lack of self-insight
Limbic structures		
Anterior cingulate	Inhibition	Failure to withhold an antisocial response
	Errors /conflict processing	Difficulty in dealing with conflictual situations
Posterior cingulated	Moral decision-making	Noncompliance with societal rules
	Self-referencing	Poorer attribution of negative life outcomes to self
Amygdala	Fear conditioning	Lack of affect and poor conscience development
	Social-emotion judgments	Misinterpreting others' motives/feelings
	Moral emotion	Noncompliance with societal rules
	Judging trustworthiness	Hypersociability and victimization
Hippocampus	Contextual fear conditioning	Not placing punished responses into social context
Temporal cortex		
Temporal pole–superior temporal gyrus	Theory of mind, social perception	Misattribution of other's motives
Posterior superior temporal gyrus	Moral judgment	Noncompliance with societal rules
Parietal cortex		
Angular gyrus	Moral judgment	Noncompliance with societal rules
	Sense of responsibility for actions	Irresponsible behavior

in the neural circuit normally activated during moral decision making. Areas include the medial prefrontal cortex (PFC), ventral PFC, angular gyrus, posterior cingulate, and amygdala—all areas implicated in antisocial behavior. The overlap of structures implicated in antisocial populations and moral-judgment tasks generates the hypothesis that *some* of the brain impairments in antisocial individuals disrupt moral emotion and decision making, in turn predisposing the individual to rule-breaking, antisocial behavior.

FROM *ENVIRONMENT* TO GENES TO BRAIN TO ANTISOCIAL BEHAVIOR?

Despite arguments for a direct causal pathway from genes to brain to antisocial behavior, psychosocial processes cannot be ruled out and could be critical. Environmental influences early in development could directly change gene expression (the way in which a gene's DNA sequence is translated into neuronal structure and function), in turn altering brain functioning and resulting in antisocial behavior. Separating rat pups from the mother in the first 3 weeks of life results in fearlessness and a reduced stress response in adulthood, resulting in an increase in glucocorticoid gene expression in the hippocampus and prefrontal cortex, two brain areas critically involved in regulation of the HPA stress response (Weaver, Meaney, & Szyf, 2006). Conduct-disordered children have a reduced cortisol stress response and a more fearless temperament. As such, early environmental influences can alter gene expression, which then gives rise to the cascade of brain and behavior events outlined above. The exciting idea is that, although 50% of the variance in antisocial behavior is genetic in origin, genes are not fixed, static, and immutable; psychosocial influences can result in structural modifications to DNA that have profound influences on neuronal functioning and, hence, antisocial behavioral outcome.

The social environment can interact with genetics and biological risk factors for antisocial behavior in other ways (Raine, 2002). Antisocial behavior is exponentially increased when social and biological risk factors combine. Studies from several countries have shown that birth complications (including anoxia, known to particularly damage the hippocampus) interact with negative home environments (e.g., early maternal rejection of the child) in predisposing to adult violent offending. There is also replicated evidence that an abnormality in the *MAOA* gene interacts with early child abuse in predisposing to adult antisocial behavior (Caspi et al., 2002).

Social processes can also moderate the relationship between biology and antisocial behavior. Reduced prefrontal glucose metabolism particularly predisposes to violence in those from benign home backgrounds. Low physiological arousal is particularly associated with antisocial behavior in individuals from benign home backgrounds. In these cases, where the individual *lacks* social risk factors that "push" them toward antisocial behavior, biological factors have a greater explanatory role (Raine, 2002). In contrast, the link between antisocial behavior and biological risk factors in those from negative home environments may be weaker because social causes of crime "camouflage" the biological contribution.

TREATMENT, MORAL JUDGMENT, AND NEUROETHICS

Biology is not destiny and it should ultimately be possible to remediate neurobiological risk factors. The fundamental question is: "If antisocial individuals have broken brains, can they be fixed?" Ultimate solutions could be both natural and surprisingly simple. Poor nutrition in the first 3 years of life has been associated with long-term antisocial behavior throughout childhood and late adolescence (Liu, Raine, Venables, Dalais, & Mednick, 2004). Low IQ was associated with both poor nutrition and antisocial behavior, and controlling for IQ abolished the relationship between poor early nutrition and later antisocial behavior. This mediating effect of IQ supports the model that poor nutrition leads to poor brain functioning, resulting in neurocognitive (brain) impairments that predispose to antisocial behavior. Fish oil is rich in omega-3, a long-chain fatty acid making up 40% of cell membrane, and dietary supplementation has been associated both with increased IQ and reduced antisocial behavior in prisoners (Gesch, Hammond, Hampson, Eves, & Crowder, 2002). Prevention programs that manipulate nutrition early in life have resulted in reduced delinquency (Olds et al., 1998) and criminality (Raine, Mellingen, Liu, Venables, & Mednick, 2003). Environmental manipulations can in theory reverse brain risk factors for antisocial behavior.

An alternative approach is to remediate the neurotransmitter abnormalities produced by gene abnormalities, although it must be recognized that such treatments are downstream from genes—we do not yet know how to directly reverse genetic predispositions to antisocial behavior. Nevertheless, genes regulating serotonin's transportation back to the cell body from the synaptic cleft have recently been linked to antisocial-aggressive behavior in children and adults. Given that antisocial-aggressive individuals have low serotonin, medications that increase the availability of serotonin, such as Prozac (an SSRI, or selective serotonin reuptake inhibitor), ought to lower antisocial behavior *if* there is a causal connection. There is evidence to support this prediction in both aggressive adults and children (Connor, Boone, Steingard, Lopez, & Melloni, 2003).

Despite this positive evidence, the fact remains that society is reluctant to use medication to treat antisocial behavior, while at the same time being comfortable in medicating other behavioral conditions. Paradoxically, because the environment influences gene expression, our neurobiological makeup is ever-changing, whether we like it or not. Should society move toward grasping the biological nettle in order to snuff out crime and violence and reduce suffering? Or should it instead turn a blind eye to new clinical neuroscience knowledge and prohibit tampering with humankind's biological essence, even if this results in lives being lost which could have been saved by biological prevention efforts?

An additional neuroethical concern is that of responsibility and punishment. If a murderer suffers brain impairments predisposing him to commit impulsive violence, are we to hold him fully accountable for his behavior? From a moral-judgment standpoint, given the evidence that the neural circuits underlying moral feeling and decision making are impaired in antisocial populations (Raine & Yang, 2006), are such individuals as capable as the rest of us to know—and do—what is

111

right? Psychopaths may know the legal difference between right and wrong, but do they have the *feeling* of what is right and wrong? Emotions are believed to be central to moral judgment, and they provide the driving force to act morally. In this context, how moral is it for us to punish many criminals as harshly as we do? On the other hand, are there not significant dangers in loosening our concept of accountability? The very concept of "from genes to brain to antisocial behavior" raises neuroethical questions that need to be aired in order for prevention science to progress.

CONCLUSIONS AND FUTURE DIRECTIONS

A new generation of clinical neuroscience research that encapsulates brain imaging and molecular genetics is giving rise to the concept that specific genes result in structural and functional brain impairments that predispose to antisocial, violent, and psychopathic behavior. A critical next step in testing the "from genes to brain to antisocial behavior" hypothesis is to conduct molecular-genetic and brain-imaging research on the same population in order to identify the genes coding both for brain structural and functional abnormalities and for antisocial behavior. The next empirical step is to ascertain whether antisocial, psychopathic individuals evidence abnormal processing of moral dilemmas. How we will deal with this new knowledge at societal and legal levels is a significant neuroethical challenge. The more we learn about the neurobiological causes of criminal behavior, the more difficult questions arise concerning culpability, punishment, and freedom of will. The future scientific and neuroethical challenges for the emerging field of neurocriminology can best be met by integrative cross-disciplinary research that bridges traditional macrosocial theories (emphasizing broad social constructs) with new perspectives from clinical and social neuroscience to better understand, and ultimately prevent, antisocial behavior in both children and adults.

Recommended Reading

Damasio, A. (1994). (See References). A ground-breaking book linking the ventral prefrontal cortex with emotion, cognition, and antisocial behavior.

Kim-Cohen, J. Caspi, A., Taylor, A., Williams, B., Newcombe, R., Craig, I.W., & Moffitt, T.E. (2006). (See References). A review of molecular genetic studies indicating replicability of the antisocial–*MAOA* association.

Moffitt, T.E. (2005). (See References). A key review of gene–environment interactions in relation to antisocial behavior.

Raine, A. (2002). (See References). A review of studies demonstrating an interaction between biological factors and social factors in predisposing to antisocial behavior.

Raine, A., & Yang, Y. (2006). (See References). A review of brain imaging research on antisocial populations arguing for impairments in the circuitry underlying moral decision making in psychopaths.

Acknowledgments—Preparation of this article was supported by a grant from the National Institute of Child Health and Human Development (1 RO1 HD42259).

Note

1. Address correspondence to Adrian Raine, Departments of Criminology, Psychiatry, and Psychology, McNeal Building, Suite 486, 3718 Locust Walk, University of Pennsylvania, Philadelphia, PA 19104-6286; e-mail: araine@sas.upenn.edu.

References

Cases, O., Seif, I., Grimsby, J., Gaspar, P., Chen, K., Pournin, S., et al. (1995). Aggressive behavior and altered amounts of brain serotonin and norepinephrine in mice lacking MAOA. *Science, 268,* 1763–1766.

Caspi, A., McClay, J., Moffitt, T., Mill, J., Martin, J., Craig, I.W., et al. (2002). Role of genotype in the cycle of violence in maltreated children. *Science, 297,* 851–854.

Connor, D.F., Boone, R.T., Steingard, R.J., Lopez, I.D., & Melloni, R.H. (2003). Psychopharmacology and aggression: II. A meta-analysis of nonstimulant medication effects on overt aggression-related behaviors in youth with SED. *Journal of Emotional and Behavioral Disorders, 11,* 157–168.

Damasio, A. (1994). *Descartes' error: Emotion, reason, and the human brain.* New York: GP Putnam's Sons.

Gesch, C.B., Hammond, S.M., Hampson, S.E., Eves, A., & Crowder, M.J. (2002). Influence of supplementary vitamins, minerals and essential fatty acids on the antisocial behaviour of young adult prisoners: Randomised, placebo-controlled trial. *British Journal of Psychiatry, 181,* 22–28.

Kim-Cohen, J., Caspi, A., Taylor, A., Williams, B., Newcombe, R., Craig, I.W., & Moffitt, T.E. (2006). MAOA, maltreatment, and gene–environment interaction predicting children's mental health: New evidence and a meta-analysis. *Molecular Psychiatry, 11,* 903–913.

Liu, J.H., Raine, A., Venables, P.H., Dalais, C., & Mednick, S.A. (2004). Malnutrition at age 3 years and externalizing behavior problems at ages 8, 11 and 17 years. *American Journal of Psychiatry, 161,* 2005–2013.

Meyer-Lindenberg, A., Buckholtz, J.W., Kolachana, B., Hariri, A.R., Pezawas, L., Blasi, G., et al. (2006). Neural mechanisms of genetic risk for impulsivity and violence in humans. *Proceedings of the National Academy of Sciences, U.S.A., 103,* 6269–6274.

Moffitt, T.E. (2005). The new look of behavioral genetics in developmental psychopathology: Gene–environment interplay in antisocial behaviors. *Psychological Bulletin, 131,* 533–554.

Olds, D., Henderson, C.R.J., Cole, R., Eckenrode, J., Kitzman, H., Luckey, D., et al. (1998). Long-term effects of nurse home visitation on children's criminal and antisocial behavior: 15-year follow-up of a randomized controlled trial. *JAMA: The Journal of the American Medical Association, 280,* 1238–1244.

Raine, A. (2002). Biosocial studies of antisocial and violent behavior in children and adults: A review. *Journal of Abnormal Child Psychology, 30,* 311–326.

Raine, A., Buchsbaum, M., & LaCasse, L. (1997). Brain abnormalities in murderers indicated by positron emission tomography. *Biological Psychiatry, 42,* 495–508.

Raine, A., Lencz, T., Bihrle, S., LaCasse, L., & Colletti, P. (2000). Reduced prefrontal gray matter volume and reduced autonomic activity in antisocial personality disorder. *Archives of General Psychiatry, 57,* 119–127.

Raine, A., Mellingen, K., Liu, J.H., Venables, P.H., & Mednick, S.A. (2003). Effects of environmental enrichment at 3–5 years on schizotypal personality and antisocial behavior at ages 17 and 23 years. *American Journal of Psychiatry, 160,* 1627–1635.

Raine, A., & Yang, Y. (2006). Neural foundations to moral reasoning and antisocial behavior. *Social, Cognitive, and Affective Neuroscience, 1,* 203–213.

Thompson, P.M., Cannon, T.D., Narr, K.L., van Erp, T., Poutanen, V.P., & Huttunen, M. (2001). Genetic influences on brain structure. *Nature Neuroscience, 4,* 1253–1258.

Weaver, I.C.G., Meaney, M.J., & Szyf, M. (2006). Maternal care effects on the hippocampal transcriptome and anxiety-mediated behaviors in the offspring that are reversible in adulthood. *Proceedings of the National Academy of Sciences, U.S.A., 103,* 3480–3485.

Section 3: Critical Thinking Questions

1. In the gene-environment interaction effect, which is the "causal" variable and which is the context that moderates the causal effect? Does it matter?

2. Belsky, Bakermans-Kranenburg, and van IJzendoorn argue that the survival of the human species has been enhanced by the diversity of genes related to susceptibility to environmental effects. Under what conditions is a highly-susceptible individual likely to flourish, and under what conditions is a low-susceptibility individual likely to flourish?

3. How does the discovery of the gene-environment interaction effect resolve or fuel the nature-nurture debate in psychology?

This article has been reprinted as it originally appeared in *Current Directions in Psychological Science*. Citation information for this article as originally published appears above.

Section 4: Externalizing Behavior Disorders

Externalizing behavior disorders are at the base of an array of problems in childhood, including aggressive behavior, substance abuse, and school dropout. The past decade has witnessed greater advances in our understanding of the development and prevention of these disorders than the entire previous century. We now know that specific genes and specific environmental experiences each make essential contributions to this development. We know that these factors interact with each other, and they cumulate across development. Some of these factors can be the target of preventive intervention.

It had been known that about half of the individual differences in externalizing disorders could be attributable to inheritance, but only since the mapping of the human genome have we been able to identify which specific genes are correlated with these behavior problems. Dick reviews several of the major genes (e.g., GABRA2 and CHRM2) that have been identified and opens a discussion of the possible mechanisms through which they might operate. She concludes that these genes confer general risk for numerous externalizing problems rather than risk for a single problem such as alcoholism or aggression. van Goozen, Fairchild, and Harold identify some of the key mechanisms that through early conduct problems grow into serious adolescent disorder, in the form of neurobiological deficits. They suggest that deficits in regulating responses to stress, based in genetic factors or perinatal experiences, may dispose some children to have difficulty with externalizing behavior. Pettit integrates these genetic and neurobiological concepts with a broader understanding of environmental factors in a general model of how antisocial behavior develops across childhood.

Steinberg considers the general problem of risk-taking in adolescence. He summarizes evidence that this behavior is related to biological developments in puberty that exacerbate impulsivity and are not matched by cognitive developments that would regulate this tendency. He suggests that rather than focusing on direct cognitive interventions, we should emphasize the management of adolescents' environments so that their opportunities for risk-taking are limited. Christenson and Thurlow consider the problem of dropping out of school. They apply models of development to propose strategies for intervention and prevention.

Together, these articles communicate the dramatic discoveries that have been made in our understanding of externalizing disorders and the potential for prevention that this knowledge provides.

Identification of Genes Influencing a Spectrum of Externalizing Psychopathology

Danielle M. Dick[1]
Virginia Institute for Psychiatric and Behavioral Genetics,
Virginia Commonwealth University

Abstract

Alcohol dependence, drug dependence, childhood conduct disorder, and adult antisocial behavior commonly occur in combination. Data from multiple literatures, including twin/family studies and electrophysiological studies, suggest that the overlap of these disorders is largely due to a shared genetic liability that contributes to a spectrum of externalizing psychopathology. These findings suggest that some genes will not be specific to any one externalizing disorder but will predispose individuals broadly to a spectrum of externalizing psychopathology. Here we review evidence for specific, identified genes, GABRA2 and CHRM2, that follow this pattern and confer risk for a spectrum of externalizing disorders. These findings confirm the etiological structure of psychopathology suggested by psychological research and suggest exciting new roles that psychologists can play in understanding the pathways underlying associations between genes and behavior.

Keywords

genetics; externalizing psychopathology; GABRA2; CHRM2

Substance-use disorders and antisocial behavior very commonly occur together (comorbidity), as demonstrated in data from several large epidemiological surveys. For example, in the National Epidemiological Survey on Alcohol and Related Conditions (NESARC), individuals with alcohol-use disorders are at nearly 16 times the risk of also having a drug dependence and are at 6.5 times the risk of meeting criteria for antisocial personality disorder (Hasin, Stinson, Ogburn, & Grant, 2007). The observation of extensive comorbidity (co-occurrence) across these disorders has been long-standing; however, more recently, quantitative methods have been applied to investigate patterns of comorbidity across psychiatric disorders. Using these sophisticated analytic methods, a number of studies have concluded that alcohol dependence, drug dependence, childhood conduct disorder, and antisocial personality disorder all fall on a single dimension that reflects a range of disinhibitory behavior and that has been referred to as externalizing psychopathology (Krueger & Markon, 2006a).

Furthermore, there is evidence from twin and family studies that this pattern may reflect shared underlying influences. Twin data are able to tease apart the extent to which comorbidity across disorders is due to genetic and/or environmental factors. The most extensive study of the factors contributing to the overlap across psychiatric disorders was conducted using data from the Virginia Twin Registry (Kendler, Prescott, Myers, & Neale, 2003). Kendler and colleagues found that alcohol dependence, drug abuse/dependence, childhood conduct disorder, and adult antisocial behavior overlap largely due to an underlying shared genetic liability

(Kendler et al., 2003). This has been a remarkably consistent finding, demonstrated both in adult and adolescent samples, across a diversity of independent twin studies (Krueger et al., 2002; Young, Stallings, Corley, Krauter, & Hewitt, 2000). Although each disorder shows some disorder-specific genetic influence, the majority of the genetic liability appears to be shared across externalizing psychopathology.

The idea of a shared underlying susceptibility to a spectrum of externalizing disorders is further supported by the electro-physiological literature. Electro-physiological abnormalities have been observed in individuals with a variety of externalizing disorders, as well as in their unaffected children, suggesting that these abnormalities may be markers of a genetic vulnerability. These markers are thought to be intermediary in the pathway from genes to the eventual manifestation of a complex behavior, and have been called endophenotypes (Gottesman & Gould, 2003). For example, a reduced amplitude of the P3 component of the electrocortical event-related potential (an index of brain-wave activity in response to a stimulus that is thought to reflect inhibition) has been observed in alcohol-dependent individuals and their children, suggesting this is a marker for a genetic predisposition to alcohol dependence. However, the abnormal P3 response is not specific to alcohol dependence but, rather, appears to be associated with a variety of disinhibitory disorders, including other forms of substance dependence, childhood externalizing disorders, and adult antisocial personality disorder—again suggesting a shared underlying origin across this spectrum of disorders (Hicks et al., 2007).

Although these literatures provide strong evidence suggesting that externalizing disorders share an underlying genetic origin, the studies reviewed above do not explicitly measure specific genes. Rather, they infer patterns of genetic influence based on comparisons of different types of relatives. So while the findings strongly suggest that some genes broadly predispose a person to a variety of disinhibitory behavioral problems, until this point it has remained hypothetical; it has not actually been demonstrated for any specific genes.

GENES INFLUENCING EXTERNALIZING PSYCHOPATHOLOGY

The field of genetics has undergone rapid growth in recent years. After early years of disappointment and difficulty, it is finally becoming possible to identify genes for a variety of clinical phenotypes (Cardon, 2006). This has been made possible by a number of factors. Technological advances have dramatically lowered the cost of genotyping, making scans of the entire genome possible. The completion of the Humane Genome Project, the HapMap Project, and other government- and privately funded endeavors have made a wealth of information cataloging variation in the human genome publicly available. These developments have been complemented by advances in the statistical analysis of genetic data. With large collaborative projects to identify genes involved in most major mental disorders underway, we have entered a new era of gene discovery in relation to behavioral disorders. However, most large-scale gene-identification projects reflect the historical, categorical model of psychopathology, in which mental disorders have been thought of as discrete entities. They largely do not take into account advances in our understanding of the underlying structure of psychopathology.

Thus, the search mostly consists of separate projects to identify genes involved in differentially classified disorders—one project to identify genes involved in alcohol dependence, another for illicit drug dependence, and so on.

The Collaborative Study on the Genetics of Alcoholism (COGA) is a large, family-based study with the goal of identifying specific genes involved in the predisposition to alcohol dependence and related disorders. COGA has employed a systematic strategy for gene identification, first conducting genome-wide linkage analyses to identify chromosomal regions likely to be involved in alcohol dependence, and then conducting association analyses on plausible biological candidate genes located within regions of linkage in order to identify the specific genes (see Dick & Foroud, 2003, for a review of genetic strategies). In 2004, the COGA group published highly significant evidence of association between a gene called GABRA2—located on chromosome 4 and coding for a receptor for the neurotransmitter GABA-A—and adult alcohol dependence (Edenberg et al., 2004). The relationship between the GABRA2 genotype and alcohol dependence in the COGA sample is illustrated in Figure 1. The odds ratio associated with GABRA2 is 1.4 (Dick, Agrawal, et al., 2006), indicating that individuals who carry the genotype associated with an elevated risk are at nearly one and a half times the risk of developing alcohol dependence as those with the lower-risk genotype. This suggests that GABRA2 is a gene of small effect, typical of the effect size associated with most specific genes identified for complex disorders. The association

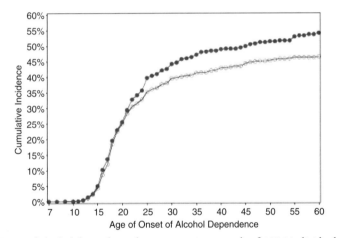

Fig. 1. Rates of alcohol dependence by genotype in a sample of 4014 individuals studied as part of the Collaborative Study on the Genetics of Alcoholism project. The red line with closed circles represents individuals with the high-risk genotype at GABRA2, and the blue line with open circles represents individuals with the low-risk genotype. These lines clearly diverge in adulthood, with higher rates of alcohol dependence in individuals with the high-risk genotype, demonstrating an association between GABRA2 and adult alcohol dependence. Reprinted from "The Role of GABRA2 in Risk for Conduct Disorder and Alcohol and Drug Dependence Across Developmental Stages," by D.M. Dick, L. Bierut, A.L. Hinrichs, L. Fox, K.K. Bucholz, J.R. Kramer, et al., 2006, *Behavior Genetics*, 36, pp. 577–590. Copyright 2006, Springer Science and Business Media. Reprinted with permission.

between *GABRA2* and alcohol dependence subsequently has been replicated in multiple independent data sets, providing strong evidence that this is a gene involved in the predisposition to alcohol dependence.

Although the focus in the COGA project is on identifying genes involved in alcohol dependence, the literature reviewed above would suggest that a number of the genes involved in the predisposition to alcohol dependence will also be associated more broadly with a spectrum of externalizing psychopathology. In the COGA project, extensive phenotypic information was collected on all subjects, including a full semi-structured psychiatric interview. There are high rates of externalizing disorders in the sample—higher than general population rates, as would be expected for a selected sample in which 48% of individuals are affected with alcohol dependence. Thirty percent also meet criteria for illicit drug dependence, 15% report childhood conduct disorder, and 11% meet criteria for adult antisocial personality disorder. Accordingly, this presented an opportunity to examine the association between *GABRA2* and other forms of externalizing psychopathology.

When the analyses were expanded to test for association with drug dependence (marijuana or other illicit drugs; according to *Diagnostic and Statistical Manual of Mental Disorders*–3rd ed. criteria), COGA found evidence of significant association with *GABRA2* (Agrawal et al., 2006). Furthermore, the association was strongest in the group of individuals who had both alcohol and illicit-drug dependence. The association between *GABRA2* and illicit-drug dependence was also replicated in a sample of individuals from control families (Dick, Bierut, et al., 2006), and although the overall rates of drug dependence were considerably lower in the control families, the magnitude of the effect associated with the genotype was nearly identical.

In order to study the relationship between *GABRA2* and childhood conduct disorder, an additional sample of children and adolescents, who were interviewed between the ages of 7 and 17, were genotyped. Childhood conduct disorder is characterized by a persistent pattern of rule-breaking behavior, including aggression toward people and animals, destruction of property, and theft. A significant relationship between *GABRA2* and conduct disorder was observed in this child/adolescent sample: Of individuals who carried the genotype associated with an increased risk of alcohol dependence in the adult COGA sample, 17.5% reported three or more conduct-disorder symptoms (the threshold for diagnosis), whereas only 10% of individuals who carried the low-risk genotype reported three or more conduct-disorder symptoms (Dick, Bierut, et al., 2006). These findings are particularly interesting in light of the fact that the lines illustrating the *GABRA2* risk for alcohol dependence shown in Figure 1 do not diverge until young adulthood. In other words, there is no effect of the *GABRA2* genotype on alcohol dependence in childhood/early adolescence, a finding that supports twin studies suggesting that early adolescent alcohol problems have a different origin than adult alcohol dependence and are largely influenced by environmental factors (reviewed in Dick, Bierut, et al., 2006). Rather, there is a significant effect of *GABRA2* on conduct disorder in the child/adolescent sample, suggesting conduct disorder may be an earlier manifestation of the predisposition that later contributes to alcohol dependence in adulthood.

Finally, COGA tested for association between *GABRA2* and adult antisocial personality disorder (ASPD). ASPD is a pervasive pattern of disregard for the rights of others that begins in childhood and extends into adulthood and includes behaviors such as repeated lying, physical assaults on others, impulsivity, and irresponsibility. The highly comorbid nature of alcohol dependence and ASPD makes it difficult to tease the effects of *GABRA2* on ASPD apart from those on alcohol dependence. Accordingly, a relationship between *GABRA2* and ASPD was tested among individuals in the COGA sample who did not meet criteria for alcohol dependence: The rates of ASPD were higher among individuals with the high-risk genotype (5.3%) as compared to individuals with the low-risk genotype (2.5%; Dick, Bierut, et al., 2006). This association was replicated in an independent control sample, providing further support for the role of this gene in ASPD.

DIMENSIONAL MODELS OF EXTERNALIZING PSYCHOPATHOLOGY

With preparation for the fifth edition of the *Diagnostic and Statistical Manual of Mental Disorders* underway, there is active discussion about whether psychopathology should be classified categorically or dimensionally (Krueger, Watson, & Barlow, 2005). A number of studies have suggested that the phenotypic patterns of co-occurrence among externalizing disorders indicate a coherent underlying domain; for example, in a recent comparison of categorical and continuous models of externalizing data from NESARC, the best-fitting model suggested that diagnoses of alcohol dependence, other substance dependence, and ASPD were best represented by a single continuous liability (Markon & Krueger, 2005). To the extent that these disorders can be phenotypically represented by a single dimension, genetic studies may benefit from examining a quantitative index of externalizing psychopathology, rather than separately testing for association with the categorical diagnoses that make up the spectrum of externalizing psychopathology. This was done in a genome-wide linkage analysis of adolescents, in which a composite index of antisocial drug dependence was used to search for genomic regions that contain genes conferring risk for externalizing psychopathology. One such region was identified on chromosome 9q, suggesting that there is a gene in that region that contributes to the overlap across substance dependence and antisocial behavior (Stallings et al., 2005).

The COGA project also adopted the approach of examining a quantitative index of externalizing psychopathology in following up another gene, *CHRM2*, that was associated with alcohol dependence in the sample (Wang et al., 2004) and replicated in other samples. *CHRM2* codes for a muscarinic acetylcholine receptor and is located on chromosome 7, near a region showing linkage to an electrophysiological endophenotype and alcohol dependence in the COGA sample. Preliminary analyses suggested that this gene was also associated with symptoms of illicit-drug dependence, antisocial personality disorder, and conduct disorder, as well as disinhibitory personality traits related to the externalizing spectrum (Krueger et al., 2002, Young et al., 2000). Subsequent analyses demonstrated that the evidence for association was strongest when considering a single quantitative factor of externalizing psychopathology (Dick et al., in press).

These findings provide further evidence of another specific gene that predisposes to a spectrum of externalizing psychopathology and demonstrate that dimensional models of psychopathology can be useful in gene identification (this was suggested by Krueger & Markon, 2006b); these analyses now provide proof of principle.

CONCLUSIONS AND FUTURE DIRECTIONS

The development of more sophisticated quantitative models has allowed psychologists to make substantial progress in understanding the structure and etiology of clinical disorders (Krueger & Markon, 2006a). The results summarized here provide the first evidence of specific genes that confer risk for a spectrum of externalizing psychopathology, and they confirm the utility of psychological models of risk factors in genetic research. They challenge us to rethink traditional, simple gene–disorder association studies, and they raise questions about the pathways by which specific genes affect clinical outcomes. For example, *GABRA2* was originally thought to be a good candidate gene for study in relation to alcohol dependence because multiple lines of evidence suggest that the neurotransmitter it codes for, GABA, is involved in many of the behavioral effects of alcohol. Although *GABRA2* was associated with alcohol dependence, the follow-up analyses demonstrating involvement in a broader spectrum of externalizing suggest that the gene does not confer risk specific to alcohol dependence but, rather, is involved via more general disinhibitory pathways. What might be the underlying behavioral, physiological, or neural mechanisms responsible for a general externalizing risk?

Clues about the underlying mechanism may be found from the association with electrophysiological traits. COGA colleagues have previously proposed that the electrophysiological abnormalities evident in individuals at risk for various forms of externalizing psychopathology represent a deficit of central nervous system (CNS) inhibition and/or an excess of CNS excitation (Begleiter & Porjesz, 1999). This CNS hyperexcitability reflects a disequilibrium in the homeostatic mechanisms responsible for maintaining a balance between excitation and inhibition. For example, the P3 amplitude is thought to reflect CNS inhibition; the inverse relationship between severity of alcohol dependence and P3 amplitude supports the idea that an imbalance in CNS excitation/inhibition has implications for behavior. Variations in *GABRA2* and *CHRM2* may be involved in creating this homeostatic imbalance, which may in turn increase risk for a number of outcomes.

The next challenge will be to map the behavioral traits that reflect this hypothesized CNS imbalance. For example, a general risk for externalizing psychopathology may be conferred through personality traits, cognitive response styles, or emotional liability. Understanding these intermediary risk factors may suggest new targets for developing more effective prevention and intervention programs. With our rich tradition of exploring pathways and mechanisms of risk for behavioral outcomes, psychologists are well poised to make important contributions to understanding *how* genes affect risk. Integrating genetic information with the wealth of phenotypic data often collected in longitudinal psychological studies will raise new analytic challenges. Careful, hypothesis-driven research will be necessary to ensure that the literature does not become littered with genotype–phenotype associations that fail to replicate. Nonetheless, studying endophenotypes to better understand the pathways by which genes affect behavior has become a hot topic in gene identification (Gottesman & Gould, 2003). As geneticists pay increasing attention to phenotype, psychologists can play a pivotal role in advancing our understanding of genetic influences on behavior.

Recommended Reading

Dick, D.M., & Foroud, T. (2003). (See References). Provides a basic introduction to genetic strategies, intended for a general audience.

Kendler, K.S., Prescott, C., Myers, J., & Neale, M.C. (2003). The structure of genetic and environmental risk factors for common psychiatric and substance use disorders in men and women. *Archives of General Psychiatry, 60,* 929–937. One of the first and largest studies to demonstrate a general externalizing and internalizing structure for genetic influences on adult psychiatric disorders.

Krueger, R.F., & Markon, K.E. (2006a). (See References). A clearly written, comprehensive paper on understanding comorbidity across clinical disorders.

Porjesz, B., Rangaswamy, M., Kamarajan, C., Jones, K., Padmanabhapillai, A., & Begleiter, H. (2005). The utility of neurophysiological markers in the study of alcoholism. *Clinical Neurophysiology, 116,* 993–1018. A comprehensive overview of the literature on neuroelectric measures as related to alcoholism.

Acknowledgments—The Collaborative Study on the Genetics of Alcoholism (COGA), Co-Principal Investigators B. Porjesz, V. Hesselbrock, H. Edenberg, L. Bierut, includes nine different centers where data collection, analysis, and storage take place. The nine sites and Principal Investigators and Co–Investigators are: University of Connecticut (V. Hesselbrock); Indiana University (H.J. Edenberg, J. Nurnberger Jr., P.M. Conneally, T. Foroud); University of Iowa (S. Kuperman, R. Crowe); SUNY Downstate (B. Porjesz); Washington University in St. Louis (L. Bierut, A. Goate, J. Rice); University of California at San Diego (M. Schuckit); Howard University (R. Taylor); Rutgers University (J. Tischfield); and Southwest Foundation (L. Almasy). Zhaoxia Ren serves as the National Institute on Alcohol Abuse and Alcoholism (NIAAA) Staff Collaborator. This national collaborative study is supported by the National Institutes of Health Grant U10AA008401 from the NIAAA and the National Institute on Drug Abuse. In memory of Henri Begleiter and Theodore Reich, Principal and Co-Principal Investigators of COGA since its inception.

Note

1. Address correspondence to Danielle M. Dick, Virginia Institute for Psychiatric and Behavioral Genetics, Virginia Commonwealth University, Department of Psychiatry, PO Box 980126, Richmond, VA 23298-0126; e-mail: ddick@vcu.edu.

References

Agrawal, A., Edenberg, H.J., Foroud, T., Bierut, L., Dunne, G., Hinrichs, A.L., et al. (2006). Association of GABRA2 with drug dependence in the Collaborative Study of the Genetics of Alcoholism sample. *Behavior Genetics, 36,* 640–650.

Begleiter, H., & Porjesz, B. (1999). What is inherited in the predisposition toward alcoholism? A proposed model. *Alcoholism: Clinical and Experimental Research, 23,* 1125–1135.

Cardon, L.R. (2006). Delivering new disease genes. *Science, 314,* 1403–1405.

Dick, D.M., Agrawal, A., Schuckit, M., Bierut, L., Hinrichs, A.L., Cloninger, C.R., et al. (2006). Marital status, alcohol dependence, and GABRA2: Evidence for gene-environment correlation and interaction. *Journal of Studies on Alcohol, 67,* 185–194.

Dick, D.M., Aliev, F., Wang, J.C., Grucza, R.A., Schuckit, M., Kuperman, S., et al. (in press). Using dimensional models of externalizing psychopathology to aid in gene identification. *Archives of General Psychiatry.*

Dick, D.M., Bierut, L., Hinrichs, A.L., Fox, L., Bucholz, K.K., Kramer, J.R., et al. (2006). The role of GABRA2 in risk for conduct disorder and alcohol and drug dependence across developmental stages. *Behavior Genetics, 36,* 577–590.

Dick, D.M., & Foroud, T. (2003). Overview of genetic strategies to detect genes involved in alcoholism and related traits. *Alcohol Research & Health, 26,* 172–180.

Edenberg, H.J., Dick, D.M., Xuei, X., Tian, H., Almasy, L., Bauer, L.O., et al. (2004). Variations in GABRA2, encoding the $\alpha 2$ subunit of the GABA-A receptor are associated with alcohol dependence and with brain oscillations. *American Journal of Human Genetics, 74,* 705–714.

Gottesman, I.I., & Gould, T.D. (2003). The endophenotype concept in psychiatry: Etymology and strategic intentions. *American Journal of Psychiatry, 160,* 1–10.

Hasin, D.S., Stinson, F.S., Ogburn, E., & Grant, B.F. (2007). Prevalence, correlates, disability and comorbidity of DSM-IV alcohol abuse and dependence in the United States. *Archives of General Psychiatry, 64,* 830–842.

Hicks, B.M., Bernat, E.M., Malone, S.M., Iacono, W.G., Patrick, C.J., Krueger, R.F., et al. (2007). Genes mediate the association between P3 amplitude and externalizing disorders. *Psychophysiology, 44,* 98–105.

Kendler, K.S., Prescott, C., Myers, J., & Neale, M.C. (2003). The structure of genetic and environmental risk factors for common psychiatric and substance use disorders in men and women. *Archives of General Psychiatry, 60,* 929–937.

Krueger, R.F., Hicks, B.M., Patrick, C.J., Carlson, S.R., Iacono, W.G., & McGue, M. (2002). Etiologic connections among substance dependence, antisocial behavior, and personality: modeling the externalizing spectrum. *Journal of Abnormal Psychology, 111,* 411–424.

Krueger, R.F., & Markon, K.E. (2006a). Reinterpreting comorbidity: A model-based approach to understanding and classifying psychopathology. *Annual Review of Clinical Psychology, 2,* 111–133.

Krueger, R.F., & Markon, K.E. (2006b). Understanding psychopathology: Melding behavior genetics, personality, and quantitative psychology to develop and empirically based model. *Current Directions in Psychological Science, 15,* 113–117.

Krueger, R.F., Watson, D., & Barlow, D.H. (2005). Introduction to the special section: Toward a dimensionally based taxonomy of psychopathology. *Journal of Abnormal Psychology, 114,* 491–493.

Markon, K.E., & Krueger, R.F. (2005). Categorical and continuous models of liability to externalizing disorders: A direct comparison in NESARC. *Archives of General Psychiatry, 62,* 1352–1359.

Stallings, M.C., Corley, R.P., Dennehey, B., Hewitt, J.K., Krauter, K.S., Lessem, J.M., et al. (2005). A genome-wide search for quantitative trait loci that influence antisocial drug dependence in adolescence. *Archives of General Psychiatry, 62,* 1042–1051.

Wang, J.C., Hinrichs, A.L., Stock, H., Budde, J., Allen, R., Bertelsen, S., et al. (2004). Evidence of common and specific genetic effects: Association of the muscarinic acetylcholine receptor M2 (CHRM2) gene with alcohol dependence and major depressive syndrome. *Human Molecular Genetics, 13,* 1903–1911.

Young, S.E., Stallings, M.C., Corley, R.P., Krauter, K.S., & Hewitt, J.K. (2000). Genetic and environmental influences on behavioral disinhibition. *American Journal of Medical Genetics, 96,* 684–695.

This article has been reprinted as it originally appeared in *Current Directions in Psychological Science*. Citation information for this article as originally published appears above.

The Role of Neurobiological Deficits in Childhood Antisocial Behavior

Stephanie H.M. van Goozen[1] and Gordon T. Harold
School of Psychology, Cardiff University
Graeme Fairchild
Developmental Psychiatry Section, University of Cambridge

Abstract

Childhood-onset antisocial behavior is an important predictor of chronic and serious forms of antisocial behavior in later life. Both biological and social factors are involved in the development of abnormal behavior. We examine the underlying role of stress-response systems in the link between early social adversity and juvenile antisocial behavior, and propose that children with genetically and/or perinatally based neurobiological deficits have problems in activating these systems and therefore experience difficulties in regulating affect and behavior. Underactivity or attenuated reactivity of the stress-response systems may predispose antisocial individuals to seek out stimulation or take risks, and thereby explain deficits in learning and socialization. Further investigations of neurobiological functioning in antisocial children might not only indicate which children are more likely to persist in behaving antisocially but also guide the development of new interventions.

Keywords

antisocial behavior; stress; cortisol; autonomic arousal; children

Antisocial behavior is a significant social and clinical concern. Every year, more than 1.6 million people are killed as a result of violence, and many more suffer from physical or mental health problems stemming from violence (World Health Organization, 2002). Antisocial behavior committed by youths is an issue of particular concern. A recent survey showed that citizens of European nations see themselves as having "significant" difficulties with antisocial behavior, and that the problem is above all associated with people under 25 years of age ("Bad behaviour," 2006).

The term *antisocial behavior* refers to the fact that people who are on the receiving end of the behavior are disadvantaged by it, and that social norms and values are violated. Not only aggression but also activities such as theft, vandalism, lying, truancy, running away from home, and oppositional behaviors are involved.

Most normally developing children will occasionally exhibit negative and disobedient behavior toward adults and engage in lying, fighting, and bullying other children. When antisocial behavior forms a pattern that goes beyond the "normal" realm and starts to have adverse effects on the child's functioning, psychiatrists tend to make a diagnosis of conduct disorder (CD) or oppositional defiant disorder (ODD; American Psychiatric Association, 1994). These disorders are relatively common in children, with estimated prevalences ranging from 5 to 10%.

The extent to which these disorders can be treated via therapy is limited, and, as a result, these children are at risk for a host of negative outcomes in adolescence and adulthood, including dropping out of school, criminality, unemployment, dependence on welfare, and substance abuse (Hill & Maughan, 2001).

There is a growing consensus that both child-specific (i.e., genetic, temperamental) and social (e.g., early adversity) factors contribute to the development and maintenance of antisocial behavior, although most research has focused on identifying specific contextual factors that impinge on the developing child. For example, negative life events, family stress, and parental relationship problems have been associated with antisocial-behavior problems in children. However, there is increasing evidence that factors organic to individual children exacerbate the risk of antisocial behavior to those who live with social adversity. Here, we review evidence relating to the role of neurobiological factors in accounting for the link between early adversity and childhood antisocial behavior and propose that consideration of biological factors underlying this stress–distress link significantly advances understanding of the mechanisms explaining individual differences in the etiology of antisocial behavior.

Research suggests that neurobiological deficits related to the functioning of the stress systems in children with CD are linked to antisocial behavior. We argue that familial factors (e.g., genetic influences, early adversity) are linked to negative outcomes through the mediating and transactional interplay with neurobiological deficits (see Fig. 1) and propose that stress hyporeactivity is an index of persistent and serious antisocial behavior.

STRESS-RESPONSE SYSTEMS

There are clear indications that stress plays an important role in explaining individual differences in antisocial behavior. The systems involved in the regulation of stress are the neuroendocrine hypothalamic-pituitary-adrenal (HPA) axis and the psychophysiological autonomic nervous system (ANS). Cortisol is studied in relation to HPA-axis activation, and heart rate (HR) and skin-conductance (SC) responses are used as markers of ANS (re)activity.

The starting point of our approach is that antisocial individuals are less sensitive to stress. This can be deduced from the fact that antisocial individuals engage in risky or dangerous behavior more often than other people do and seem less deterred by its possible negative consequences. There are two explanations for the proposed relationship between lower stress sensitivity and antisocial behavior. One theory claims that antisocial individuals are fearless (Raine, 1996). A lack of fear leads to antisocial behavior because individuals are less sensitive to the negative consequences of their own or other people's behavior in general and to the receipt of punishment in particular. The implications for treatment are clear: Antisocial individuals will have problems learning the association between behavior and punishment, such that pointing out the negative consequences of behavior, or punishing unacceptable behavior, is likely to have little or no effect.

The second explanation focuses on stress thresholds and sensation-seeking behavior (Zuckerman, 1979), and argues that antisocial individuals have elevated

Independent Influences
(Early Familial Factors)

Mediating/Moderating Mechanism(s)
(e.g., HPA-Axis Dysfunction)

Dependent Outcome
(Behavioral Dysfunction)

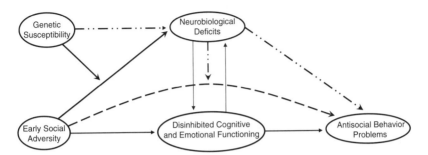

Fig. 1. Theoretical model relating early social adversity to later antisocial behavior problems. It is hypothesized that this relationship is explained by the underlying mediating and moderating role of neurobiological factors. The dashed-dotted lines emanating from genetic susceptibility to neurobiological deficits and from neurobiological deficits to antisocial behavior problems represent an indirect (or mediating) pathway between these factors. The bold line emanating from genetic susceptibility to the pathway linking early social adversity to neurobiological deficits, and the dashed-dotted line from neurobiological deficits to the pathway linking early social adversity to antisocial behavior problems, represent proposed moderating influences from each source variable (i.e., genetic susceptibility and neurobiological deficits). A moderating influence is the equivalent of statistical interaction between two theoretical constructs. Bold and dashed-dotted lines in all other instances represent direct and indirect pathways linking primary theoretical constructs. For a full exposition of this model, see van Goozen, Fairchild, Snoek, and Harold (2007).

thresholds for stress. They are more easily bored and less easily put off by situations that normal people find stressful or dangerous.

What evidence is there that dysfunctional stress systems play a role in antisocial behavior? Several studies (e.g., Virkkunen, 1985) have found that antisocial adults have low resting levels of cortisol, SC, and HR. There is also evidence of inverse relationships between these physiological variables and the severity of the behavioral problems shown. Studies investigating the relation between biological stress parameters and antisocial behavior have also been performed in children (e.g., van Goozen et al., 1998), and the predicted (inverse) relations have been found.

Stress variables can also predict antisocial behavior over time. Raine, Venables, and Mednick (1997) measured HR in more than 1,700 three-year-old children. Aggressive behavior was assessed at age 11. Raine et al. found that low resting HR at age 3 predicted aggressive behavior at age 11. In a study of criminals' sons (who are at risk of becoming delinquent), Brennan et al. (1997) found that boys who did not become delinquent had higher HR and SC than did boys who became delinquent. The authors concluded that the boys in the former group were biologically protected by their heightened autonomic responsivity.

Studies of youths who engage in antisocial behavior show that they, like antisocial adults, have less reactive stress systems than do youths who do not engage in antisocial behavior. The question is whether the same applies to children with serious antisocial behavior who have been diagnosed with CD or ODD.

STRESS STUDIES IN CD CHILDREN

Most studies collect stress data under resting conditions rather than during stress exposure. Antisocial individuals might be different from normal individuals in two respects: A low resting stress level could result in failing to avoid, or even approaching, stressful situations; and low stress reactivity implies that one is more fearless and cares less about possible negative consequences.

Our studies use a paradigm in which psychosocial stress is evoked by exposing children to frustration, provocation, and competition (e.g., van Goozen et al., 1998). The participant competes against a fictitious videotaped "opponent" who behaves in an antagonistic manner. The participant and opponent perform computerized tasks on which they can earn points. The participant is told that the person who earns the most points will receive an attractive prize. Some tasks are impossible to complete, which induces frustration. HR and SC are measured continuously, and cortisol is collected repeatedly in saliva.

CD children show lower HR, SC, and cortisol reactivity to stress than do normal children. Although CD children appear to be less affected at a biological level, they react more angrily and aggressively to provocation than do non-CD children and report feeling quite upset. It is known that CD children are impulsive, have hostile appraisal patterns, and engage in conflictual situations. It is striking that this pattern of appraisal and behavior is not accompanied by contextually appropriate somatic changes.

Genetic factors likely play a role in the functioning of the HPA axis and ANS. There is also evidence that stressful events—by which we mean serious stressors like neglect and traumatization—play an important role in "programming" the stress systems, particularly the HPA axis. This evidence comes mainly from nonhuman animal studies, but the neurobiological consequences of the types of severe stress that can be manipulated in animal studies also occur in humans.

EARLY EXPERIENCE AND FAMILY ADVERSITY

Physical and biological problems during important phases in development (e.g., birth complications, stress or illness during pregnancy), together with early adversity (e.g., malnutrition, neglect, abuse), contribute importantly to the development of personality and psychopathology. There is increasing evidence that interactions between biological and environmental factors affect the developing brain (Huizink, Mulder, & Buitelaar, 2004).

Nonhuman animal studies show that stressors in early life can have permanent effects on the functioning of the HPA axis, resulting in altered basal and stress-reactivity levels. For example, Liu et al. (1997) varied the amount of licking and grooming behavior in mothers of newborn rats. In adulthood, offspring who had been exposed to normal maternal care were more capable of handling stress than were rats that had received less care. The former also expressed more stress-hormone receptors in the hippocampus, an area important for stress regulation, than did rats that had received less care. Thus, maternal behavior had a direct and lasting effect on the development of the stress systems of the offspring.

Such conclusions are based on data from nonhuman animals, and for obvious reasons it is difficult to conduct similar studies on humans. However, evidence from a handful of studies involving institutionalized children suggests that the processes at work are similar (Carlson & Earls, 1997; Gunnar, Morison, Chisolm, & Schuder, 2001).

Antisocial children are more likely to come from adverse rearing environments involving atypical caregiver–child interactions (Rutter & Silberg, 2002). It is known that CD children are more likely to experience compromised pre- or perinatal development due to maternal smoking, poor nutrition, or exposure to alcohol and/or drugs. It is possible that these factors have affected such children's stress-response systems and resulted in children with a difficult temperament.

STRESS HYPOREACTIVITY AS A MEDIATING FACTOR

We have suggested that physiological hyporeactivity may reflect an inability to generate visceral signals to guide behavior and, in particular, to regulate anger and reactive aggression (van Goozen, Fairchild, Snoek, & Harold, 2007). Evidence from nonhuman animals indicates that abolishing the hormonal response to stress may impair processing of social signals and lead to abnormal patterns of aggression (Haller, Halász, Mikics, & Kruk, 2004). These studies also showed that abnormal aggressive behavior can be prevented by mimicking the hormonal response normally seen during aggressive encounters. These findings have clear parallels with abnormal aggression in humans, in the sense that the behavior is not only excessive but also often risky, badly judged, and callous.

We have proposed an integrative theoretical model linking genetic factors, early adversity, cognitive and neurobiological regulatory mechanisms, and childhood antisocial behavior (van Goozen et al., 2007; see Fig. 1). Interactions between genetic predispositions and the environment in which they are expressed appear to be crucial in the etiology of antisocial-behavior problems. A genetic predisposition toward antisocial behavior may be expressed in adverse rearing environments in which the child receives harsh or inconsistent discipline or is exposed to high levels of interparental conflict or marital breakdown (Moffitt, 2005). It is likely that the origin of antisocial behavior in young children lies in this combination of a difficult temperament and a harsh environment in which there is ineffective socialization: A difficult child elicits harsh, inconsistent, and negative socialization behaviors, as a result of which a difficult temperament develops into antisocial behavior (Lykken, 1995). Conversely, the effects of a genetic predisposition may be minimized if the child is raised in an environment in which the parents express warmth or adopt a consistent, authoritative parenting style.

Some children are born with a more easygoing temperament than others. In cases of "hard-to-manage" children, a child's genotype can evoke negative behavior from the environment because genetic influences lead the individual to create, seek out, or otherwise end up in environments that match the genotype (Rutter & Silberg, 2002). These active, evocative gene–environment processes are extremely important in understanding the development and continuity of antisocial behavior (Moffitt, 2005). Social factors occurring independently of the child's genetic makeup or temperament can serve as contributory factors (Harold, Aitken, & Shelton, 2008).

We noted above that early brain development is vulnerable to the effects of environmental stress (Huizink et al., 2004), and that CD children are likely to have been exposed to early stress. A down-regulation of the stress-response system in the face of chronic stress in early life would be an adaptive mechanism, avoiding chronic arousal and excessive energy expenditure that could ultimately result in serious pathophysiological consequences. Given what we know about the background of CD children, it is plausible that these processes have occurred.

We propose that physiological hyporeactivity is a mediating and/or moderating factor for persistent and severe antisocial behavior and that the effects of variations in genetic makeup and early adversity on childhood antisocial behavior occur via this deficit. The primary pathway by which familial factors are linked to antisocial outcome is the reciprocal interplay with neurobiological deficits and resulting disinhibited cognitive (e.g., impulsivity, hostile bias) and emotional (e.g., increased anger) processing, with the latter serving as the psychological gateway through which neurobiological deficits find their expression in antisocial behavior.

CONCLUSION

Antisocial behavior in children can be persistent and difficult to treat. Although behavioral interventions have been shown to be effective in milder forms of problem behavior, they have limited effectiveness in more seriously disturbed children (Hill & Maughan, 2001).

At present, we do not know what causes the pattern of neurobiological impairments observed in antisocial children, although it is clear that genetic factors are involved (Caspi et al., 2002). An important line of research suggests that psychosocial adversity affects brain development. Knowing that many CD children have problematic backgrounds, it seems possible that exposure to severe stress has had an effect on the development of their stress systems. Longitudinal research in high-risk children is needed to shed more light on this issue.

Future interventions and treatments should benefit from a neurobiological approach: Neurobiological assessment of high-risk children could indicate whether their deficits are such that interventions involving "empathy induction" or "learning from punishment," for example, are unlikely to work. In such cases, pharmacological interventions could be considered as a treatment option. An important line of future research is to establish whether CD children with attenuated stress (re)activity would be more effectively treated by using pharmacological therapies that reinstate normal HPA-axis functioning.

Current interventions for childhood antisocial behavior have limited success because we lack knowledge of the cognitive–emotional problems of these children and their neurobiological bases. We also fail to assess the environmental risk factors that affect individual neurodevelopment. Furthermore, available treatment options do not target the individual's specific neurobiological vulnerabilities. It seems prudent to identify subgroups of children in whom different causal processes initiate and maintain behavioral problems. This should result in a better match between patient and treatment.

A final point is that the understandable tendency to focus on persistence of antisocial behavior runs the risk of overlooking the fact that a substantial proportion of antisocial children do not grow up to be antisocial adults (with prevalence rates for antisocial children who persist into adulthood ranging from 35 to 75%). Neurobiological factors could also account for this: Promising data from a handful of studies show that neurobiological factors differ between children who persist in and desist from antisocial behavior (Brennan et al., 1997; van de Wiel, van Goozen, Matthys, Snoek, & van Engeland, 2004). Expanding on this research base is essential if we are to reach a more adequate understanding of the causes, course, and consequences of childhood antisocial behavior and, most importantly, devise effective ways of reducing the negative consequences for society.

Recommended Reading

Hill, J., & Maughan, B. (2001). *Conduct disorders in childhood and adolescence.* Cambridge, UK: Cambridge University Press. A clearly written and comprehensive review for readers who wish to expand their knowledge on conduct disorders in youngsters.

Moffitt, T.E. (2005). The new look of behavioral genetics in developmental psychopathology: Gene–environment interplay in antisocial behaviors. *Psychological Bulletin, 131,* 533–554. Explains and discusses the gene–environment interplay in antisocial behavior in more detail.

van Goozen, S.H.M., Fairchild, G., Snoek, H., & Harold, G.T. (2007). The evidence for a neurobiological model of childhood antisocial behavior. *Psychological Bulletin, 133,* 149–182. Discusses the neurobiological basis of antisocial behavior in greater detail than the current paper.

Note

1. Address correspondence to Stephanie H.M. van Goozen, School of Psychology, Cardiff University, Tower Building, Park Place, Cardiff CF10 3AT, United Kingdom; e-mail: vangoozens@cardiff.ac.uk.

References

American Psychiatric Association. (1994). *Diagnostic and statistical manual of mental disorders* (4th ed.). Washington, DC: Author.

Bad behaviour 'worst in Europe'. (2006). BBC News. Downloaded April 30, 2008, from http://news.bbc.co.uk/1/hi/uk/4751315.stm

Brennan, P.A., Raine, A., Schulsinger, F., Kirkegaard-Sorensen, L., Knop, J., Hutchings, B., et al. (1997). Psychophysiological protective factors for male subjects at high risk for criminal behavior. *American Journal of Psychiatry, 154,* 853–855.

Carlson, M., & Earls, F. (1997). Psychological and neuroendocrinological sequelae of early social deprivation in institutionalized children in Romania. *Annals of the New York Academy of Sciences, 807,* 419–428.

Caspi, A., McClay, J., Moffitt, T.E., Mill, J., Martin, J., Craig, I.W., et al. (2002). Role of the genotype in the cycle of violence in maltreated children. *Science, 297,* 851–854.

Gunnar, M.R., Morison, S.J., Chisholm, K., & Schuder, M. (2001). Salivary cortisol levels in children adopted from Romanian orphanages. *Development and Psychopathology, 13,* 611–628.

Harold, G.T., Aitken, J.J., & Shelton, K.H. (2008). Inter-parental conflict and children's academic attainment: A longitudinal analysis. *Journal of Child Psychology and Psychiatry, 48,* 1223–1232.

Haller, J., Halász, J., Mikics, E., & Kruk, M.R. (2004). Chronic glucocorticoid deficiency-induced abnormal aggression, autonomic hypoarousal, and social deficit in rats. *Journal of Neuroendocrinology, 16,* 550–557.

Hill, J., & Maughan, B. (2001). *Conduct disorders in childhood and adolescence.* Cambridge, UK: Cambridge University Press.

Huizink, A.C., Mulder, E.J.H., & Buitelaar, J.K. (2004). Prenatal stress and risk for psychopathology: Specific effects or induction of general susceptibility. *Psychological Bulletin, 130,* 115–142.

Liu, D., Diorio, J., Tannenbaum, B., Caldji, C., Francis, D., Freedman, A., et al. (1997). Maternal care, hippocampal glucocorticoid receptors, and hypothalamic-pituitary-adrenal responses to stress. *Science, 277,* 1659–1662.

Lykken, D.T. (1995). *The antisocial personalities.* Hillsdale, NJ: Erlbaum.

Moffitt, T.E. (2005). The new look of behavioral genetics in developmental psychopathology: Gene-environment interplay in antisocial behaviors. *Psychological Bulletin, 131,* 533–554.

Raine, A. (1996). Autonomic nervous system activity and violence. In D.M. Stoff & R.B. Cairns (Eds.), *Aggression and violence: Genetic, neurobiological and biological perspectives* (pp. 145–168). Mahwah, NJ: Erlbaum.

Raine, A., Venables, P.H., & Mednick, S.A. (1997). Low resting heart rate at age 3 years predisposes to aggression at age 11 years: Evidence from the Mauritius Child Health Project. *Journal of the American Academy of Child and Adolescent Psychiatry, 36,* 1457–1464.

Rutter, M., & Silberg, J. (2002). Gene-environment interplay in relation to emotional and behavioral disturbance. *Annual Review of Psychology, 53,* 463–490.

van de Wiel, N.M.H., van Goozen, S.H.M., Matthys, W., Snoek, H., & van Engeland, H. (2004). Cortisol and treatment effect in children with disruptive behavior disorders: A preliminary study. *Journal of the American Academy of Child and Adolescent Psychiatry, 43,* 1011–1018.

van Goozen, S.H.M., Fairchild, G., Snoek, H., & Harold, G.T. (2007). The evidence for a neurobiological model of childhood antisocial behaviour. *Psychological Bulletin, 133,* 149–182.

van Goozen, S.H.M., Matthys, W., Cohen-Kettenis, P.T., Gispen-de Wied, C., Wiegant, V.M., & van Engeland, H. (1998). Salivary cortisol and cardiovascular activity during stress in oppositional-defiant disorder boys and normal controls. *Biological Psychiatry, 43,* 531–539.

Virkkunen, M. (1985). Urinary free cortisol secretion in habitually violent offenders. *Acta Psychiatrica Scandinavica, 72,* 40–44.

World Health Organization (2002). *World report on violence and health.* E.G. Krug, L.L. Dahlman, J.A. Mercy, A.B. Zwi, & R. Lozano (Eds.). Geneva, Switzerland: Author.

Zuckerman, M. (1979). *Sensation seeking: Beyond the optimum level of arousal.* Hillsdale, NJ: Erlbaum.

This article has been reprinted as it originally appeared in *Current Directions in Psychological Science*. Citation information for this article as originally published appears above.

Violent Children in Developmental Perspective: Risk and Protective Factors and the Mechanisms Through Which They (May) Operate

Gregory S. Pettit[1]
Department of Human Development and Family Studies, Auburn University

Abstract

This article describes some of the current research and thinking about developmental pathways leading to youth violence and the risk and protective factors that play a contributory role. Considerable support can be found for theoretical models positing that life experiences, including harsh and inconsistent parenting, rejection by peers, school failure, and affiliation with an antisocial peer group, cumulate to increase the risk of antisocial and violent behavior and serve as a means through which early dispositions and sociocultural contexts exert an impact on development of antisocial behavior. Emotional and cognitive processes may provide a key connecting link between developmental risk factors and antisocial behavior and violence.

Keywords

childhood violence; risk factors; development

Interest in the factors contributing to violent behavior in children and adolescents continues to be high, as researchers, practitioners, and policymakers search for both tools to identify at-risk children and empirically based intervention strategies that might reduce violent behavior. Recent government statistics suggest that criminal violence in this country has leveled off, or even declined. Still, childhood violence exacts substantial costs to individuals, institutions, and society at large. What, then, can be said about progress in understanding the development of antisocial and violent youth? Can children who are at risk for later violence be identified in early childhood? What pathways characterize the developmental course of violence? What role do life experiences, in combination with personal attributes and sociocultural factors, play in the development and maintenance of violent behavior? These and related questions have been the focus of extensive inquiry in recent years. The aim of this article is to summarize some of the key findings in this area, and to highlight some of the issues yet to be resolved.

DEVELOPMENTAL PROGRESSIONS

For the purposes of this article, *violent behavior* refers to behavioral acts that lead to harm and injury to the victim and are perpetrated with the aim of inflicting such harm. There is considerable ambiguity in the conceptualization and measurement of the more general construct of antisocial behavior and its most frequently studied component, aggressive behavior (Rutter, 2003; Tremblay, 2000). Although not every instance of aggressive behavior is antisocial (as in the "aggressive" tennis player), and although there are forms of antisocial behavior that are not aggressive (vandalism, truancy, shoplifting, e.g.), it is reasonable to conclude that violent behavior is both antisocial and aggressive.

Some degree of physical aggression is normative in young children, but children who deviate from these normative patterns, whether by being excessively aggressive or by being aggressive in age-inappropriate ways, are on a developmental pathway that may culminate in physically violent behavior. Socialization experiences likely play an important role in altering the normative course of aggressive behavior. As children get older, parents and teachers show less tolerance for aggression and punish it (or redirect it) more consistently than they did at earlier ages.

Individual variations in the development of aggression can be characterized in terms of age of onset, severity, and persistence. A small group of children show early, persistent, and severe (e.g., violent) forms of antisocial behavior. This pattern is thought to originate in acquired or inherited neuropsychological problems, manifested as cognitive deficits, difficult temperament, and hyperactivity, in conjunction with a high-risk social environment of inept parenting, family discord, and poverty. A second developmental pattern is characterized by the emergence of less violent forms of antisocial behavior in adolescence, with a substantial decrease in such behavior by early adulthood (Moffitt, 1993). This is a relatively common pattern, thought to reflect normative adolescent struggles with autonomy and identity, and a heightened interest in peers. Youths following this pathway may find delinquent activities a means of distancing themselves from their parents and gaining peer approval. Because their preadolescent development was relatively normal, such youths typically leave the delinquent lifestyle in early adulthood as they begin to take on more conventional adult roles and responsibilities.

Existence of these two pathways—one beginning in childhood and continuing through adolescence, one beginning (and for the most part ending) in adolescence—suggests that antisocial behavior should peak in adolescence, which would be consistent with the common finding that crime rates peak during adolescence and then decrease in adulthood. However, recent longitudinal data paint a different picture. Broidy et al. (2003), drawing on data generated from six different ongoing studies, found that physical aggression, a likely behavioral forerunner of violent delinquency, at least for boys, showed a high level of consistency and stability across childhood, with no uptick in adolescence. Results from other longitudinal studies (e.g., Shaw, Gilliom, Ingoldsby, & Nagin, 2003) suggest that overt antisocial behavior declines across time, at least in the early childhood years.

RISK AND PROTECTIVE FACTORS

There is abundant evidence that antisocial and violent behavior in childhood and adolescence is associated with a variety of personal, social, and socioeconomic risk factors. Owing to the lack of demonstrable causal connections, Rutter (2003) suggested that such factors may best be construed as "contributory." In the personal domain, a partial list of risk factors includes deficits in problem solving and cognitive functioning, difficulty in regulating emotional arousal, and irritable, control-resistant temperament. Social risks include exposure to harsh and inept parenting, aggressive siblings, peer rejection, and an antisocial peer group. Contextual risks include growing up in a violent neighborhood, living in poverty, and being a member of a repressed ethnic minority group.

Protective factors, which decrease the likelihood of antisocial outcomes, given exposure to risk, have been identified in the same three domains. They include having an agreeable, adaptable temperament (personal); having a warm, supportive relationship with a caregiver (social); and growing up in a low-violence, cohesive neighborhood (contextual). How risk and protective factors from the three domains coalesce and interact with one another to increase (or decrease) the probability of violent behavior has been a central theme in recent research on the developmental course of antisocial behavior.

MECHANISMS OF INFLUENCE

Genetic Factors

Some children inherit from their parents traits and characteristics that may be directly involved in the development of criminality and violent behavior (e.g., aggressiveness, attention deficits). Genetic factors also may operate indirectly by instigating some of the environmental risk conditions known to be associated with antisocial behavior, as when a child with a genetic predisposition to be irritable elicits harsh treatment from his or her parents and peers. Life experiences, then, may be the means through which inherited dispositions exert an impact on later antisocial outcomes. Genetic predispositions also may interact with environmental factors; that is, antisocial predispositions may be manifested in problem behavior only when environmental risk is high. For example, Caspi et al. (2002) recently found a specific gene that confers increased vulnerability to the negative effects of early maltreatment.

Interplay of Risk Factors Across Development

One way in which personal and contextual risk factors may exert an impact on the development of antisocial behavior is through intervening life experiences (Dodge & Pettit, 2003). This point of view is consistent with the notion, mentioned earlier, that genetic factors instigate environmental risk conditions, and with the notion that social experiences (e.g., harsh, inconsistent discipline) serve as a connecting link between social-ecological stressors, such as poverty, and subsequent antisocial behavior. The impact of early life experiences on adolescent antisocial behavior and violence may, in turn, be explained through subsequent life experiences (e.g., Kokko & Pulkkinen, 2000). Patterson's (1982) well-known social-interactional theory of the development of antisocial behavior provides a compelling illustration. A difficult-to-manage child growing up in a family in which parents lack key child-management skills learns that if he or she actively resists his or her parent's demands, the parent will eventually capitulate. Children who successfully use such coercive behavior to escape their parents' attempts to control them may subsequently apply such tactics in school settings, when confronted with a directive or demanding teacher or peer. Lacking opportunities for learning and practicing positive and constructive interpersonal skills, and lacking connections with mainstream peers, such children eventually gravitate to an antisocial peer group that models and reinforces violent and nonviolent delinquent activity. Thus, experiences later in development (i.e., with peers) help to explain the link between earlier experiences (i.e., with parents) and antisocial and violent behavior in adolescence.

A reading of current literature suggests that later life experiences account for some, but not all, of the impact of early life experiences on the development of antisocial behavior. Depending on one's emphasis, this evidence can be viewed as support for the idea that specific risks independently add up to produce total risk or for the idea that risks interact, such that some affect the eventual impact of others.

Factors Contributing to the Development Versus Maintenance of Antisocial Behavior

For the most part, current data do not distinguish between factors that predict (or co-occur with) the initial appearance of antisocial behavior and those that predict (or co-occur with) longitudinal patterns of antisocial behavior once it has been manifested. This is a shortcoming because understanding the factors associated with subsequent declines in antisocial behavior among children who display highly antisocial behavior at a given point in time may prove critical for uncovering protective factors that help to reroute the developmental trajectories of at-risk children. The study of children whose antisocial-behavior problems escalate over time and comparisons of early-problem children with those who develop problems only later in life provide opportunities for fine-tuning prediction models to better distinguish between factors that set the stage for the initial development of antisocial behavior (e.g., harsh parental treatment) and factors that co-occur with and serve to maintain the problem behavior (e.g., involvement with antisocial peers). The former may be especially useful for understanding what precipitates antisocial behavior, the latter for understanding what experiences and dispositions serve to moderate growth and development of antisocial behavior.

Through What Mechanisms Do Life Experiences Influence Violent Behavior?

Researchers increasingly have turned their attention to the social-cognitive mechanisms that may help to account directly for the association between social experiences and children's aggressive behavior. The findings from several studies implicate emotional and cognitive processes during social events as crucial factors that mediate the relation between risk factors and antisocial behavior (Dodge & Pettit, 2003). Dispositions, context, and life experiences may contribute to the development of antisocial behavior because they lead children to develop particular kinds of social knowledge about their world. Such knowledge guides interpretation of social events (such as a provocation by a peer or adult authority figure), such that each child has a characteristic pattern of processing these events based on his or her social knowledge. A child's pattern of processing social information may in turn lead directly to specific social (or antisocial) behaviors, thereby mediating the effect of early life experiences on later antisocial behavior.

Numerous theories in social, cognitive, clinical, and developmental psychology suggest that the acquisition of knowledge structures provides a critical link between life experiences and future behavior. Dodge and I suggested that such structures, in the form of belief systems, expectations about relationships, and memories of past social encounters, serve as guides for children's interpretation of, and response to, the behavior of peers (and other people) during ongoing social exchanges (Dodge & Pettit, 2003). Consider an adolescent boy who is being teased in the school hallway by peers. This boy's immediate response can be viewed as a function of a sequential set of emotional and mental processes, which include (a) attending to relevant cues (e.g., the peers' facial expressions); (b) mentally representing and interpreting these cues in a meaningful way (e.g., interpreting them either as a provocation or as a harmless prank); (c) accessing one or more potential responses to this situation (such as getting angry, laughing, or walking away) from a long-term memorial repertoire; (d) evaluating accessed responses, perhaps by anticipating whether they are likely to lead to desired outcomes or not; and, finally, (e) enacting a selected response. Processing at each step alters the probability that the boy will react aggressively. For example, this probability is increased if he pays particular attention to cues that might indicate his peers are being hostile, if he interprets the other youngsters as being hostile toward him, if he rapidly accesses aggressive responses, and if he evaluates aggressive responses as likely to result in a positive outcome.

There is substantial evidence that children's predispositions (e.g., temperament, physiological reactions to stress), environment (e.g., poverty, racism), and experiences (e.g., harsh parenting, rejection by peers) influence the characteristic processing patterns that they develop, and that such acquired processing patterns partially account for the effect of early life experiences on later conduct problems. My colleagues and I found that certain processing patterns during the early elementary-school years were predictable from early experiences of harsh physical discipline and physical abuse, and that, in turn, these processing patterns predicted later chronic conduct problems, accounting for about half of the effect of those early-life experiences on later conduct problems (Dodge, Pettit, Bates, & Valente, 1995).

This evidence suggests one avenue through which experience exerts an impact on subsequent antisocial and violent behavior, but it is not the only possible avenue of influence. It remains for future research to specify which processes will be linked with which life experiences for which kinds of outcomes. It may be, for example, that individual differences in interpretation of social cues stem from one type of early experience (e.g., exposure to harsh punishment), whereas being inclined to evaluate aggressive responses as likely to lead to desired outcomes may stem from a different type of early experience (e.g., observing one's parents behave in aggressive ways). Each of these social-information processing components may in turn be associated with increased risk for distinct types of antisocial behavior. Tests of these possibilities should be conducted within a developmental framework because it is likely that different processes become operative at different ages. It also will be important to understand how physiological arousal (e.g., rapid heart rate during potentially conflictual social exchanges) influences processing skill and accuracy. There is some evidence that processing errors are associated with arousal and that induced arousal leads to a reduction in children's skillfulness in reading and responding to interpersonal cues (Dodge & Pettit, 2003).

CONCLUSIONS

Research on violent children has made great strides in recent years, with growing recognition of the complex interplay of biological, social, and contextual factors. Longitudinal databases are making it possible to chart the development of anti-social behavior over time and to identify those factors that may "launch" a child on a pathway leading to violence, as well as those factors that may redirect a child toward a different pathway. Accumulating evidence suggests that emotional and cognitive processes may account for a significant portion of the relation between risk factors and subsequent aggressive and violent behavior.

As with most aspects of social behavior, there are still gaps in understanding that remain to be filled. One largely unexplored area is the means through which protective factors confer their putative protection. How does a protective factor create a buffer between the child and the risk to which the child has been exposed? In addition, as is the case for indicators of risk, protective factors often are studied singly, and it is not clear whether some combinations of protective factors work better than others (Criss, Pettit, Bates, Dodge, & Lapp, 2002).

A child's behavior and environment are dynamic and reciprocally related, with each providing feedback to the other and instigating change in the other (Dodge & Pettit, 2003). But charting the course of such coordinated changes remains a daunting task, and the identification of the mechanisms through which such changes occur has proven elusive. That children's characteristics exert an impact on their environments is now accepted orthodoxy. But only recently have researchers developed analytic tools, and conceptual models, that enable the testing of hypotheses about the mechanisms that underlie these reciprocal relationships. One hypothesis, in need of further testing, is that life experiences with key social agents provide the medium through which children's behavior and environment influence each other (Dodge & Pettit, 2003).

That risk and protective factors interact with one another is a central theme of this article. But, as noted elsewhere (e.g., Dodge & Pettit, 2003), it is one thing to posit interactive models but quite another to find evidence consistent with them. This is because interaction effects are difficult to detect in nonexperimental research contexts. In laboratory settings, factors of interest can be manipulated independently, but in natural settings, risk factors tend to co-occur. The high positive correlation between risk factors (and their high negative correlation with protective factors) makes it difficult to locate sufficient numbers of individuals receiving a high score on one risk factor and a low score on another (or a high score on a protective factor). To better understand how risk and protective factors operate in relation to one another, investigators need research designs that oversample children with unexpected or unusual combinations of risk and protective factors.

Recommended Reading

Dodge, K.A., & Pettit, G.S. (2003). (See References)

Moore, M.H., Petrie, C.V., Braga, A.A., & McLaughlin, B.L. (Eds.). (2002). *Deadly lessons: Understanding lethal school violence*. Washington, DC: National Research Council.

Reid, J.B., Patterson, G.R., & Snyder, J.J. (2002). *Antisocial behavior in children and adolescents: A developmental analysis and model for intervention*. Washington, DC: American Psychological Association.

Weist, M.D., & Cooley-Quille, M. (2001). Advancing efforts to address youth violence involvement. *Journal of Clinical Child Psychology, 30,* 147–151.

Acknowledgments—Preparation of this article was supported in part by National Institute of Mental Health Grant MH57095.

Note

1. Address correspondence to Gregory Pettit, Human Development and Family Studies, 203 Spidle Hall, Auburn University, AL 36849; e-mail: gpettit@auburn.edu.

References

Broidy, L.M., Nagin, D.S., Tremblay, R.E., Brame, B., Dodge, K.A., Fergusson, D., Horwood, J., Loeber, R., Laird, R., Lynam, D., Moffitt, T., Bates, J.E., Pettit, G.S., & Vitaro, F. (2003). Developmental trajectories of childhood disruptive behaviors and adolescent delinquency: A six site, cross-national study. *Developmental Psychology, 39,* 222–245.

Caspi, A., McClay, J., Moffitt, T.E., Mill, J., Martin, J., Craig, I.W., Taylor, A., & Poulton, R. (2002). Role of genotype in the cycle of violence in maltreated children. *Science, 297,* 851–854.

Criss, M.M., Pettit, G.S., Bates, J.E., Dodge, K.A., & Lapp, A.L. (2002). Family adversity, positive peer relationships, and children's externalizing behavior: A longitudinal perspective on risk and resilience. *Child Development, 73,* 1220–1237.

Dodge, K.A., & Pettit, G.S. (2003). A biopsychosocial model of the development of chronic conduct problems in adolescence. *Developmental Psychology, 39,* 189–190.

Dodge, K.A., Pettit, G.S., Bates, J.E., & Valente, E. (1995). Social-information-processing patterns partially mediate the effect of early physical abuse on later conduct problems. *Journal of Abnormal Psychology, 104,* 632–643.

Kokko, K., & Pulkkinen, L. (2000). Aggression in childhood and long-term unemployment in adulthood: A cycle of maladaptation and protective factors. *Developmental Psychology, 36,* 463–472.

Moffitt, T.E. (1993). Adolescence-limited and life-course-persistent antisocial behavior: A developmental taxonomy. *Psychological Review, 100,* 674–701.

Patterson, G.R. (1982). *Coercive family processes*. Eugene, OR: Castalia.

Rutter, M. (2003). Commentary: Causal processes leading to antisocial behavior. *Developmental Psychology, 39,* 372–378.

Shaw, D.S., Gilliom, M., Ingoldsby, E.M., & Nagin, D.S. (2003). Trajectories leading to school-age conduct problems. *Developmental Psychology, 39,* 189–200.

Tremblay, R.E. (2000). The development of aggressive behavior during childhood: What have we learned in the past half century? *International Journal of Behavioral Development, 24,* 129–141.

Risk Taking in Adolescence: New Perspectives From Brain and Behavioral Science

Laurence Steinberg[1]

Temple University

Abstract

Trying to understand why adolescents and young adults take more risks than younger or older individuals do has challenged psychologists for decades. Adolescents' inclination to engage in risky behavior does not appear to be due to irrationality, delusions of invulnerability, or ignorance. This paper presents a perspective on adolescent risk taking grounded in developmental neuroscience. According to this view, the temporal gap between puberty, which impels adolescents toward thrill seeking, and the slow maturation of the cognitive-control system, which regulates these impulses, makes adolescence a time of heightened vulnerability for risky behavior. This view of adolescent risk taking helps to explain why educational interventions designed to change adolescents' knowledge, beliefs, or attitudes have been largely ineffective, and suggests that changing the contexts in which risky behavior occurs may be more successful than changing the way adolescents think about risk.

Keywords

adolescence; decision making; risk taking; brain development

Adolescents and college-age individuals take more risks than children or adults do, as indicated by statistics on automobile crashes, binge drinking, contraceptive use, and crime; but trying to understand why risk taking is more common during adolescence than during other periods of development has challenged psychologists for decades (Steinberg, 2004). Numerous theories to account for adolescents' greater involvement in risky behavior have been advanced, but few have withstood empirical scrutiny (but see Reyna & Farley, 2006, for a discussion of some promising approaches).

FALSE LEADS IN RISK-TAKING RESEARCH

Systematic research does not support the stereotype of adolescents as irrational individuals who believe they are invulnerable and who are unaware, inattentive to, or unconcerned about the potential harms of risky behavior. In fact, the logical-reasoning abilities of 15-year-olds are comparable to those of adults, adolescents are no worse than adults at perceiving risk or estimating their vulnerability to it (Reyna & Farley, 2006), and increasing the salience of the risks associated with making a potentially dangerous decision has comparable effects on adolescents and adults (Millstein & Halpern-Felsher, 2002). Most studies find few age differences in individuals' evaluations of the risks inherent in a wide range of dangerous behaviors, in judgments about the seriousness of the consequences that might result from risky behavior, or in the ways that the relative costs and benefits of risky activities are evaluated (Beyth-Marom, Austin, Fischoff, Palmgren, & Jacobs-Quadrel, 1993).

Because adolescents and adults reason about risk in similar ways, many researchers have posited that age differences in actual risk taking are due to differences in the information that adolescents and adults use when making decisions. Attempts to reduce adolescent risk taking through interventions designed to alter knowledge, attitudes, or beliefs have proven remarkably disappointing, however (Steinberg, 2004). Efforts to provide adolescents with information about the risks of substance use, reckless driving, and unprotected sex typically result in improvements in young people's thinking about these phenomena but seldom change their actual behavior. Generally speaking, reductions in adolescents' health-compromising behavior are more strongly linked to changes in the contexts in which those risks are taken (e.g., increases in the price of cigarettes, enforcement of graduated licensing programs, more vigorously implemented policies to interdict drugs, or condom distribution programs) than to changes in what adolescents know or believe.

The failure to account for age differences in risk taking through studies of reasoning and knowledge stymied researchers for some time. Health educators, however, have been undaunted, and they have continued to design and offer interventions qof unproven effectiveness, such as Drug Abuse Resistance Education (DARE), driver's education, or abstinence-only sex education.

A NEW PERSPECTIVE ON RISK TAKING

In recent years, owing to advances in the developmental neuroscience of adolescence and the recognition that the conventional decision-making framework may not be the best way to think about adolescent risk taking, a new perspective on the subject has emerged (Steinberg, 2004). This new view begins from the premise that risk taking in the real world is the product of both logical reasoning and psychosocial factors. However, unlike logical-reasoning abilities, which appear to be more or less fully developed by age 15, psychosocial capacities that improve decision making and moderate risk taking—such as impulse control, emotion regulation, delay of gratification, and resistance to peer influence—continue to mature well into young adulthood (Steinberg, 2004; see Fig. 1). Accordingly, psychosocial immaturity in these respects during adolescence may undermine what otherwise might be competent decision making. The conclusion drawn by many researchers, that adolescents are as competent decision makers as adults are, may hold true only under conditions where the influence of psychosocial factors is minimized.

Evidence From Developmental Neuroscience

Advances in developmental neuroscience provide support for this new way of thinking about adolescent decision making. It appears that heightened risk taking in adolescence is the product of the interaction between two brain networks. The first is a socioemotional network that is especially sensitive to social and emotional stimuli, that is particularly important for reward processing, and that

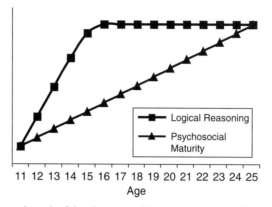

Fig. 1. Hypothetical graph of development of logical reasoning abilities versus psychosocial maturation. Although logical reasoning abilities reach adult levels by age 16, psychosocial capacities, such as impulse control, future orientation, or resistance to peer influence, continue to develop into young adulthood.

is remodeled in early adolescence by the hormonal changes of puberty. It is localized in limbic and paralimbic areas of the brain, an interior region that includes the amygdala, ventral striatum, orbitofrontal cortex, medial prefrontal cortex, and superior temporal sulcus. The second network is a cognitive-control network that subserves executive functions such as planning, thinking ahead, and self-regulation, and that matures gradually over the course of adolescence and young adulthood largely independently of puberty (Steinberg, 2004). The cognitive-control network mainly consists of outer regions of the brain, including the lateral prefrontal and parietal cortices and those parts of the anterior cingulate cortex to which they are connected.

In many respects, risk taking is the product of a competition between the socioemotional and cognitive-control networks (Drevets & Raichle, 1998), and adolescence is a period in which the former abruptly becomes more assertive (i.e., at puberty) while the latter gains strength only gradually, over a longer period of time. The socioemotional network is not in a state of constantly high activation during adolescence, though. Indeed, when the socioemotional network is not highly activated (for example, when individuals are not emotionally excited or are alone), the cognitive-control network is strong enough to impose regulatory control over impulsive and risky behavior, even in early adolescence. In the presence of peers or under conditions of emotional arousal, however, the socioemotional network becomes sufficiently activated to diminish the regulatory effectiveness of the cognitive-control network. Over the course of adolescence, the cognitive-control network matures, so that by adulthood, even under conditions of heightened arousal in the socioemotional network, inclinations toward risk taking can be modulated.

It is important to note that mechanisms underlying the processing of emotional information, social information, and reward are closely interconnected. Among adolescents, the regions that are activated during exposure to social and emotional stimuli overlap considerably with regions also shown to be sensitive to

142

variations in reward magnitude (cf. Galvan, et al., 2005; Nelson, Leibenluft, McClure, & Pine, 2005). This finding may be relevant to understanding why so much adolescent risk taking—like drinking, reckless driving, or delinquency—occurs in groups (Steinberg, 2004). Risk taking may be heightened in adolescence because teenagers spend so much time with their peers, and the mere presence of peers makes the rewarding aspects of risky situations more salient by activating the same circuitry that is activated by exposure to nonsocial rewards when individuals are alone.

The competitive interaction between the socioemotional and cognitive-control networks has been implicated in a wide range of decision-making contexts, including drug use, social-decision processing, moral judgments, and the valuation of alternative rewards/costs (e.g., Chambers, Taylor, & Potenza, 2003). In all of these contexts, risk taking is associated with relatively greater activation of the socioemotional network. For example, individuals' preference for smaller immediate rewards over larger delayed rewards is associated with relatively increased activation of the ventral striatum, orbitofrontal cortex, and medial prefrontal cortex—all regions linked to the socioemotional network—presumably because immediate rewards are especially emotionally arousing (consider the difference between how you might feel if a crisp $100 bill were held in front of you versus being told that you will receive $150 in 2 months). In contrast, regions implicated in cognitive control are engaged equivalently across decision conditions (McClure, Laibson, Loewenstein, & Cohen, 2004). Similarly, studies show that increased activity in regions of the socioemotional network is associated with the selection of comparatively risky (but potentially highly rewarding) choices over more conservative ones (Ernst et al., 2005).

Evidence From Behavioral Science

Three lines of behavioral evidence are consistent with this account. First, studies of susceptibility to antisocial peer influence show that vulnerability to peer pressure increases between preadolescence and mid-adolescence, peaks in mid-adolescence—presumably when the imbalance between the sensitivity to socioemotional arousal (which has increased at puberty) and capacity for cognitive control (which is still immature) is greatest—and gradually declines thereafter (Steinberg, 2004). Second, as noted earlier, studies of decision making generally show no age differences in risk processing between older adolescents and adults when decision making is assessed under conditions likely associated with relatively lower activation of brain systems responsible for emotion, reward, and social processing (e.g., the presentation of hypothetical decision-making dilemmas to individuals tested alone under conditions of low emotional arousal; Millstein, & Halpern-Felsher, 2002). Third, the presence of peers increases risk taking substantially among teenagers, moderately among college-age individuals, and not at all among adults, consistent with the notion that the development of the cognitive-control network is gradual and extends beyond the teen years. In one of our lab's studies, for instance, the presence of peers more than doubled the number of risks teenagers took in a video driving game and increased risk taking by 50% among college undergraduates but had no effect at all among adults

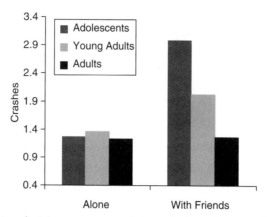

Fig. 2. Risk taking of adolescents, young adults, and adults during a video driving game, when playing alone and when playing with friends. Adapted from Gardner & Steinberg (2004).

(Gardner & Steinberg, 2005; see Fig. 2). In adolescence, then, not only is more merrier—it is also riskier.

What Changes During Adolescence?

Studies of rodents indicate an especially significant increase in reward salience (i.e., how much attention individuals pay to the magnitude of potential rewards) around the time of puberty (Spear, 2000), consistent with human studies showing that increases in sensation seeking occur relatively early in adolescence and are correlated with pubertal maturation but not chronological age (Steinberg, 2004). Given behavioral findings indicating relatively greater reward salience among adolescents than adults in decision-making tasks, there is reason to speculate that, when presented with risky situations that have both potential rewards and potential costs, adolescents may be more sensitive than adults to variation in rewards but comparably sensitive (or perhaps even less sensitive) to variation in costs (Ernst et al., 2005).

It thus appears that the brain system that regulates the processing of rewards, social information, and emotions is becoming more sensitive and more easily aroused around the time of puberty. What about its sibling, the cognitive-control system? Regions making up the cognitive-control network, especially prefrontal regions, continue to exhibit gradual changes in structure and function during adolescence and early adulthood (Casey, Tottenham, Liston, & Durston, 2005). Much publicity has been given to the finding that synaptic pruning (the selective elimination of seldom-used synapses) and myelination (the development of the fatty sheaths that "insulate" neuronal circuitry)—both of which increase the efficiency of information processing—continue to occur in the prefrontal cortex well into the early 20s. But frontal regions also become more integrated with other brain regions during adolescence and early adulthood, leading to gradual improvements in many aspects of cognitive control such as response inhibition; this integration may be an even more important change than changes

144

within the frontal region itself. Imaging studies using tasks in which individuals are asked to inhibit a "prepotent" response–like trying to look away from, rather than toward, a point of light—have shown that adolescents tend to recruit the cognitive-control network less broadly than do adults, perhaps overtaxing the capacity of the more limited number of regions they activate (Luna et al., 2001).

In essence, one of the reasons the cognitive-control system of adults is more effective than that of adolescents is that adults' brains distribute its regulatory responsibilities across a wider network of linked components. This lack of cross-talk across brain regions in adolescence results not only in individuals acting on gut feelings without fully thinking (the stereotypic portrayal of teenagers) but also in thinking too much when gut feelings ought to be attended to (which teenagers also do from time to time). In one recent study, when asked whether some obviously dangerous activities (e.g., setting one's hair on fire) were "good ideas," adolescents took significantly longer than adults to respond to the questions and activated a less narrowly distributed set of cognitive-control regions (Baird, Fugelsang, & Bennett, 2005). This was not the case when the queried activities were not dangerous ones, however (e.g., eating salad).

The fact that maturation of the socioemotional network appears to be driven by puberty, whereas the maturation of the cognitive-control network does not, raises interesting questions about the impact—at the individual and at the societal levels—of early pubertal maturation on risk-taking. We know that there is wide variability among individuals in the timing of puberty, due to both genetic and environmental factors. We also know that there has been a significant drop in the age of pubertal maturation over the past 200 years. To the extent that the temporal disjunction between the maturation of the socioemotional system and that of the cognitive-control system contributes to adolescent risk taking, we would expect to see higher rates of risk taking among early maturers and a drop over time in the age of initial experimentation with risky behaviors such as sexual intercourse or drug use. There is evidence for both of these patterns (Collins & Steinberg, 2006; Johnson & Gerstein, 1998).

IMPLICATIONS FOR PREVENTION

What does this mean for the prevention of unhealthy risk taking in adolescence? Given extant research suggesting that it is not the way adolescents think or what they don't know or understand that is the problem, a more profitable strategy than attempting to change how adolescents view risky activities might be to focus on limiting opportunities for immature judgment to have harmful consequences. More than 90% of all American high-school students have had sex, drug, and driver education in their schools, yet large proportions of them still have unsafe sex, binge drink, smoke cigarettes, and drive recklessly (often more than one of these at the same time; Steinberg, 2004). Strategies such as raising the price of cigarettes, more vigilantly enforcing laws governing the sale of alcohol, expanding adolescents' access to mental-health and contraceptive services, and raising the driving age would likely be more effective in limiting adolescent smoking, substance abuse, pregnancy, and automobile fatalities than strategies aimed at making adolescents wiser, less impulsive, or less shortsighted. Some things just take time to develop, and, like it or not, mature judgment is probably one of them.

The research reviewed here suggests that heightened risk taking during adolescence is likely to be normative, biologically driven, and, to some extent, inevitable. There is probably very little that can or ought to be done to either attenuate or delay the shift in reward sensitivity that takes place at puberty. It may be possible to accelerate the maturation of self-regulatory competence, but no research has examined whether this is possible. In light of studies showing familial influences on psychosocial maturity in adolescence, understanding how contextual factors influence the development of self-regulation and knowing the neural underpinnings of these processes should be a high priority for those interested in the well-being of young people.

Recommended Reading

Casey, B.J., Tottenham, N., Liston, C., & Durston, S. (2005). (See References)
Johnson, R., & Gerstein, D. (1998). (See References)
Nelson, E., Leibenluft, E., McClure, E., & Pine, D. (2005). (See References)
Spear, P. (2000). (See References)
Steinberg, L. (2004). (See References)

Acknowledgments—Thanks to Nora Newcombe for comments on an earlier draft and to Jason Chein for his expertise in developmental neuroscience.

Note

1. Address correspondence to Laurence Steinberg, Department of Psychology, Temple University, Philadelphia, PA 19122; lds@temple.edu.

References

Baird, A., Fugelsang, J., & Bennett, C. (2005, April). *"What were you thinking?": An fMRI study of adolescent decision making*. Poster presented at the annual meeting of the Cognitive Neuroscience Society, New York.

Beyth-Marom, R., Austin, L., Fischoff, B., Palmgren, C., & Jacobs-Quadrel, M. (1993). Perceived consequences of risky behaviors: Adults and adolescents. *Developmental Psychology, 29*, 549–563.

Casey, B.J., Tottenham, N., Liston, C., & Durston, S. (2005). Imaging the developing brain: What have we learned about cognitive development? *Trends in Cognitive Science, 9*, 104–110.

Chambers, R.A., Taylor, J.R., & Potenza, M.N. (2003). Developmental neurocircuitry of motivation in adolescence: A critical period of addiction vulnerability. *American Journal of Psychiatry, 160*, 1041–1052.

Collins, W.A., & Steinberg, L. (2006). Adolescent development in interpersonal context. In W. Damon & R. Lerner (Series Eds.) & N. Eisenberg (Vol. Ed.), *Handbook of Child Psychology: Social, emotional, and personality development* (Vol. 3, pp. 1003–1067). New York: Wiley.

Drevets, W.C., & Raichle, M.E. (1998). Reciprocal suppression of regional cerebral blood flow during emotional versus higher cognitive processes: Implications for interactions between emotion and cognition. *Cognition and Emotion, 12*, 353–385.

Ernst, M., Jazbec, S., McClure, E.B., Monk, C.S., Blair, R.J.R., Leibenluft, E., & Pine, D.S. (2005). Amygdala and nucleus accumbens activation in response to receipt and omission of gains in adults and adolescents. *Neuroimage, 25*, 1279–1291.

Galvan, A., Hare, T., Davidson, M., Spicer, J., Glover, G., & Casey, B.J. (2005). The role of ventral frontostriatal circuitry in reward-based learning in humans. *Journal of Neuroscience, 25*, 8650–8656.

Gardner, M., & Steinberg, L. (2005). Peer influence on risk-taking, risk preference, and risky decision-making in adolescence and adulthood: An experimental study. *Developmental Psychology, 41,* 625–635.

Johnson, R., & Gerstein, D. (1998). Initiation of use of alcohol, cigarettes, marijuana, cocaine, and other substances in US birth cohorts since 1919. *American Journal of Public Health, 88,* 27–33.

Luna, B., Thulborn, K.R., Munoz, D.P., Merriam, E.P., Garver, K.E., Minshew, N.J., et al. (2001). Maturation of widely distributed brain function subserves cognitive development. *Neuroimage, 13,* 786–793.

McClure, S.M., Laibson, D.I., Loewenstein, G., & Cohen, J.D. (2004). Separate neural systems value immediate and delayed monetary rewards. *Science, 306,* 503–507.

Millstein, S.G., & Halpern-Felsher, B.L. (2002). Perceptions of risk and vulnerability. *Journal of Adolescent Health, 31S,* 10–27.

Nelson, E., Leibenluft, E., McClure, E., & Pine, D. (2005). The social re-orientation of adolescence: A neuroscience perspective on the process and its relation to psychopathology. *Psychological Medicine, 35,* 163–174.

Reyna, V., & Farley, F. (2006). Risk and rationality in adolescent decision-making: Implications for theory, practice, and public policy. *Psychological Science in the Public Interest, 7,* 1–44.

Spear, P. (2000). The adolescent brain and age-related behavioral manifestations. *Neuroscience and Biobehavioral Reviews, 24,* 417–463.

Steinberg, L. (2004). Risk-taking in adolescence: What changes, and why? *Annals of the New York Academy of Sciences, 1021,* 51–58.

This article has been reprinted as it originally appeared in *Current Directions in Psychological Science*. Citation information for this article as originally published appears above.

School Dropouts: Prevention Considerations, Interventions, and Challenges

Sandra L. Christenson[1] and Martha L. Thurlow
University of Minnesota

Abstract

Preventing school dropout and promoting successful graduation is a national concern that poses a significant challenge for schools and educational communities working with youth at risk for school failure. Although students who are at greatest risk for dropping out of school can be identified, they disengage from school and drop out for a variety of reasons for which there is no one common solution. The most effective intervention programs identify and track youth at risk for school failure, maintain a focus on students' progress toward educational standards across the school years, and are designed to address indicators of student engagement and to impact enrollment status—not just the predictors of dropout. To leave no child behind, educators must address issues related to student mobility, alternate routes to school completion, and alternate time lines for school completion, as well as engage in rigorous evaluation of school-completion programs.

Keywords

dropout; graduation; at-risk; engagement

No one questions the seriousness of the school-dropout problem in the United States. Attention to graduation and dropout rates has increased significantly, and is reflected in current federal priorities. Most recently, graduation rate has been targeted in Title I of No Child Left Behind (NCLB), which identifies schools as needing improvement if their overall performance does not improve from year to year or if subgroups, including students who need to learn English and youth with disabilities, do not make adequate yearly progress. Along with test performance, graduation rate, defined as the percentage of ninth graders receiving a standard diploma in 4 years, is a required indicator in calculations of adequate yearly progress for high schools.

Thousands of American youth are school dropouts, with an estimated 1 in 8 children never graduating from high school. In fact, high school graduation rates have not changed significantly since 1990 (National Educational Goals Panel, 2002). The startling statistic that one high school student drops out every 9 seconds illustrates the magnitude of the problem (Children's Defense Fund, 2002).

Most states are far from the 90% graduation rate that was targeted in the early 1990s (National Educational Goals Panel, 2002). Furthermore, students with disabilities are much more likely to drop out of school than their general-education peers. Also, dropout rates are disproportionately high for students from Hispanic, African American, Native American, and low-income backgrounds; students who live in single-parent homes; and those who attend large urban schools (National Center for Education Statistics, 2002). Dropout rates are highest among students with emotional and behavioral disabilities; half of these students dropped out of school in 1998–1999 (U.S. Department of Education, 2001). Although these marker variables identify students who may be at risk for dropout, predicting who will drop out is not foolproof. For example, in a study of middle and high school dropout-prevention programs for students with two or more risk factors, no single risk factor predicted who would drop out (Dynarski & Gleason, 2002).

Dropout statistics are particularly alarming because jobs that pay living wages and benefits have virtually disappeared for youth without a high school diploma. For society, the costs of dropout are staggering, estimated in the billions of dollars in lost revenues, welfare programs, unemployment programs, under-employment, and crime prevention and prosecution (Christenson, Sinclair, Lehr, & Hurley, 2000). Given these individual and societal consequences, facilitating school completion for all students must be a critical concern for researchers, pol-icymakers, and educators across the country.

Promoting successful school completion for students who are at risk of drop-ping out is recognized as especially challenging in light of current national reform efforts to achieve high academic standards, end social promotion, and ratchet up educational accountability. The need for schools and the broader educational com-munity to create opportunities for success and to provide necessary supports for all youth to meet educational standards is complicated by requirements in many states that students must pass state high school exit exams to earn a standard diploma. Although these exams may ensure that students have attained specific competencies prior to receiving a diploma, a potential unintended consequence is increases in the number of students who drop out.

CRITICAL CONSIDERATIONS IN DROPOUT PREVENTION

Educators designing dropout-prevention programs will want to attend to five crit-ical considerations: dropout as a process, the role of context, alterable variables, an orientation toward completion and engagement, and the importance of empir-ical evidence.

Dropout as a Process

Early and sustained intervention is integral to the success of students because the decision to leave school without graduating is not an instantaneous one, but rather a process that occurs over many years. Teaching students to read is vital for them to become engaged learners. Research shows that leaving school early is the outcome of a long process of disengagement from school (Christenson, Sinclair, Lehr, & Godber, 2001); dropout is preceded by indicators of withdrawal (e.g., poor attendance) or unsuccessful school experiences (e.g., academic or behavioral difficulties) that often begin in elementary school. Overt indicators of disengagement are generally accompanied by feelings of alienation, a poor sense of belonging, and a general dislike for school.

The Role of Context

The problem of school dropout cannot be understood in isolation from contex-tual factors. Early school withdrawal reflects a complex interplay among student, family, school, and community variables, as well as risk and protective factors. School and family policies and practices are critical (Christenson et al., 2000). For example, schools with the greatest holding power tend to have relatively small enrollment, fair discipline policies, caring teachers, high expectations, and opportunities for meaningful participation. Policies that support suspension and grade retention for students who are deemed not ready to advance have been linked to higher dropout rates. Family factors associated with reduced dropout rates include parental support, monitoring and supervision, high regard for education, and positive expectations regarding school performance.

Alterable Variables

The dichotomy between predictors that are more versus less easy to influence provides a suggested course of action for educators. Finn (1989) made an important distinction when he contrasted *status* predictor variables such as socioeconomic status, which educators have little ability to change, and *behavioral* or alterable predictor variables such as out-of-school suspensions and course failures, which are more readily influenced by educators. Recently, there has been a shift toward investigating alterable variables—behaviors and attitudes that reflect students' connection to school as well as family and school practices that support children's learning—because they have greater utility for interventions.

Completion and Engagement

School dropout and school completion are considered two sides of the same coin; however, school completion is the preferred term given its positive orientation and emphasis on the development of student competencies. School-completion programs require a primary focus on student engagement, particularly on finding ways to enhance students' interest in and enthusiasm for school, sense of belonging at school, motivation to learn, and progress in school, as well as the value they place on school and learning (Christenson et al., 2001). Engagement is multidimensional (Sinclair, Christenson, Lehr, & Anderson, in press). *Academic and behavioral engagement* refers to observable indicators; sustained attention to and completion of academic work and accrual of credits exemplify academic engagement, and attendance, number of suspensions, and classroom participation are measures of behavioral engagement. *Cognitive and psychological engagement* refers to internal indicators; processing academic information, thinking about how to learn, and self-monitoring progress toward task completion exemplify cognitive engagement, and identification with school, a sense of belonging and connection, and positive relationships with peers and teachers characterize psychological engagement.

Conceptually, promoting school completion encompasses more than preventing dropout. For example, it is characterized by school personnel emphasizing development of students' competencies rather than dwelling on their deficits. Successful programs are comprehensive, interfacing family, school, and community efforts rather than offering a single, narrow intervention in one environment; are implemented over time rather than at a single period in time; and make an effort to tailor interventions to fit individual students rather than adopting a programmatic "one size fits all" orientation. School-completion programs have a longitudinal focus, aiming to promote a "good" outcome, not simply prevent a "bad" outcome for students and society (Christenson et al., 2001).

Empirical Evidence

Schools across the nation have implemented dropout-prevention programs. The National Dropout Prevention Center at Clemson University has studied the issue of dropout for nearly two decades and has developed a database cataloguing such programs (Schargel & Smink, 2001). Although these programs provide general guidelines and appear promising, continued empirical study is required to determine those variables that influence the effectiveness of interventions. However, despite the importance of school completion for individuals and society as a whole, and despite the complexity of the problem, few such studies have been published. A comprehensive review of dropout interventions (Lehr, Hanson, Sinclair, & Christenson, 2003) indicated that dropout research has been overwhelmingly predictive or descriptive (i.e., there have been few controlled studies), and the methodology used to evaluate the effectiveness of the majority of dropout interventions has been judged to be of low quality or poor scientific merit. For example, many studies have not reported the statistical significance of results, and even fewer have reported effect sizes to help determine practical significance. Aptly, the need for more rigorous studies was highlighted in a recent report from the U.S. General Accounting Office (2002), which stated that "although there have been many federal, state, and local dropout prevention programs over the last 2 decades, few have been rigorously evaluated" (p. 31).

Currently, we know considerably more about who drops out than we do about efficacious intervention programs. Most interventions have been designed to remediate specific predictors of dropout, such as poor attendance and poor academic performance. Although research supports the idea that these variables should be targeted, there is little evidence to suggest that these programs change dropout rates (Dynarski & Gleason, 2002). On a more optimistic note, there are promising signs that comprehensive, personalized, long-term interventions yield positive results for students (e.g., Fashola & Slavin, 1998; Sinclair et al., in press).

INTERVENTIONS

What are the characteristics of school-based dropout-prevention interventions? An integrative review of 45 prevention and intervention studies addressing dropout or school completion, described in professional journals from 1983 through 2000 (Lehr et al., 2003), identified many similarities among the interventions, including their focus on changing the student, beginning with a *personal-affective focus* (e.g., individual counseling, participation in an interpersonal-relations class) and then shifting to an *academic focus* (e.g., specialized courses or tutoring), and their efforts to address alterable variables (e.g., poor grades, attendance, and attitude toward school). Most interventions were implemented with secondary students with a history of poor academic performance and dropping out, poor attendance, and teacher referral for supplemental support; students with disabilities were targeted in only two programs and specifically excluded from two. Interventions that yielded moderate to large effects on at least one dependent variable provided early reading programs, tutoring, counseling, and mentoring; they emphasized creating caring environments and relationships, used block scheduling, and offered community-service opportunities.

There is consensus that successful interventions do more than increase student attendance—they help students and families who feel marginalized in their relations with teachers and peers to be connected at school and with learning. Student engagement across the school years depends on the degree to which there is a match between the student's characteristics and the school environment so that the student is able to handle the academic and behavioral demands of school. For more than a decade, we and our colleagues have field-tested the Check & Connect model of student engagement among students with and without disabilities. Our field tests have been conducted in kindergarten through grade 12 and in both urban and suburban schools (Sinclair et al., in press). Applications of this evidence-based intervention approach have underscored the critical need to keep education and learning the salient issue for many students and their families. We have used the concept of "persistence-plus" to show students that there is someone who is not going to give up on them or allow them to be distracted from school; that there is someone who knows them and is available to them throughout the school year, the summer, and into the next school year; and that caring adults want them to learn, do the work, attend class regularly, be on time, express frustration constructively, stay in school, and succeed. Furthermore, McPartland (1994) cogently addressed the need for school-completion programs to be adapted to fit local circumstances when he argued, "It is unlikely that a program developed elsewhere can be duplicated exactly in another site, because local talents and priorities for school reform, the particular interests and needs of the students to be served, and the conditions of the school to be changed will differ" (p. 256).

Consensus is emerging with respect to essential intervention components. In particular, the "personalization" of education—striving to understand the nature of academic, social, and personal problems affecting students and tailoring services to address individualized concerns—is an essential component. Effective programs aimed at promoting school completion focus on building students' relationships with teachers, parents, and peers and include systematic monitoring of the students' performance; they work to develop students' problem-solving skills, provide opportunities for success in schoolwork, create a caring and supportive environment, communicate the relevance of education to future endeavors, and help with students' personal problems (McPartland, 1994; Sinclair et al., in press). In a comprehensive review of federal dropout-prevention evaluations, Dynarski and Gleason (2002) identified smaller class sizes, more personalized settings, and individualized learning plans as characteristics that lowered dropout rates in both General Educational Development (GED) programs for older students and alternative middle school programs. Of particular importance is the need for a more intensive intervention approach. Although low-intensity supplemental services such as tutoring or occasional counseling were relatively easy to implement, they had little to no impact on student outcomes, such as grades, test scores, attendance, or the dropout rate.

CHALLENGES

New federal initiatives have made it clear that decisions about educational programs should be based on empirical evidence. Research is only beginning to address the critical need for programs that promote student engagement and school completion, and thereby reduce dropout rates. Educators and policymakers are in need of sound research to guide best practice.

As programs are developed and evaluated, we must address the challenge of *student mobility*, which is significantly associated with school failure (Rumberger & Larson, 1998). High rates of mobility seriously undermine the potential for youth to value school or develop a sense of belonging. Even if a school offers services well suited to meet the needs of disenfranchised students, the potential benefit can be lost if youth do not remain in the school long enough or trust someone enough to participate. If we are to reduce significantly the dropout rate and promote the successful completion of school, we must grapple with the question of how to ensure that the protective factors of sustained intervention and continuity of relationships with teachers and peers exist when students move frequently. There may be a need for interventions that coordinate the efforts of multiple schools and multiple school districts and perhaps a mechanism for educators and mentors to track student performance and partner with families within and across states.

Another challenge that must be addressed is the acceptability of the current array of exit documents, ranging from honors diplomas to certificates of completion, attendance diplomas, and special education diplomas. The options recognize different ways in which students complete school, and which option students are encouraged to pursue has often been based on educators' expectations for their success. Yet current federal law (NCLB) indicates that for purposes of school accountability, only those students who have earned a standard diploma in 4 years will be counted in the percentage of students graduating. We must examine the consequences of this definition. Is the value of earning a diploma within 5 years or completing school via other options discounted? It will be important for the nation to consider its definition of successful school completion to ensure that the requirement for a standard diploma does not provide an incentive for students to drop out.

CONCLUDING REMARKS

The dropout problem in the United States is solvable, provided student performance is systematically monitored to ensure students are provided with realistic opportunities for academic and reading success, supported as learners by educators and families, encouraged to see the relevance of school and learning in their personal lives and future goals, and helped with personal problems across the school years. Increasing students' engagement and enthusiasm for school requires much more than simply having them stay in school—it involves supporting students to help them meet the defined academic standards of their schools, as well as the underlying social and behavioral standards. If students are engaged at school and with learning, they should not only graduate but also demonstrate academic and social competence at school completion.

NCLB demands and provides unique opportunities for educators and parents to partner in order to foster the learning of all students across school years and settings. To improve outcomes for youth at high risk for school failure, further research and evaluation must systematically document strategies that actively engage youth in the learning process and help youth to stay in school and on track to graduate while developing academic and behavioral skills. The educational success of all students will require explicit attention to social and emotional learning as well as academics, through a focus on cognitive, psychological, and behavioral engagement, along with academic engagement.

Recommended Reading

Doll, B., Hess, R., & Ochoa, S.H. (Eds.). (2001). Contemporary psychological perspectives on school completion [Special issue]. *School Psychology Quarterly, 16*(4).

Gleason, P., & Dynarski, M. (1998). *Do we know whom to serve? Issues in using risk factors to identify dropouts.* Princeton, NJ: Mathematica Policy Research.

Prevatt, F., & Kelly, F.D. (2003). Dropping out of school: A review of intervention programs. *Journal of School Psychology, 41,* 377–395.

Rosenthal, B.S. (1998). Non-school correlates of dropout: An integrative review of the literature. *Children & Youth Services Review, 20,* 413–433.

University of Minnesota, College of Education and Human Development, Institute on Community Integration. (2002). *Check & Connect.* http://www.ici.umn.edu/checkandconnect/

Note

1. Address correspondence to Sandra Christenson, University of Minnesota, School Psychology Program, 350 Elliott Hall, 75 East River Rd., Minneapolis, MN 55455; e-mail: chris002@umn.edu.

References

Children's Defense Fund. (2002). *Twenty-five facts about American children from the State of America's Children Yearbook 2001.* Retrieved October 17, 2002, from http://www.childrensdefense.org/keyfacts.htm

Christenson, S.L., Sinclair, M.F., Lehr, C.A., & Godber, Y. (2001). Promoting successful school completion: Critical conceptual and methodological guidelines. *School Psychology Quarterly, 16,* 468–484.

Christenson, S.L., Sinclair, M.F., Lehr, C.A., & Hurley, C.M. (2000). Promoting successful school completion. In K. Minke & G. Bear (Eds.), *Preventing school problems—promoting school success: Strategies and programs that work* (pp. 377–420). Bethesda, MD: National Association of School Psychologists.

Dynarski, M., & Gleason, P. (2002). How can we help? What we have learned from recent federal dropout prevention evaluations. *Journal of Education for Students Placed at Risk, 7*(1), 43–69.

Fashola, O.S., & Slavin, R.E. (1998). Effective dropout prevention and college attendance programs for students placed at risk. *Journal of Education for Students Placed at Risk, 3*(2), 159–183.

Finn, J.D. (1989). Withdrawing from school. *Review of Educational Research, 59,* 117–124.

Lehr, C.A., Hanson, A., Sinclair, M.F., & Christenson, S.L. (2003). Moving beyond dropout prevention towards school completion: An integrative review of data-based interventions. *School Psychology Review, 32,* 342–364.

McPartland, J.M. (1994). Dropout prevention in theory and practice. In R.J. Rossi (Ed.), *Schools and students at risk: Context and framework for positive change* (pp. 255–276). New York: Teachers College.

National Center for Education Statistics. (2002). *The condition of education 2002* (NCES 2002-025). Washington, DC: U.S. Department of Education, Office of Educational Research and Improvement.

National Educational Goals Panel. (2002). *Find out how the nation is doing.* Retrieved May 23, 2003, from http://www.negp.gov

Rumberger, R.W., & Larson, K.A. (1998). Student mobility and the increased risk of high school dropout. *American Journal of Education, 107,* 1–35.

Schargel, F.P., & Smink, J. (2001). *Strategies to help solve our school dropout problem.* Larchmont, NY: Eye on Education.

Sinclair, M.F., Christenson, S.L., Lehr, C.A., & Anderson, A.R. (in press). Facilitating student engagement: Lessons learned from Check & Connect longitudinal studies. *Journal of California Association of School Psychologists.*

U.S. Department of Education. (2001). *Twenty-third annual report to Congress on the implementation of the Individuals With Disabilities Education Act.* Washington, DC: Author.

U.S. General Accounting Office. (2002). *School dropouts: Education could play a stronger role in identifying and disseminating promising prevention strategies.* Washington, DC: Author.

Section 4: Critical Thinking Questions

1. These articles point toward a vast array of factors in the development of externalizing disorders. What gaps remain in our understanding, that is, what factors, if any, need to be added to achieve a truly comprehensive understanding?

2. Does the biological basis for externalizing disorders limit the potential for preventive intervention? What are the most exciting avenues for prevention?

This article has been reprinted as it originally appeared in *Current Directions in Psychological Science.* Citation information for this article as originally published appears above.

Section 5: Neurodevelopmental Disorders

We have come a long way in understanding the commonalities and distinctions among cognitive disorders such as autism, learning disabilities, and attention deficits. Improved assessments distinguish among these disorders, research has identified common and distinct neurodevelopmental paths, and interventions have been identified to cope with or offset these disorders. The concept of gene-environment interaction organizes even these seemingly biological disorders.

Autism has received a great deal of attention in the popular media. New theories of its development are promulgated almost yearly. Although naïve theories about the role of early parenting have been debunked, the origins of this disorder remain vexing. One of the most plausible notions has been the hypothesis that children with autism have deficits in theory-of-mind concepts. Tager-Flusberg evaluates this hypothesis and concludes that the patterns displayed by children with autism are consistent with this hypothesis but also go well beyond it to include other aspects of social-affective information processing. Gernsbacher, Dawson, and Goldsmith take up the popular notion that the prevalence rate of autism is increasing in our society. They provide a sense of sanity for this field by suggesting three reasons that the rate of autism has not increased. Their treatise is a tutorial in scientific reasoning.

Yeo, Gengestad, and Thoma suggest an intriguing hypothesis that seemingly diverse neurodevelopmental disorders might share a common process of developmental instability which accounts for shared features. Their hypothesis suggests areas of research that need to be pursued.

Dyslexia is no longer a mysterious disorder, thanks to research in brain imaging that has identified the locus of the disorder in left-hemisphere posterior neural systems. This exciting work paves the way for translation to interventions and education policies.

Kovas and Plomin revisit the question of whether single genes are responsible for single cognitive skills such as reading, mathematics, spatial ability, and memory. They conclude that the same genes are involved in all of these cognitive skills, a phenomenon they identify as "generalist genes." In contrast, they suggest that specific environments account for differences in skills across the domains of reading, mathematics, and language.

Evaluating the Theory-of-Mind Hypothesis of Autism

Helen Tager-Flusberg[1]
Boston University School of Medicine

Abstract

Two decades ago, the theory-of-mind hypothesis of autism was introduced by Baron-Cohen and his colleagues; this theory provided a unified cognitive explanation for the key social and communication symptoms in that disorder. I evaluate the theory-of-mind hypothesis in light of studies that have addressed several key questions: Do children with autism develop theory-of-mind concepts? How can we explain why some children with autism pass theory-of-mind tasks? Do deficits in theory of mind account for the major impairments that characterize autistic disorder? Current research supports the view that autism involves delays and deficits not only in the development of a theory of mind but also in additional aspects of social-affective information processing that extend beyond the traditional boundaries of theory of mind.

Keywords

autism; theory of mind; social cognition; communication

Daily social life depends on the ability to evaluate the behavior of other people on the basis of their mental states, such as their goals, emotions, and beliefs. This is accomplished by dedicated cognitive systems, collectively referred to as *theory of mind*. By age four, children normally pass tasks that tap mental-state understanding, including the hallmark false-belief tasks that require a child to distinguish between the world as it really is and the way it might be represented (incorrectly) in the mind of another person. In the classic Sally–Anne false-belief task, a child is told the following story, accompanied by supporting pictures or toy props: Sally places her ball in a basket and goes out to play; while she is gone, Anne takes the ball from the basket and hides it inside a box. The child is then asked where Sally will look for the hidden ball (or where she thinks it will be located) when she returns to play with it again (see Fig. 1).

Two decades ago, Baron-Cohen and his colleagues revolutionized autism research when they introduced the theory-of-mind hypothesis to explain the main behavioral symptoms that characterize this neurodevelopmental disorder. Their initial studies showed that most children with autism whose mental and verbal abilities were well beyond the 4-year-old level nevertheless failed the Sally–Anne task and other related tasks (Baron-Cohen, Leslie, & Frith, 1985). Deficits in the acquisition of a theory of mind provided a plausible explanation for the major symptoms of autism, especially impairments in social reciprocity and communication, thus providing the first integrated account of the cognitive mechanisms that might underlie several key behaviors that define the disorder. The original studies have been replicated many times by different research teams, and there is

Fig. 1. The Sally–Anne false-belief task. To test theory-of-mind skills, children are presented with a story in which (from the top frame to the bottom) Sally (left) has a basket and Ann (right) has a box; Sally puts her marble in the basket; Sally leaves; Ann takes the marble from the basket and puts it in the box; and Sally returns to look for the marble. Subjects are then asked whether Sally will look for the marble in the basket or the box. Reprinted from *Autism: Explaining the Enigma,* by U. Frith, 1989, Blackwell Publishers, p. 83. Copyright 1989, Blackwell Publishers. Reprinted with permission.

little doubt that children with autism have difficulty attributing mental states to themselves or to other people.

Yet despite the robustness of the empirical findings, there is now less excitement and increasing skepticism among many investigators about the significance of the theory-of-mind hypothesis of autism. Questions about the universality and uniqueness of theory-of-mind impairments in autism, and about how this hypothesis could account for the earliest manifestations of autistic symptoms, have been raised (Tager-Flusberg, 2001). Autism is generally defined on the basis of impairments not only in social and communicative functioning but also in restricted or repetitive behavior patterns. The theory-of-mind hypothesis does not extend to explaining these areas of impairment; nor does it explain some of the strengths that are characteristic of people with autism, such as their superior visual-attention skills.

The past decade has witnessed an exponential increase in research on autism. Today, autism is clearly understood to be a complex and heterogeneous set of related developmental disorders in which no single cognitive mechanism or cause can account for the variety of symptoms and range in their expression. Even the social-communication impairments cannot be explained exclusively on the basis of theory-of-mind impairments. Nevertheless, current research supports the view that children and adults with autism have problems processing mental-state information; that when they are able to infer mental states, they tend not to use the same neurocognitive systems as do nonautistic people; and that performance on theory-of-mind tasks can account for some, though not all, of the severity of the social and communication symptoms that define this disorder.

A DEVELOPMENTAL PERSPECTIVE ON THEORY OF MIND IN AUTISM

Most studies investigating theory of mind in autism focused on the transition that takes place at the age of four, when children typically first understand false belief. This narrow perspective appeared to reduce a complex social-cognitive developmental progression to a categorical capacity indexed by passing or failing a single task, thus encouraging the notion that autism could be defined as the "absence" of a theory of mind. Yet in all studies that have been conducted, some children with autism pass false-belief tasks. At the same time, research has shown that older children with different disorders (e.g., nonsigning deaf children; Peterson, Wellman, & Liu, 2005) fail these tasks—evidence that challenges the notion that theory-of-mind deficits are universal and specific to autism.

More recent studies have taken a developmental approach by including a wider range of tasks that tap a child's ability to reason about mental states from the early preschool years to adolescence. For example, Steele, Joseph, and Tager-Flusberg (2003) conducted a longitudinal study in a large sample of children with autism; the participants were administered a battery of nine developmentally sequenced reasoning tasks ranging from tasks appropriate for toddlers (assessing the ability to understand the concept of pretense and the ability to attribute desire to others), young children (assessing the ability to correctly match others' emotions to situations and to understand others' knowledge and false beliefs), or older children and young adolescents (assessing understanding of others' second-order false belief, nonliteral language, traits and intentions, and moral judgments). Over two thirds of the children made some gains over the course of 1 year, and although all the children were delayed relative to their age, a small number of the most able adolescents passed some of the more advanced tasks. Peterson and her colleagues (Peterson et al., 2005) used a set of five tasks that formed a coherent scale of theory-of-mind concepts, from desire to false belief and hidden emotions. The children with autism were generally similar to the other groups in their ability to pass the tasks according to their developmental sequence, but unlike the other groups, children with autism found false belief harder than hidden emotions. While children with autism develop some understanding of desire and emotion, belief and other cognitive states seem to pose a unique challenge to this population.

EXECUTIVE FUNCTIONS, LANGUAGE, AND THEORY OF MIND IN AUTISM

An important question that has generated considerable research focuses on how some children with autism pass theory-of-mind tasks. For nonautistic children, performance on classic theory-of-mind tasks reflects intuitive social insights into people or conceptual knowledge of mental states coupled with general cognitive skills that support the verbal processing, memory of key narrative events, and inhibition of spontaneous responses that are central to the tasks. In contrast, studies of children with autism suggest that such children treat theory-of-mind tasks as logical-reasoning problems, relying primarily on language and other nonsocial cognitive processes in lieu of social insight.

Children with autism generally have executive-function deficits that require planning, flexibility, or working memory combined with inhibitory control (Ozonoff et al., 2004). Performance on false-belief tasks by both typically developing children and children with autism is significantly related to these aspects of executive control (Joseph & Tager-Flusberg, 2004).

Children with better planning skills and inhibitory control are more likely to pass false-belief tasks, supporting the view that successful performance on false-belief tasks requires one to maintain a false representation of an event in working memory while resisting the tendency to predict a person's action on the basis of what one knows to be true.

Language ability has also been closely linked to the development of theory-of-mind skills (see Astington & Baird, 2005). Children with autism who are able to use language to communicate are nevertheless usually delayed in acquiring language and continue to lag behind their peers in basic linguistic abilities. Studies of children with autism report that higher vocabulary-test scores correlate with performance on false-belief tasks (e.g., Happé, 1995). Semantic and grammatical knowledge, as well as more specific knowledge of complex embedded sentence structures, are the most significant predictors of who will pass false-belief tasks (Tager-Flusberg & Joseph, 2005). Children with autism are especially dependent on mastering the syntax and semantics of verbs of communication (for example, "John *said* that Mary is sleeping") for building theory-of-mind skills. These linguistic constructions provide a format for representing the content of mental states by analogy to the content of speech. For both mental states and speech, the content may differ from reality (e.g., Mary may not be sleeping, even though John said she was, or believed she was). So, through listening and speaking about what people say, some children with autism develop the knowledge that people may represent the world in ways that do not match reality.

Language is important for the development of a consciously mediated explicit theory of mind. About 1 year before they are able to pass false-belief test questions, typically developing toddlers will reliably look to the correct location where Sally will search for the hidden ball (the basket), even while saying that she will look in the box. This eye-gaze behavior is taken as an implicit measure of false-belief understanding, which is the foundation for later-developing explicit knowledge. Ruffman and his colleagues found that, in contrast to well-matched children with mental retardation, children with autism did not look at the correct location on theory-of-mind tasks, although the two groups performed at the same level when answering the verbal test questions (Ruffman Garnham & Ridout, 2001). Like typically developing toddlers, the children with mental retardation were more likely to pass the implicit measure (eye-gaze) than they were to pass the explicit one (verbal-response), whereas the opposite pattern was found for the children with autism. Ruffman et al. (2001) argue that the implicit measure taps social insight that appears to be lacking in most children with autism, even those who pass false-belief tasks.

Despite the ability of some high-functioning children with autism to pass false-belief tasks, these children still lack social "intuition." Some more able children with autism develop a linguistically mediated theory of mind that provides them with the facility to reason correctly about the social world, but their theory of mind is not based on the same foundational social insights that are provided by a domain-specific theory-of-mind mechanism. This conclusion is consistent with functional neuroimaging studies, which have shown that high-functioning adults with autism who pass theory-of-mind tasks activate different brain regions when solving such problems. When nonautistic controls process theory-of-mind tasks they typically activate areas in the medial prefrontal cortex and temporoparietal junction that are considered central to the social-cognitive neural network, as well as areas involved in executive control. In contrast, participants with autism activate only those areas associated with general problem-solving abilities (Frith & Frith, 2003).

THEORY OF MIND AND SYMPTOM SEVERITY IN AUTISM

Surprisingly little research has directly investigated whether core autism symptoms are directly related to theory-of-mind impairments. Early studies reported significant correlations between social or communicative functioning and theory-of-mind performance, but these correlations were no longer significant once age and language level were included as control variables. These negative findings fueled some of the criticisms of the theory-of-mind hypothesis of autism, but these investigations relied on small samples of children who varied widely in age and ability and assessment of theory of mind was limited to false-belief tasks.

More recently, we addressed this issue in a large group of school-aged children with autism using the battery of theory-of-mind tasks developed by Steele et al. (2003). After separating out the effects of age, IQ, and language, theory-of-mind scores were significantly related to scores on the Socialization domain of the Vineland Adaptive Behavior Scales and social- and communication-symptom severity as measured on the Autism Diagnostic Observation Schedule (Tager-Flusberg, 2003). By definition, all children with autism have core deficits in social reciprocity and communication skills that impact their everyday adaptive socialization with peers in school and other community settings. Nevertheless, variation in the severity of these social and communication impairments is partially explained by the degree of impairments in theory of mind.

BEYOND THEORY OF MIND IN AUTISM

Autism involves significant difficulties in understanding mental states. The theory-of-mind hypothesis focuses on deficits in reasoning about mental states. But social and communication developments begin long before theory-of-mind skills emerge in typically developing children. They encompass emotional and perceptual processing that serve as the foundation for social cognition. When the theory-of-mind hypothesis of autism was introduced, Hobson (1993) argued that the deficits associated with theory of mind were based on early affective impairments. Several research groups have extended studies of mental-state understanding to more naturalistic social contexts to investigate the spontaneous processing of mental-state information from faces, voices, or body gestures (e.g., Klin, Jones, Schultz, & Volkmar, 2003). Thus, the scope of the mechanisms that may underlie the core symptoms of autism has broadened to include on-line perception and responses to a wide range of social stimuli. Even when individuals with autism are able to pass theory-of-mind tasks, they often perform poorly in experiments that tap these core aspects of social/affective information. In the first year of life, social interactions are grounded in recognizing and responding to facial and vocal expression. The earliest signs of autism, including failure to orient toward social stimuli and deficits in joint attention, can be readily interpreted within a broader theory-of-mind framework that encompasses these online social-perceptual components as well as more traditional social-cognitive components (Tager-Flusberg, 2001).

FUTURE DIRECTIONS

The theory-of-mind hypothesis stimulated a surge of interest in autism, with a particular focus on how research with this population could provide important insights into the neurocognitive architecture for theory of mind. In recent years, the debate has turned toward the role played by the mirror-neuron system in accounting for the range of social-communicative deficits in autism that include not only those encompassed by theory of mind but also those that go beyond theory of mind—for example, face recognition, imitation, and empathy (Williams et al., 2006). Mirror neurons were first described when researchers noted that certain neurons located in the prefrontal motor cortex of monkeys fired when the animals carried out an action, when they observed the same action carried out by another individual, and when imitating the action, suggesting that these neurons are important for encoding the intentions of other actors (Gallese, Fadiga, Fogassi, & Rizzolatti, 1996). Since mirror neurons were initially described, researchers have proposed that the mirrorneuron system is an important component of the social-cognitive network, and there is evidence for impaired functioning of this system in autism (Oberman & Ramachandran, 2007). But there are still many questions about the relationship between the variety of processes that are subsumed under the mirror-neuron umbrella—such as imitation or empathy—and other aspects of social-information processing—including theory of mind and face processing. To investigate the emergence (or nonemergence) of the full range of behaviors that are considered key to the mirror-neuron system and theory of mind, it will be necessary to conduct longitudinal behavioral studies beginning in infancy, before the onset of major autism symptoms. More systematic neuroimaging studies should be conducted to investigate the common and distinct neural pathways that underlie the social-information-processing deficits implicated in autism, with particular sensitivity to the individual variation that can be expected in this heterogeneous population. The past two decades of research on theory of mind in autism has taught us that no single hypothesis can explain the full range of symptoms that define autism. As we move forward with a broader perspective on the neurocognitive mechanisms that are associated with social-communicative impairments in autism, it will be crucial to embrace the variability that we can expect to find in our data. Only by focusing on this variability can we hope to advance our understanding of this complex and enigmatic neurodevelopmental disorder.

Recommended Reading

Baron-Cohen, S., Tager-Flusberg, H., & Cohen, D.J. (Eds.). (2000). *Understanding other minds: Perspectives from developmental cognitive neuroscience* (2nd ed.). Oxford, UK: Oxford University Press. A comprehensive sourcebook for developmental, neurobiological, and clinical research studies on theory of mind, including chapters on theory of mind in autism.

Oberman, L.M., & Ramachandran, V.S. (2007). (See References). A detailed presentation of the mirror-neuron system and its relation to theory of mind in explaining core deficits in autism.

Ruffman, T., Garnham, W., & Rideout, P. (2001). (See References). An important study that illustrates the difference between implicit and explicit measures of theory-of-mind understanding in children with autism.

Tager-Flusberg, H. (2001). (See References). A critical analysis and defense of the theory-of-mind hypothesis of autism.

Acknowledgments—Preparation of this article was supported in part by Grant U19 DC 03610 from the National Institute on Deafness and Other Communication Disorders (NIDCD), which is part of the National Institute of Child Health and Human Development/NIDCD-funded Collaborative Programs of Excellence in Autism.

Note

1. Address correspondence to Helen Tager-Flusberg, Department of Anatomy & Neurobiology, Boston University School of Medicine, 715 Albany Street L-814, Boston, MA 02118; e-mail: htagerf@bu.edu.

References

Astington, J., & Baird, J. (Eds.). (2005). *Why language matters for theory of mind*. Oxford, UK: Oxford University Press.

Baron-Cohen, S., Leslie, A.M., & Frith, U. (1985). Does the autistic child have a "theory of mind?" *Cognition, 21,* 37–46.

Frith, U. (1989). *Autism: Explaining the Enigma.* Oxford, UK: Blackwell.

Frith, U., & Frith, C. (2003). Development and neurophysiology of mentalizing. *Philosophical Transactions of the Royal Society of London – Series B: Biological Sciences, 258,* 459–473.

Gallese, V., Fadiga, L., Fogassi, L., & Rizzolatti, G. (1996). Action recognition in the premotor cortex. *Brain, 119,* 593–609.

Happé, F. (1995). The role of age and verbal ability in the theory of mind task performance of subjects with autism. *Child Development, 66,* 843–855.

Hobson, R.P. (1993). *Autism and the development of mind.* Hove, UK: Erlbaum.

Joseph, R.M., & Tager-Flusberg, H. (2004). The relationship between theory of mind and executive functions to symptom type and severity in children with autism. *Development and Psychopathology, 16,* 137–155.

Klin, A., Jones, W., Schultz, R., & Volkmar, F. (2003). The enactive mind, or from actions to cognition: Lessons from autism. *Philosophical transactions of the Royal Society of London – Series B: Biological Sciences, 358,* 345–360.

Oberman, L., & Ramachandran, V. (2007). The simulating social mind: The role of the mirror neuron system and simulation in the social and communicative deficits of autism spectrum disorders. *Psychological Bulletin, 133,* 310–327.

Ozonoff, S., Cook, I., Coon, H., Dawson, G., Joseph, R.M., Klin, A., et al. (2004). Performance on CANTAB subtests sensitive to frontal lobe function in people with autistic disorder: Evidence from the CPEA Network. *Journal of Autism and Developmental Disorders, 34,* 139–150.

Peterson, C., Wellman, H., & Liu, D. (2005). Steps in theory of mind development for children with deafness or autism. *Child Development, 76,* 502–517.

Ruffman, T., Garnham, W., & Rideout, P. (2001). Social understanding in autism: Eye gaze as a measure of core insights. *Journal of Child Psychology and Psychiatry, 42,* 1083–1094.

Steele, S., Joseph, R.M., & Tager-Flusberg, H. (2003). Developmental change in theory of mind abilities in children with autism. *Journal of Autism and Developmental Disorders, 33,* 461–467.

Tager-Flusberg, H. (2001). A re-examination of the theory of mind hypothesis of autism. In J. Burack, T. Charman, N. Yirmiya, & P.R. Zelazo (Eds.), *Development in autism: Perspectives from theory and research* (pp. 173–193). Hillsdale NJ: Erlbaum.

Tager-Flusberg, H. (2003). Exploring the relationships between theory of mind and social-communicative functioning in children with autism. In B. Repacholi & V. Slaughter (Eds.), *Individual differences in theory of mind: Implications for typical and atypical development* (pp. 197–212). London: Psychology Press.

Tager-Flusberg, H., & Joseph, R.M. (2005). How language facilitates the acquisition of false belief understanding in children with autism. In J. Astington & J. Baird (Eds.), *Why language matters for theory of mind* (pp. 298–318). Oxford, UK: Oxford University Press.

Williams, J., Waiter, G., Gilchrist, A., Perrett, D., Murray, A., & Whiten, A. (2006). Neural mechanisms of imitation and 'mirror neuron' functioning in autism spectrum disorders. *Neuropsychologia, 44,* 610–621.

This article has been reprinted as it originally appeared in *Current Directions in Psychological Science*. Citation information for this article as originally published appears above.

Three Reasons Not to Believe in an Autism Epidemic

Morton Ann Gernsbacher[1] and H. Hill Goldsmith
University of Wisconsin-Madison

Michelle Dawson
University of Montreal, Montreal, Quebec, Canada

Abstract

According to some lay groups, the nation is experiencing an autism epidemic—a rapid escalation in the prevalence of autism for unknown reasons. However, no sound scientific evidence indicates that the increasing number of diagnosed cases of autism arises from anything other than purposely broadened diagnostic criteria, coupled with deliberately greater public awareness and intentionally improved case finding. Why is the public perception so disconnected from the scientific evidence? In this article we review three primary sources of misunderstanding: lack of awareness about the changing diagnostic criteria, uncritical acceptance of a conclusion illogically drawn in a California-based study, and inattention to a crucial feature of the "child count" data reported annually by the U.S. Department of Education.

Keywords

autism; epidemiology; epidemic

If you have learned anything about autism lately from the popular media, you most likely have learned—erroneously—that there is "a mysterious upsurge" in the prevalence of autism (*New York Times*, October 20, 2002, Section 4, p. 10), creating a "baffling . . . outbreak" (CBSnews.com, October 18, 2002), in which new cases are "exploding in number" (*Time*, May 6, 2002, p. 48), and "no one knows why" (*USA Today*, May 17, 2004, p. 8D). At least a handful of U.S. Congress members decree on their .gov Web sites that the nation is facing an autism epidemic. Several national media have erroneously concluded that a set of data from California "confirms the autism epidemic," and the largest autism-advocacy organization in the world has expressed alarm over astronomical percentage increases in the number of autistic children served in the public schools since 1992. However, no sound scientific evidence indicates that the increase in the number of diagnosed cases of autism arises from anything other than intentionally broadened diagnostic criteria, coupled with deliberately greater public awareness and conscientiously improved case finding. How did public perception become so misaligned from scientific evidence? In this article, we review three major sources of misunderstanding.

THE CHANGING DIAGNOSIS OF AUTISM

The phenomenon of autism has existed most likely since the origins of human society. In retrospect, numerous historical figures—for instance, the 18th-century "wild boy of Aveyron"—fit autism diagnostic criteria but were not so diagnosed in their day (Frith, 1989). Only in the 1940s did a constellation of differences in social interaction, communication, and focused interests come to be categorized by Leo Kanner as "autism." However, another 40 years would elapse before American psychiatric practice incorporated criteria for autism into what was by then the third edition of its *Diagnostic and Statistical Manual of Mental Disorders* (*DSM-III*; American Psychiatric Association, APA, 1980). Thus, estimates of the prevalence of autism prior to 1980 were based on individual clinicians' (e.g., Kanner & Eisenberg, 1956) or specific researchers' (e.g., Rutter, 1978) conceptions—and fluctuated because of factors that continue to introduce variation into current-day estimates (e.g., variation in the size of the population sampled and the manner of identification).

Autism has remained in the *DSM* (under the title, Pervasive Developmental Disorders), but not without modification through subsequent editions. Whereas the 1980 *DSM-III* entry required satisfying six mandatory criteria, the more recent 1994 *DSM-IV* (APA, 1994) offers 16 optional criteria—only half of which need to be met. Moreover, the severe phrasing of the 1980 mandatory criteria contrasts with the more inclusive phrasing of the 1994 optional criteria. For instance, to qualify for a diagnosis according to the 1980 criteria an individual needed to exhibit "*a pervasive lack of responsiveness* to other people" (emphasis added; APA, 1980, p. 89); in contrast, according to 1994 criteria an individual must demonstrate only "a lack of spontaneous seeking to share . . . achievements with other people" (APA, 1994, p. 70) and peer relationships less sophisticated than would be predicted by the individual's developmental level. The 1980 mandatory criteria of "*gross deficits* in language development" (emphasis added; APA, 1980, p. 89) and "if speech is present, peculiar speech patterns such as immediate and delayed echolalia, metaphorical language, pronominal reversal" (APA, 1980, p. 89) were replaced by the 1994 options of difficulty "sustain[ing] a conversation" (APA, 1994, p. 70) or "lack of varied . . . social imitative play" (p. 70). "*Bizarre responses* to various aspects of the environment" (emphasis added; APA, 1980, p. 90) became "persistent preoccupation with parts of objects" (APA, 1994, p. 71).

Furthermore, whereas the earlier 1980 (*DSM-III*) entry comprised only two diagnostic categories (infantile autism and childhood onset pervasive developmental disorder), the more recent 1994 (*DSM-IV*) entry comprises five. Three of those five categories connote what is commonly called autism: Autistic Disorder, Pervasive Developmental Disorder Not Otherwise Specified (PDDNOS), and Asperger's Disorder. Autistic Disorder requires meeting half of the 16 criteria, but Asperger's Disorder, which did not enter the *DSM* until 1994, involves only two thirds of that half, and PDDNOS, which entered the *DSM* in 1987, is defined by subthreshold symptoms. Therefore, Asperger's Disorder and PDDNOS are often considered "milder variants." These milder variants can account for nearly three fourths of current autism diagnoses (Chakrabarti & Fombonne, 2001). Consider also the recent practice of codiagnosing autism alongside known medical and genetic conditions (e.g., Down syndrome, Tourette's syndrome, and cerebral palsy; Gillberg & Coleman, 2000); the contemporary recognition that autism can exist among people at every level of measured intelligence (Baird et al., 2000), the deliberate efforts to identify autism in younger and younger children (Filipek et al., 2000), and the speculation that many individuals who would meet present-day criteria were previously mis- or undiagnosed (Wing & Potter, 2002), including some of the most accomplished, albeit idiosyncratic, historical figures such as Isaac Newton, Lewis Carroll, W.B. Yeats, Thomas Jefferson, and Bill Gates (Fitzgerald, 2004).

THE CALIFORNIA DATA

In California, persons diagnosed with autism (and other developmental disabilities) qualify for services administered by the statewide Department of Developmental Services (DDS). In 1999, the California DDS reported that from 1987 to 1998 the number of individuals served under the category of "autism" had increased by 273% (California DDS, 1999). Alarmed by this 273% increase, the California legislature commissioned the University of California Medical Investigation of Neurodevelopmental Disorders (M.I.N.D.) Institute to determine whether the increase could be explained by changes in diagnostic criteria. The M.I.N.D. Institute (2002) concluded, on the basis of data we describe next, that there was "no evidence that a loosening in the diagnostic criteria has contributed to the increased number of autism clients served by the [California DDS] Regional Centers" (p. 5). Although this unrefereed conclusion made national headlines and continues to be articulated on innumerable Web sites, it is unwarranted.

The study involved two samples of children who had been served under the California DDS category of "autism": One sample was born between 1983 and 1985 (the earlier cohort); the other sample was born between 1993 and 1995 (the more recent cohort). Both cohorts were assessed with the same autism diagnostic instrument (an interview conducted with care providers). However, the autism diagnostic instrument was based on *DSM-IV* criteria—criteria that were not even published until 1994. When the same percentage of children in the earlier and the more recent cohort met the more recent *DSM-IV* criteria, the researchers imprudently concluded that the "observed increase in autism cases cannot be explained by a loosening in the criteria used to make the diagnosis" (M.I.N.D. Institute, 2002, p. 7).

To understand the fallacy of the conclusion, consider the following analogy, based on male height and graphically illustrated in Figure 1. Suppose the criterion for "tall" was 74.5 in. and taller in the mid-1980s, but the criterion was loosened to 72 in. and taller in the mid-1990s. A diagnostic instrument based on the looser, more recent criterion of 72 in. would identify males who met the 74.5-in. criterion as well as those who met the 72-in. criterion.[2] Although a perfectly reliable diagnostic instrument based on a looser criterion would identify 100% of the individuals who meet the looser criterion along with 100% of the individuals who meet the more restricted criterion, a highly reliable instrument might identify about 90% of each group; this is the percentage of each cohort in the California study who met the more recent autism criteria.

Most crucially, broadening the criterion will result in a dramatic increase in diagnosed cases. For instance, census data allow us to estimate that 2,778 males in McClennan County, Texas would be called tall by the more restricted 74.5-in.

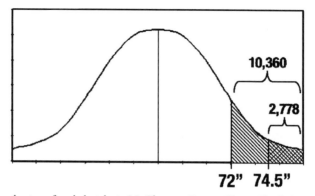

Fig. 1. Distribution of male height in McClennan County, Texas. Shaded areas represent segments of the population defined as "tall" according to two standards: men over 74.5 in. (2,778) versus men over 72 in. (10,360).

criterion, and 10,360 males would be called tall by the broader 72-in. criterion; if those two criteria had been applied a decade apart, a 273% increase in the number of males called tall would have emerged—without any real increase in Texans' height. In the same way, the 273% increase from 2,778 versus 10,360 California children who received services for "autism" in 1987 versus 1998 could well be a function of broadened criteria.

As we have already detailed, the commonly applied diagnostic criteria for autism broadened nationally from the 1980s to the 1990s; thus, it would be unusual if the criteria used for eligibility in California had not also broadened during this time. Two further aspects of the California data suggest that the criteria must have broadened. First, children in the more recent cohort were dramatically less likely to have intellectual impairment: Whereas 61% of the children in the earlier cohort were identified as having intellectual impairments, only 27% of the children in the more recent cohort were so identified. The lower rate of intellectual impairment in the more recent cohort matches recent epidemiological data, and the difference between the two rates suggests a major difference between the two cohorts (e.g., that the more recent cohort was drawn from a less cognitively impaired population).

Second, on two of the three dimensions measured by the autism diagnostic instrument, the children in the more recent cohort were, on average, less symptomatic than the children from the earlier cohort. The researchers stated that although these differences were statistically significant (i.e., they exceeded the criterion of a statistical test), they were likely not clinically significant (i.e., they were likely not of significance to the clinical presentation); therefore, the researchers suggested that these differences should not be taken as evidence that the diagnostic criteria had broadened. However, refer again to the tallness analogy: Comparing two cohorts of males in McClennan County diagnosed according to our more restricted (74.5-in.) versus our broader (72-in.) criterion would probably result in a statistically significant difference between the two cohorts' average height—but the difference would be just about an inch (i.e., most likely not a clinically significant difference).

THE "CHILD COUNT" DATA

The purpose of the federal Individuals With Disabilities Education Act (IDEA), passed in 1991, is to ensure that all children with disabilities are provided a free, appropriate, public education including an individually designed program. Schools comply with the IDEA by reporting to the federal Department of Education an annual "child count" of the number of children with disabilities served. It is the data from these annual child counts that have been the most egregiously misused in arguments for an autism epidemic.

For example, in October 2003, the Autism Society of America sent its 20,000 members the following electronic message: "Figures from the most recent U. S. Department of Education's 2002 Report to Congress on IDEA reveal that the number of students with autism [ages 6 to 21] in America's schools *jumped an alarming 1,354% in the eight-year period from the school year 1991-92 to 2000-01*" (emphasis added). What the Autism Society failed to note is the following fact (available in the *Report to Congress,* immediately under the autism data entries): Prior to the 1991–1992 school year, there was no child count of students with autism; autism did not even exist as an IDEA reporting category. Moreover, in 1991–1992, use of the autism reporting category was optional (it was required only in subsequent years).

Whenever a new category is introduced, if it is viable, increases in its usage will ensue. Consider another IDEA reporting category introduced along with autism in 1991–1992: "traumatic brain injury." From 1991–1992 to 2000–2001, this category soared an astronomical 5,059%. Likewise, the reporting category "developmental delay," which was introduced only in 1997–1998, grew 663% in only 3 years.

After the initial year, the number of children reported under the IDEA category of autism has increased by approximately 23% annually. Why the continuing annual increase? As is the case with new options in the marketplace, like cellular phones and high-speed Internet, new reporting categories in the annual child count are not capitalized upon instantaneously; they require incrementally magnified awareness and augmentation or reallocation of resources. Currently no state reports the number of children with autism that would be expected based on the results of three recent, large-scale epidemiological studies, which identified 5.8 to 6.7 children per 1,000 for the broader autism spectrum (Baird et al., 2000; Bertrand et al., 2001; Chakrabarti & Fombonne, 2001). In 2002–2003, front-runners Oregon and Minnesota reported 4.3 and 3.5 children with autism per 1,000, respectively, while Colorado, Mississippi, and New Mexico reported only 0.8, 0.7, and 0.7 children with autism per 1,000. Thus, most likely IDEA child counts will continue to increase until the number reported by each state approaches the number of children identified in the epidemiological studies.

Why do states vary so widely in the number of children reported (or served)? Each state's department of education specifies its own diagnostic criteria, and states differ (as do school districts within states, and individual schools within school districts) in the value given to a diagnosis in terms of services received. States also vary from year to year in the number of children served and reported. For instance, Massachusetts historically reported the lowest percentage of children with autism: only 0.4 or 0.5 per 1,000 from 1992 through 2001. Then, in 2002, Massachusetts reported a 400% increase in one year, when it began using student-level data (i.e., actually counting the students) rather than applying a ratio, which was calculated in 1992, based on the proportion of students in each disability classification as reported in 1992. In their 2002 IDEA report to Congress, Massachusetts state officials warned that the increase will continue for several years as "districts better understand how to submit their data at the student level" (IDEA, 2002, p. 4) and "all districts comply completely with the new reporting methods" (IDEA, 2002, p. 4).

OTHER REASONS NOT TO BELIEVE IN AN AUTISM EPIDEMIC

In this article we have detailed three reasons why some laypersons mistakenly believe that there is an autism epidemic. They are unaware of the purposeful broadening of diagnostic criteria, coupled with deliberately greater public awareness; they accept the unwarranted conclusions of the M.I.N.D. Institute study; and they fail to realize that autism was not even an IDEA reporting category until the early 1990s and incremental increases will most likely continue until the schools are identifying and serving the number of children identified in epidemiological studies. Apart from a desire to be aligned with scientific reasoning, there are other reasons not to believe in an autism epidemic.

Epidemics solicit causes; false epidemics solicit false causes. Google *autism* and *epidemic* to witness the range of suspected causes of the mythical autism epidemic. Epidemics also connote danger. What message do we send autistic children and adults when we call their increasing number an epidemic? A pandemic? A scourge? Realizing that the increasing prevalence rates are most likely due to noncatastrophic mechanisms, such as purposely broader diagnostic criteria and greater public awareness, should not, however, diminish societal responsibility to support the increasing numbers of individuals being diagnosed with autism. Neither should enthusiasm for scientific inquiry into the variety and extent of human behavioral, neuroanatomical, and genotypic diversity in our population be dampened.

Recommended Reading

Fombonne, E. (2003). Epidemiological surveys of autism and other pervasive developmental disorders: An update. *Journal of Autism and Developmental Disorders, 33,* 365–382.
Institute of Medicine. (2004). *Immunization safety review: Vaccines and autism.* Washington, DC: National Academies Press.
Wing, L., & Potter, D. (2002). (See References)

Notes

1. Address correspondence to Morton Ann Gernsbacher, Department of Psychology, University of Wisconsin-Madison, 1202 W. Johnson St., Madison, WI 53706; e-mail: MAGernsb@wisc.edu.

2. Wing and Potter (2002) provide a similar illustration. The same percentage of children who met Kanner's earlier, more restricted criteria met *DSM-IV's* more recent, broadened criteria; if the child was autistic according to Kanner's restricted criteria, the child was autistic according to *DSM-IV's* broadened criteria. Of course, the reverse was not true. Only 33 to 45% of the children who met more recent *DSM-IV* criteria met earlier Kanner criteria.

References

American Psychiatric Association. (1980). *Diagnostic and statistical manual of mental disorders* (3rd ed.). Washington, DC: Author.

American Psychiatric Association. (1994). *Diagnostic and statistical manual of mental disorders* (4th ed.). Washington, DC: Author.

Baird, G., Charman, T., Baron-Cohen, S., Cox, A., Swettenham, J., Wheelwright, S., & Drew, A. (2000). A screening instrument for autism at 18 months of age: A 6 year follow-up study. *Journal of the American Academy of Child and Adolescent Psychiatry, 39*, 694–702.

Bertrand, J., Mars, A., Boyle, C., Bove, F., Yeargin-Allsopp, M., & Decoufle, P. (2001). Prevalence of autism in a United States population: The Brick Township, New Jersey, investigation. *Pediatrics, 108*, 1155–1161.

California Department of Developmental Services. (1999). *Changes in the population with autism and pervasive developmental disorders in California's developmental services system: 1987–1998. A report to the legislature.* Sacramento, CA: California Health and Human Services Agency.

Chakrabarti, S., & Fombonne, E. (2001). Pervasive developmental disorders in preschool children. *Journal of the American Medical Association, 285*, 3093–3099.

Filipek, P.A., Accardo, P.J., Ashwal, S., Baranek, G.T., Cook, E.H. Jr., Dawson, G., Gordon, B., Gravel, J.S., Johnson, C.P., Kallen, R.J., Levy, S.E., Minshew, N.J., Ozonoff, S., Prizant, B.M., Rapin, I., Rogers, S.J., Stone, W.L., Teplin, S.W., Tuchman, R.F., & Volkmar, F.R. (2000). Practice parameter: Screening and diagnosis of autism: Report of the Quality Standards Subcommittee of the American Academy of Neurology and the Child Neurology Society. *Neurology, 55*, 468–479.

Fitzgerald, M. (2004). *Autism and creativity: Is there a link between autism in men and exceptional ability?* London: Brunner-Routledge.

Frith, U. (1989). *Autism: Explaining the enigma.* Oxford, England: Blackwell.

Gillberg, C., & Coleman, M. (2000). *The biology of the autistic syndromes* (3rd ed.). London: MacKeith Press.

IDEA. (2002). *Data Notes for IDEA, Part B.* Retrieved April 22, 2005, from IDEAdata Web side: http://www.ideadata.org/docs/bdatanotes2002.doc

Kanner, L., & Eisenberg, J. (1956). Early infantile autism 1943–1955. *American Journal of Orthopsychiatry, 26*, 55–65.

M.I.N.D. Institute. (2002). *Report to the Legislature on the principal findings from The Epidemiology of Autism in California: A Comprehensive Pilot Study.* Davis: University of California-Davis.

Rutter, M. (1978). Diagnosis and definition. In M. Rutter & E. Schopler (Eds.), *Autism: A reappraisal of concepts and treatments* (pp. 1–25). New York: Plenum Press.

U.S. Department of Education. (2002). *Twenty-fourth annual report to Congress on the implementation of the Individuals With Disabilities Education Act.* Washington, DC: Author.

Wing, L., & Potter, D. (2002). The epidemiology of autistic spectrum disorders: Is the prevalence rising? *Mental Retardation and Developmental Disabilities Research Reviews, 8*, 151–162.

This article has been reprinted as it originally appeared in *Current Directions in Psychological Science*. Citation information for this article as originally published appears above.

Neural Mechanisms in Dyslexia

Sally E. Shaywitz[1] and Bennett A. Shaywitz

Yale Center for the Study of Learning, Reading, and Attention, Department of Pediatrics, Yale University School of Medicine

Maria Mody

Athinoula A. Martinos Center for Biomedical Imaging, Massachusetts General Hospital–Harvard Medical School

Abstract

Within the last two decades, evidence from many laboratories has converged to indicate the cognitive basis for dyslexia: Dyslexia is a disorder within the language system and, more specifically, within a particular subcomponent of that system, phonological processing. Converging evidence from a number of laboratories using functional brain imaging indicates that there is a disruption of left-hemisphere posterior neural systems in child and adult dyslexic readers when they perform reading tasks. The discovery of a disruption in the neural systems serving reading has significant implications for the acceptance of dyslexia as a valid disorder—a necessary condition for its identification and treatment. Brain-imaging findings provide, for the first time, convincing, irrefutable evidence that what has been considered a hidden disability is "real," and these findings have practical implications for the provision of accommodations, a critical component of management for older children and young adults attending postsecondary and graduate programs. The utilization of advances in neuroscience to inform educational policy and practices provides an exciting example of translational science being used for the public good.

Keywords

dyslexia; reading; fMRI; neural systems; accommodations; translational science

Developmental dyslexia is defined as an unexpected difficulty in reading in children and adults who otherwise possess the intelligence and motivation considered necessary for accurate and fluent reading and who also have had reasonable reading instruction. Dyslexia may be contrasted with other reading difficulties that are not unexpected—for example, in children with low intelligence or with very limited or inadequate reading instruction. In contrast to dyslexia or specific reading retardation, such reading difficulties have been referred to as general reading backwardness.

Though dyslexia was first described over a century ago, it has only been in the last two decades that neuroscientists have determined the neural systems influencing reading and dyslexia. To a significant extent, this explosion in understanding the neural bases of reading and dyslexia has been driven by the development of functional neuroimaging—technologies such as positron emission tomography (PET) and functional magnetic resonance imaging (fMRI) that measure changes in metabolic activity and blood flow in specific brain regions while subjects are engaged in cognitive tasks (Frackowiak et al., 2004).

To a large degree, these advances in understanding the neurobiological underpinnings of reading and dyslexia have been informed by progress in understanding the cognitive basis of reading and dyslexia. Though a number of theories of dyslexia have been proposed, there is now a strong consensus supporting the phonological theory, a theory recognizing that speech is natural whereas reading is acquired and must be taught. In order to read, a child has to acquire the alphabetic principle. This is the insight that spoken words can be pulled apart into smaller units of speech—for example, syllables, and the smallest particles of speech, phonemes—and that the letters in a written word represent these sounds. Results from large and well-studied populations confirm that a deficit in phonology is the most robust and specific correlate of dyslexia and form the basis for the most successful and evidence-based interventions designed to improve reading (summarized in S. Shaywitz, 2003).

Languages vary in the consistency and predictability of letter–sound linkages, with some such as Finnish and Italian having highly predictable mappings and others, for example English and Danish, having much more inconsistency (Ziegler & Goswami, 2005). Such differences in consistency have many consequences, including developmental differences in the size of word segments (e.g., syllables, rimes, phonemes) represented in the mental lexicon, the ease of and preferred strategies in learning to read, and manifestations of dyslexia. However, what is uniform across languages is that learning to read depends on the development of phonological awareness, the sensitivity to the sound structure of spoken words.

NEUROBIOLOGICAL STUDIES OF DISABLED READERS

Though brain-imaging studies of dyslexia are relatively recent, neural systems influencing reading were first proposed over a century ago, based on studies of adults who had suffered strokes with subsequent acquired alexia, the sudden loss of the ability to read. These neuropathological studies, which implicated left-hemisphere posterior regions, have now been confirmed using functional brain imaging. Such imaging studies have begun to describe the brain organization for reading—specifically, the identification and localization of specific neural systems serving reading and their differences in typical and dyslexic readers; a neural system for skilled, fluent reading; plasticity in the systems, that is, that they are malleable and able to respond to an effective reading intervention; and the existence of two types of reading disability, one hypothesized as primarily genetic in origin, the other as primarily influenced by environmental factors.

A range of studies converge to demonstrate three left-hemisphere neural systems for reading (see Fig. 1; reviewed in Price & Mechelli, 2005; S. Shaywitz & B. Shaywitz, 2005). Brain-imaging investigations further demonstrate differences in activation patterns between good and struggling readers at all ages. Nonimpaired younger children demonstrate significantly greater activation in the three left-hemisphere neural systems than do dyslexic children. With maturation, there appears to be compensation in anterior regions around the inferior frontal gyrus, so that differences between older nonimpaired and dyslexic children are confined to two posterior regions, the parieto-temporal and occipito-temporal systems (B. Shaywitz et al., 2002).

175

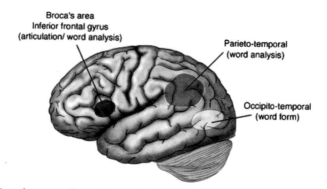

Fig. 1. Neural systems for reading in the brain's left hemisphere. An anterior system in the region of the inferior frontal gyrus (Broca's area) is believed to serve articulation and word analysis. A system in the parieto-temporal region is believed to serve word analysis, and a second in the occipito-temporal region (termed the word-form area) is believed to be responsible for the rapid, automatic, fluent identification of words. Reprinted from *Overcoming Dyslexia: A New and Complete Science-Based Program for Reading Problems at Any Level,* by Sally E. Shaywitz, 2003, p. 78, New York: Alfred A. Knopf. Copyright 2003 by Alfred A. Knopf. Reprinted with permission.

These data converge with reports from many investigators showing what has been referred to as a neural signature of dyslexia: a failure of left-hemisphere posterior brain systems to function properly during reading (reviewed in Price & Mechelli, 2005; S. Shaywitz & B. Shaywitz, 2005). One of these systems, in the left occipito-temporal (LOT) region, has increasingly attracted the attention of reading researchers and is our focus in this article. Considerable research in the last 5 years has converged to indicate a computational role for this system in influencing skilled, fluent reading, with neurons in this region coding for words and letter strings; not surprisingly, the LOT region has been labeled the "visual word-form area." Specialization of a population of neurons within this area results in the rapid extraction of linguistic information from strings of letters so that, within 250 milliseconds of being viewed, they are integrated and perceived as words—a process resulting in the rapid, effortless recognition of familiar words (for discussion, see Dehaene, Cohen, Sigman, & Vinckier, 2005). Recent evidence indicates that disruption of this region in dyslexic individuals is found not only for reading words but for naming the pictures of the words, suggesting that the disruption in this region "may underlie the reading and naming deficits observed in developmental dyslexia" (McCrory, Mechelli, Frith, & Price, 2005, p. 265).

fMRI has been helpful in clarifying potentially different types of reading disability. Shaywitz et al. (2003) studied men and women from the Connecticut Longitudinal Study, a representative sample prospectively followed since 1983 when they were 5 years old and who have had their reading performance assessed yearly throughout their primary and secondary schooling. Within this population, three groups of young adults, ages 18 to 22.5 years, were identified and imaged: (a) nonimpaired readers, who had no evidence of reading problems; (b) accuracy-improved readers, who were inaccurate readers in third grade but by ninth grade had compensated to some degree so that they were accurate (but not fluent); and (c) persistently poor readers, who were inaccurate readers in third grade and remained inaccurate and not fluent in ninth grade.

A common goal of functional imaging studies of reading is to activate those neural systems used in phonological analysis; to accomplish this, one of the most useful tasks asks subjects to determine if two pseudowords rhyme—for example, "lete" and "jeat" (which do rhyme) or "mobe" and "haib" (which do not). Since pseudowords are novel and could neither have been seen before nor memorized, subjects must use phonologic analysis to perform the task. Brain-activation patterns during this task demonstrated the typical pattern of disruption of posterior neural system in both accuracy-improved and persistently poor readers. However, during a task using real words, brain-activation patterns in the two groups of disabled readers diverged. In this semantic-category task, subjects are asked to judge, for example, if *corn* and *rice* are in the same category (yes, they are both foods) or if *lion* and *tree* are in the same category (they are not). During this task, accuracy-improved readers demonstrated the typical disruption of left-hemisphere posterior systems. In contrast, similar to nonimpaired readers, persistently poor readers activated these posterior systems even though their reading performance was significantly poorer than that of nonimpaired readers on every reading task administered.

Connectivity analysis, an imaging technique assessing the correlations of activity in a source region to activity in other brain areas, showed that when the LOT area was selected as the source region, activity in LOT in nonimpaired readers was correlated with activity in the left inferior frontal gyrus, a component of the neural systems for reading. However, the same analysis in persistently poor readers demonstrated functional connectivity between LOT and right prefrontal regions often associated with memory, suggesting that in these individuals the LOT functions as part of a memory network. Further support for the hypothesis that persistently poor readers rely on memory networks was provided by results of an out-of-magnet oral reading task. Results indicated that persistently poor readers, but not accuracy-improved or nonimpaired readers, identified significantly fewer low-frequency than high-frequency words; this suggests that persistently poor readers have not learned to use phonologic strategies to analyze unfamiliar words and that they appear to rely more on memory-based strategies.

Demonstration of neurobiological differences between the groups led to the examination of the longitudinal data in an attempt to sort out other potential differences between accuracy-improved and persistently poor readers. Both groups began school with comparable reading scores, but compared to accuracy-improved readers, persistently poor readers had poorer cognitive (primarily verbal) ability; attended more disadvantaged schools; and tended to come from lower-socioeconomic-status homes. Thus, persistently poor readers resemble those with what is termed general reading backwardness, who tend to have lower cognitive ability and to come from more disadvantaged circumstances, while accuracy-improved readers appear to relate best to dyslexia, where the reading difficulties are unexpected.

Genetic studies, too, provide support for the notion that accuracy-improved and persistently poor readers may represent different etiologies. Twin studies report that subjects with relatively higher IQs, as is true of accuracy-improved readers or those with dyslexia, tend to have stronger genetic influence, whereas shared environment is a stronger influence for those with lower IQs, comparable to that found in persistently poor readers or those with general reading backwardness. Here, the investigators postulate that "poor home and educational environment could be jointly responsible for the concurrent expression of low IQ" and poor reading (Olson, 1999, p.13). In contrast, in accuracy-improved readers or those with dyslexia, reading difficulties are more likely to be unexpected and to reflect stronger genetic influences.

There is good evidence of differences in exposure to language among children growing up in less, compared to more, advantaged homes—a factor that may place some children at risk for later language and reading difficulties. This supposition is supported, in part, by brain-imaging findings indicating that persistently poor readers read real words using memory systems, suggesting brain systems for analyzing and reading words have not developed. An intriguing suggestion is that with more language experience at home and more effective reading instruction at school, persistently poor readers' phonologically based reading system would have developed.

Alternatively, accuracy-improved and persistently poor readers may both be genetically vulnerable but the higher cognitive ability, better verbal ability, and, perhaps, exposure to more effective reading instruction may serve as protective factors to help compensate for accuracy-improved readers' decoding difficulties. Thus, a larger vocabulary and strong reasoning abilities may help a struggling reader to use the context around an unknown word to figure out its meaning. Obviously, other factors may be operating as well. At this juncture, the notion of accuracy-improved and persistently poor readers as representing primarily genetic and environmental influences, respectively, is a hypothesis. At least four prominent candidate genes have been related to dyslexia (Fisher & Francks, 2006) and ongoing genetic studies of accuracy-improved and persistently poor readers may help confirm or refute this hypothesis.

Functional imaging studies, too, indicate that the neural systems for reading are malleable and respond to an effective reading intervention. Struggling readers, ages 6.1 years to 9.4 years, who received an intervention based on application of the alphabetic principle (focusing on, for example, teaching sound–symbol associations and practicing segmenting and blending phonemes in words) not only improved their reading but, compared to preintervention brain imaging, demonstrated increased activation in the neural systems for reading (B. Shaywitz et al., 2004). Other investigators, too, have found that an effective reading intervention influences neural systems in the brain (reviewed in S. Shaywitz & B. Shaywitz, 2005).

It is important to note that, from a practical perspective, it is neither necessary nor appropriate to use brain imaging as an assessment tool for the diagnosis of dyslexia in school-age children. Here, the history and diagnostic tools are both effective and economical. In the future, brain imaging may be helpful in the assessment of two very specific groups in whom diagnosis is often difficult: very young children and bright young adults. Newer methods in structural imaging (Sowell et al., 2003)—including diffusion tensor imaging, which shows connectivity of white-matter tracts and does not require the child to perform a task (such as reading) requiring cooperation of the subject during imaging—may be useful in very young at-risk children (Deutsch et al., 2005). Functional brain imaging, when perfected to allow reliable measures in *individual* subjects with dyslexia (it is only reliable currently at the group level), may prove useful in clarifying the diagnosis in bright, highly accomplished young adults who have compensated to some degree for their dyslexia and for whom current testing is often inadequate.

FUTURE DIRECTIONS AND IMPLICATIONS

Where do we go from here? With the elucidation of the neural systems for reading in typical and dyslexic readers and, in particular, the demonstration of the key role of the LOT in skilled or fluent readers, a next question is to begin to understand the specific mechanisms underlying LOT function in reading—in particular, how important information about orthography, semantics, and phonology is integrated. Brain imaging allows examination of competing hypotheses: for example, whether visual word recognition takes place serially, in a progressive, step-by-step approach (Dehaene et al., 2005), or conversely, whether the LOT functions as an interface between basic visual-form information and linguistic (semantic and phonologic) properties in a dynamic integrative process. Studies using functional imaging combined with priming are beginning to help resolve this question (Devlin, Jamison, Gonnerman, & Matthews, 2006).

To date, most studies have focused on word-level reading; an important next question concerns elucidating and understanding the more complex and distributed neural organization for comprehending connected text. Here, studies using sentence-level tasks engaging semantic or syntactic neural systems are beginning to tease apart the components of a cohesive operational system for reading comprehension.

Findings from laboratories around the world, in every language tested, indicate a neural signature for dyslexia, and these findings have implications for the acceptance of dyslexia as a valid disorder—a necessary condition for its identification and treatment. Simply put, such studies provide, for the first time, convincing, irrefutable evidence that what has been considered a hidden disability is "real."

This demonstration also has implications for the provision of accommodations for people with dyslexia, a critical component of management for older children attending postsecondary and graduate programs. Such findings should make policymakers more willing to allow children and adolescents with dyslexia to receive accommodations (such as extra time) on high-stakes tests. That would allow dyslexic readers with a disruption in the word-form area (influencing skilled, fluent reading) to be on a level playing field with their peers who do not have a reading disability. The utilization of advances in neuroscience to inform educational policy and practices provides an exciting example of translational science being used for the public good.

Recommended Reading

Dehaene, S., Cohen, L., Sigman, M., & Vinckier, F. (2005). (See References)
Mody, M. (2003). Phonological basis in reading disability: A review and analysis of the evidence. *Reading & Writing: An Interdisciplinary Journal, 16*, 21–39.

Price, C., & Mechelli, A. (2005). (See References)
Shaywitz, S. (2003). (See References)
Shaywitz, S., & Shaywitz, B. (2005). (See References)

Acknowledgments—The work described in this review was supported by grants from the National Institute of Child Health and Human Development (P50 HD25802; RO1 HD046171) to Sally Shaywitz and Bennett Shaywitz and from the Mental Illness and Neuroscience Discovery (MIND) Institute to Maria Mody.

Note

1. Address correspondence to Sally E. Shaywitz, Department of Pediatrics, Yale University School of Medicine, 333 Cedar Street, New Haven, CT 06510; e-mail: sally.shaywitz@yale.edu.

References

Dehaene, S., Cohen, L., Sigman, M., & Vinckier, F. (2005). The neural code for written words: A proposal. *Trends in Cognitive Sciences, 9,* 335–341.

Devlin, J.T., Jamison, H.L., Gonnerman, L.M., & Matthews, P.M. (2006). The role of the posterior fusiform gyrus in reading. *Journal of Cognitive Neuroscience, 18,* 911–922.

Deutsch, G., Dougherty, R., Bammer, R., Siok, W., Gabrieli, J., & Wandell, B. (2005). Children's reading performance is correlated with white matter structure measured by diffusion tensor imaging. *Cortex, 41,* 354–363.

Fisher, S.E., & Francks, C. (2006). Genes, cognition and dyslexia: Learning to read the genome. *Trends in Cognitive Sciences, 10,* 250–257.

Frackowiak, R., Friston, K., Frith, C., Dolan, R., Price, C., Zeki, S., Ashburner, J., Penny, W. (2004). *Human Brain Function* (2nd ed.). San Diego: Academic Press, Elsevier Science.

McCrory, E., Mechelli, A., Frith, U., & Price, C. (2005). More than words: A common neural basis for reading and naming deficits in developmental dyslexia? *Brain, 128,* 261–267.

Olson, R. (1999). Genes, environment, and reading disabilities. In R. Sternberg & L. Spear-Swerling (Eds.), *Perspectives on learning disabilities* (pp. 3–22). Oxford: Westview Press.

Price, C., & Mechelli, A. (2005). Reading and reading disturbance. *Current Opinion in Neurobiology, 15,* 231–238.

Shaywitz, B., Shaywitz, S., Blachman, B., Pugh, K., Fulbright, R., Skudlarski, P., et al. (2004). Development of left occipito-temporal systems for skilled reading in children after a phonologically-based intervention. *Biological Psychiatry, 55,* 926–933.

Shaywitz, B., Shaywitz, S., Pugh, K., Mencl, W., Fulbright, R., Skudlarski, P., et al. (2002). Disruption of posterior brain systems for reading in children with developmental dyslexia. *Biological Psychiatry, 52,* 101–110.

Shaywitz, S. (2003). *Overcoming dyslexia: A new and complete science-based program for reading problems at any level.* New York: Alfred A. Knopf.

Shaywitz, S., & Shaywitz, B. (2005). Dyslexia (specific reading disability). *Biological Psychiatry, 57,* 1301–1309.

Shaywitz, S., Shaywitz, B., Fulbright, R., Skudlarski, P., Mencl, W., Constable, R., et al. (2003). Neural systems for compensation and persistence: Young adult outcome of childhood reading disability. *Biological Psychiatry, 54,* 25–33.

Sowell, E.R., Peterson, B.S., Thompson, P.M., Welcome, S.E., Henkenius, A.L., & Toga, A.W. (2003). Mapping cortical change across the human life span. *Nature Neuroscience, 6,* 309–315.

Ziegler, J.C., & Goswami, U. (2005). Reading acquisition, developmental dyslexia, and skilled reading across languages: A psycholinguistic grain size theory. *Psychological Bulletin, 131,* 3–29.

Learning Abilities and Disabilities: Generalist Genes, Specialist Environments

Yulia Kovas[1] and Robert Plomin

Social, Genetic, and Developmental Psychiatry Centre, Institute of Psychiatry, King's College London, London, England

Abstract

Twin studies comparing identical and fraternal twins consistently show substantial genetic influence on individual differences in learning abilities such as reading and mathematics, as well as in other cognitive abilities such as spatial ability and memory. Multivariate genetic research has shown that the same set of genes is largely responsible for genetic influence on these diverse cognitive areas. We call these "generalist genes." What differentiates these abilities is largely the environment, especially nonshared environments that make children growing up in the same family different from one another. These multivariate genetic findings of generalist genes and specialist environments have far-reaching implications for diagnosis and treatment of learning disabilities and for understanding the brain mechanisms that mediate these effects.

Keywords

disabilities; reading; mathematics; genetics; multivariate

Why do children differ in their ability to read, to use language, or to understand mathematics? One way to answer this question is to use genetic research methods to investigate genetic and environmental causes of such differences among children. Two decades of research make it clear that genetics is a surprisingly large part of the answer for both learning abilities and learning disabilities.

A review of twin studies of language disability reported concordance (the likelihood that one twin will be affected if the other twin is affected) of 75% for monozygotic (MZ, identical) twins and 43% for dizygotic (DZ, fraternal) twins (Stromswold, 2001). For reading disability, the concordances for MZ and DZ twins are 84% and 48%, respectively. For mathematics disability, the concordances are about 70% for MZ twins and 50% for DZ twins (Oliver et al., 2004). Such studies consistently indicate substantial heritability for learning abilities as well as for disabilities.

Genetic research has moved beyond merely demonstrating the importance of genetic influence to ask more interesting questions. Multivariate genetic analysis makes it possible to ask questions about the genetic and environmental links between and within learning abilities and disabilities. The analysis focuses on the covariance (correlation) between two traits (bivariate) or multiple traits (multivariate) and uses the twin method to estimate genetic and environmental contributions to their covariance as well as the variance of each trait. In other words, multivariate genetic analysis estimates the extent to which genetic and environmental factors that affect one trait also affect another trait. Although space does not permit a detailed explanation, Figure 1 illustrates the model used in multivariate genetic analyses. Such analyses yield the *genetic correlation,* a statistic central

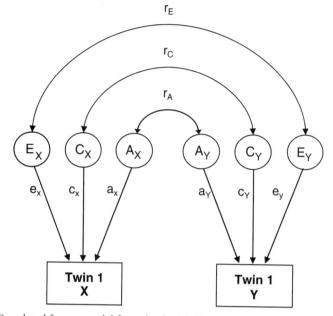

Fig. 1. Correlated factors model for individual differences on traits X and Y in one individual from a twin pair. Though not illustrated here, there are genetic and shared environmental correlations between the two members of a pair for both X and Y scores. Using the twin method that compares monozygotic (MZ, identical) and dizygotic (DZ, fraternal) twin resemblance, variance in each trait is divided into that due to latent additive genetic influences (A), shared environmental influences (C), and non-shared environmental influences (E), with the subscripts x and y to denote scores on traits X and Y, respectively. Paths, represented by lower case (a, c, and e), are standardized regression coefficients and are squared to estimate the proportion of variance accounted for. The gist of the multivariate genetic method lies in cross-trait twin correlations. Just as univariate genetic analysis compares MZ and DZ correlations for a single trait, multivariate genetic analysis compares MZ and DZ correlations across traits. If MZ cross-trait cross-twin (CTCT) correlations are greater than DZ CTCT correlations, this suggests that genetic differences account for some of the phenotypic correlation between the traits. Correlations between the latent genetic, shared environmental, and nonshared environmental influences are denoted by r_A, r_C and r_E. The genetic correlation represents the extent to which genetic influences on trait X are correlated with genetic influences on trait Y regardless of the heritabilities of traits X and Y. Bivariate heritability, which represents the genetic contribution to the phenotypic correlation between traits X and Y, is the product of the paths $a_x r_a a_y$, which weights the genetic correlation by the heritabilities of the traits.

to this article. The genetic correlation (which may range from 0, no correlation, to 1.0) indexes the extent to which genetic effects on one trait correlate with genetic effects on another trait independently of the heritability of the two traits. As shown in Figure 1, multivariate genetic analyses also yield analogous shared and nonshared environmental parameters. Multivariate genetic research has produced surprising findings with far-reaching implications. The purpose of this article is to review the results and to consider those implications.

GENERALIST GENES FOR READING, MATHEMATICS AND LANGUAGE

Multivariate genetic research on learning abilities and disabilities consistently yields high genetic correlations. In a recent review, genetic correlations varied from .67 to 1.0 for reading versus language (five studies), .47 to .98 for reading versus mathematics (three studies) and .59 to .98 for language versus mathematics (two studies; Plomin & Kovas, 2005).

These studies examined the entire distribution of individual differences in learning abilities. What about disabilities? Few multivariate genetic studies of disabilities have been reported because they require large samples of twins for both types of disabilities in order to investigate their co-occurrence. In general, genetic research comparing abilities and disabilities suggests that what we call learning disability is merely the low end of the normal distribution of learning ability and caused by the same genetic and environmental factors responsible for learning ability (Plomin & Kovas, 2005). The implication is that when large multivariate genetic studies of disabilities are conducted, they will yield similarly high genetic correlations.

These high genetic correlations indicate that the genes affecting one ability (e.g., reading) are to a surprising extent the same genes that affect other abilities (e.g., mathematics). In order to highlight this general effect of genes, we refer to them as generalist genes. When DNA research identifies genes responsible for genetic influence on reading ability and disability, for example, we predict that most of these genes will also be associated with mathematics ability and disability because the genetic correlation between reading and mathematics is .70.

If genetic correlations are so high between learning abilities, it makes sense to expect that components within each learning domain are also highly correlated genetically, and that is the case. Genetic correlations range between .60 and .90 within each of the domains of language, reading, and mathematics (Plomin & Kovas, 2005). The most recent study used Web-based testing to assess five components of mathematics, including computation, interpretation, and non-numerical processes, in a study of more than 1,000 10-year-old twin pairs (Kovas, Petrill, & Plomin, 2007). The average genetic correlation between the five components of mathematics was .91.

It is important to emphasise that conclusions regarding generalist genes apply to common abilities and disabilities whose origins involve multiple genes and multiple environmental influences, not to rare single-gene disorders such as Phenylketonuria or chromosomal disorders such as Down syndrome. Furthermore, the generalist-genes hypothesis does not extend to rare or family-specific mutations, such as the FOXP mutation in the KE family, a family with an unusual type of speech-language impairment that includes deficits in oro-facial motor control. (Lai, Fisher, Hurst, Vargha-Khadem, & Monaco, 2001). The FOXP mutation appears to be both necessary and sufficient to cause this impairment in the 15 affected KE family members but does not contribute to genetic variation in common language disabilities (Meaburn, Dale, Craig, & Plomin, 2002).

Instead of thinking about rare genetic disorders caused by a single-gene mutation of the sort that Mendel investigated in the pea plant, it is now generally accepted that common disorders are caused by many genes, which implies that each of these genes will have only a small effect. These multiple genetic variants of small effect are called *quantitative trait loci* (QTLs), referring to the loci in the DNA that contribute to the variation in continuously (quantitatively) distributed traits. If, as is now generally accepted, disorders represent the quantitative extremes of the normal variation in complex traits, QTLs contribute to disorders interchangeably and additively as probabilistic risk factors.

GENERALIST GENES FOR OTHER COGNITIVE ABILITIES

Much multivariate genetic research has focused on cognitive abilities, such as verbal, spatial, and memory abilities, rather than on learning abilities. This research consistently finds genetic correlations greater than .50 and often near 1.0 across diverse cognitive abilities (Deary, Spinath, & Bates, 2006). Similar results suggesting substantial genetic overlap have been found for more basic information-processing measures, such as speed of processing, as well as measures of brain volume (Deary et al., 2006).

Phenotypic (observed) correlations among diverse tests of cognitive abilities led Charles Spearman in 1904 to call this general factor *g* in order to avoid the many connotations of the word intelligence. To what extent do generalist genes for *g* overlap with generalist genes for learning abilities? A review of about a dozen such studies concludes that genetic correlations between *g* and learning abilities are substantial but somewhat lower than the genetic correlations among learning abilities (Plomin & Kovas, 2005). This result suggests that most (but not all) generalist genes that affect learning abilities are even more general in that they also affect other sorts of cognitive abilities included in the *g* factor.

SPECIALIST GENES AND SPECIALIST ENVIRONMENTS

As we have shown, genetic correlations among learning abilities and disabilities are substantial—about .70 on average—which suggests that what they have in common is largely genetic in origin. However, genetic correlations are less than 1.0, which means that genes also contribute to making children better at some abilities than others. In other words, some relatively specialist genes (influencing some abilities but not others) also exist. As mentioned earlier, when DNA research identifies QTLs responsible for genetic influence on reading ability, we predict that most of the QTLs will also be associated with mathematics ability. However, we also predict that some of these QTLs will not be associated with mathematics. Because genetic influence on learning abilities is substantial, such specialist genes contribute importantly to dissociations among learning abilities and disabilities even though most genes are generalists.

Multivariate genetic research also has an interesting story to tell about environmental influences on learning abilities and disabilities. Genetic research distinguishes two types of environmental influences. Those that make family members similar are called *shared environment*. The rest, those that do not contribute to resemblance among family members, are called *non-shared environment,* and this category also includes error of measurement. Multivariate genetic analyses indicate that shared environmental influences are generalists: Shared environmental correlations among learning and cognitive abilities are as high as genetic correlations. For example, in the two recent studies, the shared-environmental correlation was .74 between reading and mathematics at 7 years (Kovas, Harlaar, Petrill, & Plomin, 2005), and the average shared-environmental correlation was .86 between five components of mathematics at 10 years (Kovas et al., 2007). An obvious hypothesis that has not yet been rigorously tested is that some monolithic factors such as the family's socioeconomic status or school quality might be responsible for these generalist shared-environmental effects.

In contrast to these generalist effects of shared environment, nonshared environmental effects are specialists: Nonshared environmental correlations are low. For example, in the same two studies, the nonshared environmental correlation was .39 between reading and mathematics at 7 years (Kovas et al., 2005), and the average nonshared environmental correlation was .24 between five components of mathematics at 10 years (Kovas et al., 2007).

Nearly all research attempting to identify specific sources of nonshared environment has focused on family environments rather than school environments and on personality and behavior problems rather than learning abilities. Nonetheless, such research should be informative for future research that will attempt to identify nonshared environments that affect learning abilities. A meta-analysis of 43 papers relating differential family experience of siblings to differential outcomes concluded that "measured nonshared environmental variables do not account for a substantial portion of nonshared variability" (Turkheimer & Waldron, 2000, p. 78).

The search for nonshared environments might best begin outside the family. For example, initial research supports the hypothesis that peer influence may be an important candidate for a nonshared environment as siblings make their own individual ways in the world outside their family (Iervolino et al., 2002). However, peers would not seem to be a likely explanation for why nonshared environmental factors change so much from year to year, nor why nonshared environmental factors differ from one academic subject to another (Kovas, Haworth, Dale, & Plomin, in press). Perceptions of the environment may be an important direction for research because they are specific to the child. A recent study of 3,000 pairs of 9-year-old twin pairs found that children's perceptions of school experiences were significantly but modestly influenced by genetic factors (20% of the variance), but that most of the variance (65%) was due to nonshared environment (Walker & Plomin, 2006). However, the problem is that these nonshared environmental experiences hardly relate to nonshared environmental variance in academic achievement.

We also need to consider the possibility that chance contributes to nonshared environment in terms of random noise, idiosyncratic experiences, or the subtle interplay of a concatenation of events. However, chance might only be a label for our current ignorance about the environmental processes by which children—even pairs of MZ twins—in the same family and same classroom come to be so different.

Even though we have a long way to go to understand the nonshared environmental influences that are the source of specialist environments, there are important implications now of thinking about specialist environments in relation to education. Almost all work on school environments focuses on shared environmental factors such as family background and school and teacher quality. However, such shared environmental influences have modest effects and, at least for cognitive abilities, decline sharply in importance from childhood to adolescence (Deary et al., 2006). Moreover, shared environmental influences act as generalists. More important, and of increasing importance during development, are nonshared environmental influences. As we have described, multivariate genetic research shows that these environmental factors primarily work as specialists contributing to differences in children's performances in different areas. One implication is that educational influences might have their greatest impact on remediating discrepant performances among learning abilities (such as differences in reading and mathematics) and discrepancies between learning abilities and cognitive abilities, which is one way to view the topic of over- and underachievement.

IMPLICATIONS OF GENERALIST GENES

Definitive proof of the importance of generalist genes will come from molecular-genetic research that identifies DNA associated with learning and cognitive abilities and disabilities. The multivariate genetic research reviewed here leads to a clear prediction: Most (but not all) genes found to be associated with a particular learning ability or disability will also be associated with other learning abilities and disabilities. In addition, most (but not all) of these generalist genes for learning abilities (such as reading and mathematics) will also be associated with other cognitive abilities (such as memory and spatial ability).

A major reason why identification of genes has been slower than anticipated is that there are likely to be many more genes (QTLs) with much smaller effect sizes than had been anticipated, which means that larger studies with greater power to detect small effects are needed (Zondervan & Cardon, 2004). Optimism is warranted with the advent of completely new approaches such as whole-genome association studies involving thousands of DNA markers genotyped on microarrays (slides the size of a postage stamp that contain millions of DNA sequences to which single stranded DNA or RNA can hybridise; Carlson, Eberle, Kruglyak, & Nickerson, 2004), including microarray genotyping of DNA pooled across large samples of learning-disabled individuals and controls (Butcher, Kennedy, & Plomin, 2006). The good news from the generalist-genes theory is the prediction that the same set of genes is associated with most learning disabilities. Studies that collect data on multiple phenotypes can empirically test the generalist-genes hypothesis by testing whether genes found to be associated with one phenotype (e.g., reading) also relate to other phenotypes in the same sample.

Although no genes have as yet been reliably identified as associated with learning disabilities, several linkages to chromosomal regions have been found for learning disabilities. These QTL linkage results provide some support for the theory of generalist genes. For example, for reading disability the linkages are general. That is, the same linkages appear across measures of diverse reading processes, including orthographic coding, phonological decoding, word recognition, and rapid naming (e.g., Fisher & DeFries, 2002).

When the generalist genes are identified, they will greatly accelerate research on general mechanisms at all levels of analysis from genes to brain to behavior. We have recently discussed implications of generalist genes for cognitive and brain sciences (Kovas & Plomin, 2006). Implications of generalist genes for translational research are also far-reaching. Multivariate genetic research reviewed in this article suggests that genetic "diagnoses" of learning disabilities differ from traditional diagnoses: From a genetic perspective, learning disabilities are not distinct diagnostic entities. The same set of generalist genes affects learning abilities and disabilities. Discrepancies in children's profiles of performance are largely due to specialist environments.

Recommended Reading

Butcher, L.M., Kennedy, J.K.J., & Plomin, R. (2006). (See References)
Kovas, Y., Petrill, S.A., & Plomin, R. (2007). (See References)
Kovas, Y. & Plomin, R. (2006). (See References)
Plomin, R. & Kovas, Y. (2005). (See References)

Acknowledgments—The writing of this article and some of the research it describes was supported in part by grants from the U.K. Medical Research Council (G0500079), the U.K. Wellcome Trust (GR75492), and the U.S. National Institutes of Health (HD46167, HD44454, HD49861).

Note

1. Address correspondence to Yulia Kovas, Box Number P080, Social, Genetic, & Developmental Psychiatry Centre, Institute of Psychiatry, King's College London, De Crespigny Park, London, SE5 8AF, United Kingdom; e-mail: y.kovas@iop.kcl.ac.uk.

References

Butcher, L.M., Kennedy, J.K.J., & Plomin, R. (2006). Generalist genes and cognitive neuroscience. *Current Opinion in Neurobiology, 16*, 141–151.

Carlson, C.S., Eberle, M.A., Kruglyak, L., & Nickerson, D.A. (2004). Mapping complex disease loci in whole-genome association studies. *Nature, 429*, 446–452.

Deary, I.J., Spinath, F.M., & Bates, T.C. (2006). Genetics of intelligence. *European Journal of Human Genetics, 14*, 690–700.

Fisher, S.E., & DeFries, J.C. (2002). Developmental dyslexia: Genetic dissection of a complex cognitive trait. *Nature Reviews Neuroscience, 3*, 767–780.

Iervolino, A.C., Pike, A., Manke, B., Reiss, D., Hetherington, E.M., & Plomin, R. (2002). Genetic and environmental influences in adolescent peer socialization: Evidence from two genetically sensitive designs. *Child Development, 73*, 162–175.

Kovas, Y., Harlaar, N., Petrill, S.A., & Plomin, R. (2005). 'Generalist genes' and mathematics in 7-year-old twins. *Intelligence, 5*, 473–489.

Kovas, Y., Haworth, C.M.A., Dale, P.S., & Plomin, R. (in press). The genetic and environmental origins of learning abilities and disabilities in the early school years. *Monographs of the Society for Research in Child Development*.

Kovas, Y., Petrill, S.A., & Plomin, R. (2007). The origins of diverse domains of mathematics: Generalist genes but specialist environments. *Journal of Educational Psychology, 99*, 128–139.

Kovas, Y., & Plomin, R. (2006). Generalist genes: Implications for cognitive sciences. *Trends in Cognitive Science, 10*, 198–203.

Lai, C.S., Fisher, S.E., Hurst, J.A., Vargha-Khadem, F., & Monaco, A.P. (2001). A forkhead-domain gene is mutated in a severe speech and language disorder. *Nature, 413,* 519–523.

Meaburn, E., Dale, P.S., Craig, I.W., & Plomin, R. (2002). Language-impaired children: No sign of the FOXP2 mutation. *NeuroReport, 13,* 1075–1077.

Oliver, B., Harlaar, N., Hayiou-Thomas, M.E., Kovas, Y., Walker, S.O., Petrill, S.A., et al. (2004). A twin study of teacher-reported mathematics performance and low performance in 7-year-olds. *Journal of Educational Psychology, 96,* 504–517.

Plomin, R., & Kovas, Y. (2005). Generalist genes and learning disabilities. *Psychological Bulletin, 131,* 592–617.

Stromswold, K. (2001). The heritability of language: A review and metaanalysis of twin, adoption and linkage studies. *Language, 77,* 647–723.

Turkheimer, E., & Waldron, M. (2000). Nonshared environment: A theoretical, methodological, and quantitative review. *Psychological Bulletin, 126,* 78–108.

Walker, S.O., & Plomin, R. (2006). Nature, nurture, and perceptions of the classroom environment as they relate to teacher assessed academic achievement: A twin study of 9-year-olds. *Educational Psychology, 26,* 541–561.

Zondervan, K.T., & Cardon, L.R. (2004). The complex interplay among factors that influence allelic association. *Nature Reviews Genetics, 5,* 89–100.

Section 5: Critical Thinking Questions

1. Identify a neurodevelopmental disorder, and describe how genes and environments interact in its development.

2. Evaluate the prospect that we will eventually find a single gene that is responsible for neurodevelopmental disorders such as autism and dyslexia.

3. Kovas and Plomin suggest that genes confer general cognitive risk, but environments determine its form. What implications does this model have for intervention with children who display wide discrepancies in abilities across domains?

This article has been reprinted as it originally appeared in *Current Directions in Psychological Science*. Citation information for this article as originally published appears above.